Education and Psychology of the Gifted Series

James H. Borland, Editor

*Planning and Implementing
Programs for the Gifted*

James H. Borland

*Patterns of Influence on Gifted Learners:
The Home, the Self, and the School*

Joyce L. VanTassel-Baska and Paula Olszewski-Kubilius, Editors

Planning and Implementing Programs for the Gifted

JAMES H. BORLAND

Teachers College, Columbia University
New York and London

Published by Teachers College Press, 1234 Amsterdam Avenue
New York, NY 10027

Library of Congress Cataloging-in-Publication Data

Borland, James H.
    Planning and implementing programs for the gifted/James H.
Borland.
    p. cm.—(Education and psychology of the gifted series)
    Bibliography: p.
    Includes index.
    ISBN 0-8077-2967-1.—ISBN 0-8077-2966-3 (pbk.)
    1. Gifted children—Education—United States. I. Title.
II. Series.
LC3993.9.B67 1989   89-33665
371.95′0973—dc20   CIP

Printed on acid-free paper

Manufactured in the United States of America

96   95   94   93   92   91   90   89   8   7   6   5   4   3   2   1

This book is dedicated with love to my parents,
James H. Borland, Jr. (1913–1988) and Sara Jane Borland

If there is anything more dangerous to the life of the mind than having no independent commitment to ideas, it is having an excess of commitment to some special and constricting idea.

Richard Hofstadter,
Anti-intellectualism in
American Life

By different methods different men excel.

Charles Churchill, *An*
Epistle to William Hogarth

Contents

Foreword

This is the first volume of the Education and Psychology of the Gifted Series published by Teachers College Press. Since I am the series editor, I would like to discuss briefly the goals of the series and why I think it is needed.

One would be hard-pressed to justify a new series about the gifted on the basis of scarcity. A cursory glance at *Books in Print* or a brief visit to a bookseller will quickly disabuse anybody of the notion that insufficient ink has been spilled on this topic in recent years. Once again, it seems, gifted children are objects of interest to the educational profession and to society at large. As a result, one of the hottest topics in the professional and popular literature these days is the education of the gifted (or "gifted education," if one is willing to take some liberties with grammar and, all too often, the truth). So what possible justification could there be for adding to the glut?

I cannot claim to have read everything that has been written about gifted children and adults over the past decade, but I have managed to wade through a significant amount of it. This has led me to the conclusion that we may have too many books and too few ideas, a notion that may strike the reader as radical. But the flood of review copies that has crossed my desk recently has prompted me to ask, among other things, just how many basic texts on the nature and nurture of gifted children, texts that repeat the same ideas in the same bland uncritical manner, we really need. I suspect that the correct answer would be a fraction of the number we currently have.

I am determined, therefore, that this series will do more than merely add to the accretion of books in the field. Instead, I want the series to serve as a forum for those individuals, whatever their relationship to the field of the gifted, who have something new to say and an interesting way to say it, especially if what they have to say takes us into new areas of inquiry. Let me elaborate upon that a bit.

It was the wise Mr. Dooley who said that the proper role of the press is to comfort the afflicted and to afflict the comfortable. That, in a sense, is what I would like this series to do. I hope that by addressing and offering solutions to the critical problems that confront us, the authors who contribute to this series will offer aid and comfort to gifted children and adults and to those concerned with their education and welfare. But it is also my hope that the same authors will not hesitate to disturb us in our comfort, to challenge our orthodoxies, to rouse us from our complacency. I think we need comfort and affliction in equal doses.

As a field, we can point to some significant gains in the education of gifted children in recent years, and we can take pride in our role in bringing them about. But pride is one thing, satisfaction another. I fear that, to an extent, we have given in to the latter and become much too comfortable with our customary ways of doing things. By this I mean that we may be too willing to embrace the received wisdom and unexamined assumptions on which many of our beliefs and practices have been predicated without subjecting them to the rigorous critical scrutiny they, and we, deserve.

Ours is a small and collegial field. In most respects this is all to the good, but I wonder if it sometimes does not exact its toll. For example, it often seems that one has an easier time gaining acceptance into our professional ranks by repeating the catechism and swallowing the dogma than by main-taining an attitude of scholarly and critical skepticism. One need not be an inveterate curmudgeon to believe that comity, a desideratum in most social organizations, can, if carried too far, result in intellectual stagnation for a field of scholarship and practice.

If I am correct in suggesting that our field has at times suffered from intellectual lassitude, it may be a reflection of a parochialism on which others have commented. Sternberg (1982), for example, has argued that a "schism" has arisen between the mainstream disciplines in psychology and the field of the education of the gifted, and I think his assertion is demonstrably true. To an appreciable extent, we have for years been functioning as a field cut off from the ongoing discourse in the broader domains of psychology and education, much to our detriment. Now that education has again become a central issue in the social and intellectual debates of the day, it is even more crucial that we do more than preach to the converted, recycle the same no-tions, repeat the old jargon. We need to expand our focus and our reach; to move beyond our trivial concern with cubes, triads, totem poles, and—God help us—"McTalent Burgers"; to confront such issues as race and gender, excellence and equity, giftedness and the mission of the schools.

This means that we ought to encourage such Jeremiahs as Robert Sawyer, who, writing in the *Journal for the Education of the Gifted* (1988a,b), feels compelled to put in a few good words for academic rigor, and Richard Ronvik, who, in Volume 2 of this series, *Patterns of Influence on Gifted Learners* (VanTassel-Baska & Olszewski-Kubilius, New York: Teachers College Press, 1989), argues that our "trivialization of gifted education . . . invites the abuse it sometimes receives." It is possible, I suppose, to view such critics among us as troublemakers or traitors; I see them as our best hope for continued vitality and as a hedge against our irrelevance as a field.

I do not wish to give the impression that this series will consist of nothing but broadsides delivered by Cassandras and heretics. These volumes will be issued in the normal fashion by a respected educational publisher, not nailed to the church door. I even suspect that the reader will find more that is comfortable than controversial in the books to come. But there will always be room here for new ideas, heterodox opinions, and reasoned challenges to the status quo. I see this as positive, as contributing to the growth and maturity of a field that, if we go back to Yoder's "The Story of the Boyhood of Great Men" (1894), is just five years short of centenarian status in this country. Quite possibly, many in this field will disagree with me on this and other points. They are entitled to their opinions, and I encourage them to send me proposals for books.

Thus, I am excited by the prospect of this new series. I think it will fill a void, serve a useful purpose, and probably ruffle a few feathers. And while I cannot promise that every reader will find everything published in the series to be unexceptionable, I can promise that he or she will find little that is boring.

James H. Borland, Editor
Education and Psychology
of the Gifted Series

Preface

I worked on this book for over a decade and a half, although I actually wrote it in considerably less time. By this I mean that I have been trying to come to grips with the issues discussed here over the past 15 years, during which time I have been a teacher of the gifted; a doctoral student in special education with a concentration in the education of the gifted; a director of a college center for gifted children and of the preschool that operates under that center's auspices; a college professor teaching graduate students seeking degrees in the field of the education for the gifted; and a consultant for numerous schools and school districts.

In pursuing the various activities required by each of these roles, I have asked myself many questions about what programs for the gifted should be doing and for whom they should be doing it. To be honest, I have also asked myself whether, in fact, we ought to be doing this at all, whether programs for "gifted students," (a term to which I have never reconciled myself) have a legitimate place in our schools. I have answered every one of those questions, including the last one, many times, discovering and discarding a series of "truths" that turned out, in light of experience, to be less than or only equivocally true. Truth, I have come to realize, is rather more difficult to come by in this field than some would have us believe.

I have, however, learned from my 15 years in this field one thing that is immutable: Programs for the gifted are inordinately hard to plan, implement, defend, sustain, and improve. This is probably true of all educational programs; I doubt that the public at large has the faintest conception of how difficult the educational profession is. Nevertheless, if a competition were held to determine the aspect of the educational enterprise that is the most exacting (and exasperating) in terms of the demands placed on those who would plan and institute them in the public schools, I would place my money on programs for the gifted.

Although I despaired long ago of producing definitive, enduring answers to the questions that haunt those brave people who undertake the task of creating programs for gifted children, I have learned some things of value simply by asking myself the questions. And although I found myself, as a result of pondering the multitude of issues that confront us as a field, ever more uncertain about what (and who) was right and wrong, I also found myself, perhaps as a result of the same activity, better able to help those who sought my assistance. Paradoxically, I found that the fewer answers I had, the more I knew, and vice versa.

Perhaps throwing out the answers I had learned by rote and listening attentively to the concerns of real educators who work with real children played the greatest role in my growth as someone with something to offer to this field; for in the process, I learned that every school as well as every community is unique, each with its own needs and its own particular types of gifted children. Furthermore, I learned that those who profess to have *the* answer, the one best answer, for all these communities, schools, and children are wrong. There is no single answer; no single method for program planning, identifying children, or curriculum development; no all-purpose nostrum; no panacea. That, if anything, is the central message of this book.

I wrote this book, therefore, to help those who are trying, practically and conceptually, to come to grips with the issues that surround planning and implementing programs for the gifted. This is a group of individuals who, if they approach the task as scholars and problem solvers rather than as true believers, court confusion and uncertainty at every turn. In fact, I toyed with the idea of subtitling the book "A Guide for the Perplexed," but that title, give or take a preposition, has already been used.

The perplexed, my intended audience, consist of various groups. Most obviously, school administrators and teachers who have been charged with the task of developing a "gifted program" figure prominently here. They are the ones who, I hope, will derive the most benefit from what I have written by using this book to guide them in their difficult but rewarding undertaking.

Students of education also loomed large in the audience I envisioned while writing the chapters that follow. The issues raised in planning programs for the gifted in the schools are among the most important faced by our profession, and I would like to think that the examination of those issues here would have educational value for students preparing to enter the fray.

Parents of gifted children are among the most informed and inquisitive educational consumers that school personnel are likely to encounter. Although this is not by design a book for parents, it does cast a critical eye on the same program components that parents of gifted children should be concerned with evaluating. I believe that many of them will find the book to be accessible and useful.

Finally, there are many ideas in this book that are presented in hope that they will be read and debated by my colleagues in the field of the education of the gifted. I believe our field has been a bit stagnant of late with respect to new ideas for programs for the children whom we serve, and that much of our received wisdom deserves reexamination. I would like my challenges to some of our orthodoxies to be taken in the spirit of inquiry and collegiality in which they are offered, but more important, I would like them to be discussed.

Acknowledgments

There are so many individuals to whom I am indebted for direct and indirect contributions to this book that to attempt to acknowledge them here risks doing an injustice to those whose names I will inadvertently—and inevitably—omit. Nevertheless, it would be churlish of me not to thank the following people whose support has been indispensable. To them is due much of the credit for whatever virtues the book may possess and none of the blame for its shortcomings.

Numerous individuals at Teachers College, Columbia University, have contributed ideas, criticism, and encouragement without which I could never have finished this book. My friend and colleague, Heidi Jacobs, is owed thanks for more things than I can acknowledge here. Many of the ideas presented in this book were developed during the course of our working together. Thanks are also due to Lisa Wright, my successor at the Center for the Study and Education for the Gifted at Teachers College, who provided astute suggestions for improving the chapter on curriculum (Chapter 8). The frequency with which Abe Tannenbaum's magisterial *Gifted Children* (1983) is cited between these covers attests to the profound effect he has had on my thinking. Harry Passow and Len Blackman, distinguished senior members of the T.C. faculty, have been constant sources of wisdom and encouragement, as has Esther McGrath, and I am very grateful. Roy Campbell, the college's Media Relations Officer, tracked down the source of a quotation that had eluded my efforts.

Carole Saltz and Sarah Biondello of Teachers College Press gave me the opportunity to publish this book and to edit the series of which it is a part. Sarah had the unenviable task of trying to coax a completed manuscript from me before the number of missed deadlines reached double figures, and she deserves my undying thanks.

Special thanks are due to my graduate students at Teachers College, especially those who endured TE 5024, Planning and Implementing Programs for the Gifted, for keeping the ideas flowing, and me on my toes.

If my memory is accurate, it was Ron Rubenzer who first showed me the evaluation framework that evolved into the approach to program evaluation that appears in Chapter 9. Tami Fern's unpublished review of the literature on the evaluation of programs for the gifted was very useful in the writing of that chapter.

Most of what I have learned about programs for gifted students has been acquired through my work with various schools and school districts across the country, and I want to thank the administrators, teachers, parents, and students involved in these programs for allowing me to learn by doing. I have shown drafts of various chapters of this book to teachers and coordinators of programs for the gifted in a number of school districts; their encouragement and suggestions were invaluable.

I cannot begin to comprehend, much less acknowledge, the debt I owe to my parents, to whom this book is dedicated. My mother and my late father never wavered in their faith in me, nor have I in my love for them.

Finally, I want to thank my wife, Marcie, and my son, Max. If I had half the confidence in myself that Marcie has in me, or half the respect for myself that I have for her, I would be insufferable. As she has with everything I have done, Marcia supported and encouraged my work on this book during the seemingly interminable time I worked on it, and she uncomplainingly took care of Max on her days off so I could write. Max, being Max, made that a joy rather than a chore.

CHAPTER 1

Introduction

"Where shall I begin, please your majesty?" he asked.
   "Begin at the beginning," the King said, gravely, "and
go on till you come to the end: then stop."
Carroll, Alice's Adventures in Wonderland

This is a book about planning and implementing special-educational programs for gifted children. It is my hope that it will serve both as a guide to practice and as a basis for the discussion of issues related to such programs. I emphasize these two objectives because, although my intention was to write a handbook that could be used effectively by educators faced with the challenge of developing programs, I never intended to write a cookbook. Thus, in addition to providing recommendations for dealing with the various aspects of program planning and implementation, I have tried to illuminate the major issues and questions related to specific facets of programs for the gifted, and I have not hesitated to offer opinions about what I think is right and wrong with our current practice.

In the chapters that follow, the reader will find discussions of the components that make up programs for the gifted along with practical recommendations, derived from experience with a number of schools and school districts, for their implementation. Tying all of this together is a strategy for program development that I refer to as a *system approach*. This approach, which is discussed in detail in Chapter 3, is the heart of the book. It represents my thinking about how programs should emerge from and be compatible with the settings in which they will be implemented. I am strongly convinced that programs for the gifted should be part of, not imposed upon, the schools and school districts in which, I hope, they will take root, grow, and flourish. The recommendations and opinions contained in this book are all offered in that spirit and to that end.

Before discussing the system approach and the components of a program for the gifted, I wish to outline the major principles that inform the book, and to present an overview of what lies ahead.

GUIDING PRINCIPLES

Litotes is a rhetorical device employing understatement in which something is affirmed by negating its contrary. The statement "Special programs
for gifted children are not uncontroversial" is an example of litotes. Invariably, when individuals, be they educators or laypersons, discuss special education for gifted children, a lively exchange of ideas and opinions ensues,
and there is greater recourse to hyperbole than to litotes. Whether they support it or oppose it, people care about the education of the gifted. They may
be well informed about the topic, or they may know next to nothing; in either
case, though, they will have strong opinions that are grounded in deeply held
values and beliefs about education, excellence, equality, and a host of related
issues.

In order to understand and to evaluate fairly the ideas of anyone who
ventures to make recommendations concerning the education of gifted students, therefore, one should be aware of the principles on which those recommendations are based. The following is a statement of the major beliefs
that guided the writing of this book. The major elements of this credo will
be delineated in more detail in the appropriate sections of the chapters that
follow. I present them here in summary form to orient the reader to the
arguments and recommendations that follow.

1. *The education of the gifted is a form of special education.* I am a special
   educator whose population of interest is gifted children. I believe that the
   gifted are exceptional children to the same extent that the visually impaired
   and the learning-disabled are exceptional children. Like all exceptional
   children, those we label gifted possess special characteristics that affect
   their ability to learn to a significant degree, and they will not reach their
   full educational potential unless we modify their curricula substantially.
   No other way of conceiving of the education of the gifted, I believe, offers
   as defensible a rationale or as workable a framework for special programming.
2. *Children's current educational needs, not their prospects for future eminence,
   should guide our practice.* This means that the unfortunate label "gifted
   child," if it must be used at all, should be applied to those able children
   who have needs that are not currently being met by the existing core
   curriculum. We misplace our energies when we concern ourselves overly
   with who "deserves" the label or who is "truly gifted" by virtue of having
   certain appealing traits. Furthermore, this means that we should direct
   our efforts toward creating an appropriate educational environment for
   these children in the present, not toward making them productive in the
   future.

3. *The nature of the children served in programs for the gifted will and should vary from school district to school district.* Since school giftedness should be defined in terms of needs that are not being addressed by the school's core curriculum, and since curricula differ from one school district to another, different kinds of children will be identified for special programs in different districts. A child who is correctly placed in a program for the gifted in one school district conceivably may not require such a placement in another. This is essentially what takes place across the nation now, although it happens more by chance than by plan.

4. *No single program model can be appropriate for all school districts.* Schools and the communities in which they are located differ from one another in numerous important ways. No single approach to meeting the needs of the gifted can possibly be right for all schools and all communities. There are, unfortunately, no panaceas; this is the central theme of this book.

5. *Programs for the gifted should be based on information gleaned from formal needs assessments.* Programs for the gifted are attempts to remedy deficiencies in educational systems—systems that are not working for the gifted. They are prescriptions that are more likely to be effective if they are based upon thorough diagnoses. Without a needs assessment, one must resort to planning a program in the dark, which is closer to gambling than to sound policy-making.

6. *The needs of gifted children are best addressed in the company of their age and ability peers.* I will argue in Chapter 6 for as much homogeneous grouping of the gifted as can be effected in a given school or school district. Although it is the norm in this country to keep gifted children in the educational mainstream for the majority of their school time, it is not necessarily true that the mainstream is the least restrictive environment for the gifted. It may, in fact, be the opposite.

7. *Curricula for gifted students should stress the acquisition of important knowledge.* Knowledge, for some reason, has taken a back seat to less important things in many special curricula for the gifted. As a result, too many special programs are characterized by trivial curricula, a lack of rigor, and student indifference. The goal of education is the learning of declarative and procedural knowledge, including learning how to learn. This is not meant to limit the ways in which knowledge can be taught and learned, but to restore the pursuit of knowledge to its rightful place in the education of the gifted.

Some or all of these principles may strike the reader as radical. I will readily assent to that characterization if the term is used in its original sense deriving from the Latin *radix*, meaning *root*. My desk dictionary offers the following as the primary definitions of *radical*: "of, related to, or proceeding from a root . . . of or relating to the origin: fundamental" (*Webster's Seventh New Collegiate Dictionary*, 1972, p. 705). In light of those meanings of the word, the ideas presented in this book and the principles on which they are based are, indeed, radical. They represent my attempt to think about why and how gifted children should receive special education without making any more assumptions than are absolutely necessary. In writing this book, I have tried not to accept anything as valid simply because it is the way things are usually done. Rather, I have tried to go to the root of our theory and our practice, to reexamine the foundations upon which they are based, and to build from there. I will leave it to the reader to decide whether or not I have been successful, and whether the effort was worthwhile.

PLAN OF THE BOOK

The following is a summary of Chapters 2–10 of the book.

I focus in Chapter 2 on the need to define the target population. Although the definition of the target population is but one, albeit the most important, component of a program for the gifted, it is discussed prior to the explication of the general model into which it is incorporated because defining our population is central to every other aspect of our practice. Various approaches to defining giftedness in children are reviewed in Chapter 2, as are the many meanings that have been applied to the terms *giftedness* and *talent*. In this chapter I make a distinction between national-resources approaches to defining giftedness and special-educational approaches. The chapter concludes with a special-educational definition of a general nature that can be made specific within the context of the system approach described in the following chapter.

Chapter 3 contains the rationale for the approach to program planning and implementation that is the core of this book. The diagnostic-prescriptive system model is contrasted favorably to what I refer to as the packaged-program approach, and the components of the system model (and of a program for the gifted) are briefly described. The special-educational definition proposed in Chapter 2 is discussed and made more specific in the context of the system model. A discussion of some important initial steps, program-planning preliminaries, rounds out the chapter.

Since I argue in Chapter 3 that an assessment of local needs is requisite for the planning of a program that will work in a specific setting, in Chapter 4 I explore the whys and wherefores of needs assessment and outline some of the steps that should be incorporated into the needs-assessment process. Questions that should be answered by a needs assessment are discussed, as are likely sources of information and caveats related to the interpretation of needs-assessment data.

Chapter 5 deals with the most controversial component of a program for the gifted, the process of selecting students for the program. I argue in this chapter that identification is a matter of determining appropriate placements, not a matter of separating the truly gifted from the nongifted for purposes of labeling. Numerous issues are discussed, including the use of identification matrices, the virtues and drawbacks of various tests, effectiveness versus efficiency, and the composition of selection committees. A systematic framework for identification is proposed and explained.

In Chapter 6 I focus primarily on the issue of grouping for instruction. A range of formats is discussed, ranging from those requiring full-time homogeneous grouping to those that keep gifted students in the regular classroom. A case is made for homogeneous grouping. The models identified as effective in the Richardson Foundation Report (Cox, Daniel, & Boston, 1985) are discussed and criticized.

The elusive qualities of effective teachers of the gifted are discussed in Chapter 7, and the reader is warned not to take too seriously lists of "essential traits of teachers of the gifted." Following this warning, I present a list of essential traits of teachers of the gifted. The chapter concludes with some thoughts about supervising programs for the gifted.

Drawing heavily on Robert Sawyer's (1988a) seminal paper, "In Defense of Academic Rigor," I argue in Chapter 8 for substance in curricula for gifted students. The meanings of the ubiquitous terms *differentiated* and *defensible* are discussed, and some essential elements of a defensible, differentiated curriculum for the gifted are noted. The thorny problem of what is appropriate for the gifted and what is appropriate for all learners is explored.

Program evaluation as part of, not as something external to, the planning of special programs is the central theme of Chapter 9. The chapter opens with a discussion of the meaning and functions of evaluation. The many problems one encounters in trying to evaluate programs for the gifted are enumerated, and a framework for program evaluation is presented.

In the final chapter, I discuss program planning as an ongoing process that does not end once a program is in place. Before concluding the book, I touch upon two issues of importance that did not easily fit into earlier chapters: the need to achieve in programs for the gifted fair representation of all the groups that constitute our society and the need to attend to the affective needs of gifted students.

Now let me turn to our first concern, the meaning of giftedness and the process of defining the target population of a program for the gifted.

CHAPTER 2

Defining the Target Population

If confusion is the sign of the times, I see at the root of this
confusion a rupture between things and words, between
things and the ideas and signs that are their representation.

Artaud, *The Theater and its Double*

"When *I* use a word," Humpty Dumpty said, in a rather
scornful tone, "it means just what I choose it to mean—
neither more nor less."

"The question is," said Alice, "whether you *can* make
words mean so many things."

"The question is," said Humpty Dumpty, "which is to
be the master—that's all."

Carroll, *Through the Looking Glass*

In his landmark treatise on human intelligence, *The Abilities of Man* (1927),
the British psychologist Charles Spearman wrote, "In truth, 'intelligence' has
become a mere vocal sound, a word with so many meanings that finally it has
none" (p. 14). More recently, the words *gifted* and *giftedness* have suffered a
similar fate. These words are used so variously by so many individuals in so
many contexts that they, too, often seem to be "mere vocal sounds."

The problem is compounded when the adjective *gifted* is used to modify
the noun *child*. Although most educators would agree that there are children
in the schools who should be designated as gifted, there is very little agreement
as to *which* children should be included in this category. One person's gifted
child is another's troublemaker, while the latter's candidate is regarded as
merely a good test taker by the former. Confusion, as the quotation from
Artaud is meant to suggest, reigns supreme. There truly is a rupture between
the word *gifted* in its various usages and a clearly and consensually defined
group of children in the schools, and this state of affairs works to the detriment
of sound educational practice. Indeed, a casual observer could be forgiven
for concluding that educators have no idea of what a gifted child is. Even the
not-so-casual observer, including many working in the field of education of
the gifted, might feel inclined to support that conclusion.

In short, there is a basic problem of definition that has yet to be resolved. The problem, as I suggest above, is not one of a paucity but rather one of a surfeit of definitions. Every writer in this field seems to be a Humpty Dumpty, using the word *gifted* in a manner that suits his or her purposes. Definitions abound, but meaning is in short supply.

It would be easy to dismiss all of this as abstruse, ivory-tower hairsplitting, scholasticism taken to a ridiculous extreme, a minor annoyance but nothing that should concern those in the real world of the schools. This stance, however comforting it might be, would be mistaken. For, as recondite and petty as definitional arguments often become, their resolution or lack of resolution has profound implications for educational practice. Defining what one means by the phrase *gifted child* is a very practical undertaking, with consequences that affect the lives of real children. In fact, defining the target population is the first and in many ways the most important step that must be taken in planning a program for gifted students. I will attempt to underscore this point and to show how our confusion over the meaning of the term *giftedness* can complicate the lives of educators by using a fabricated, but far from unrealistic, example.

DEFINING GIFTEDNESS: A CAUTIONARY TALE

Let us examine the case of a fictitious school administrator who, charged with the task of planning a program for gifted students in his district, sets forth with good intentions and a blissful ignorance of the pitfalls that await. Our unwary administrator might very likely (and sensibly) set as his first task the definition of the target population, reasoning that designating the students who will receive special services is a prerequisite to planning those services. He would probably want to know what the experts agree upon as the best definition of a gifted child, and might, therefore, purchase or borrow some books on this topic and plan to attend a conference or two. If there is a college nearby with a department of education, this conscientious public servant could also be expected to get in touch with the faculty member of that college who teaches the course or courses dealing with the education of the gifted. The answer to his basic question would appear to be close at hand.

But such is not to be, as we watch our administrator begin the quest for a definition. First he examines one of the texts and finds a plausible definition of "the gifted child." Seeking to confirm this definition, he turns to a second text, only to find a quite different formulation. A third and a fourth book supply definitions that vary significantly from each other and from those found in the first two volumes. Confused by the babel of written definitions, the administrator decides to place his somewhat shaken faith in the spoken word and attend a conference on the education of the gifted. But visits to six workshops at the conference produce six more definitions and a state of utter confusion. Reeling from this vertiginous experience, he turns to the court of last resort—the local academic expert. There the hapless administrator learns that this cacaphony of definitions reflects the current state of the art. However, the professor would be only too happy to share *her* definition, one that happens to contradict all of the others.

Now our protagonist is faced with a major dilemma (and, probably, the beginnings of a transient stress disorder). He has uncovered a plethora of definitions, all with something to recommend them. From these he must choose, or fashion, a single definition that will guide the program he is planning for his district. The administrator, being rather astute, realizes that a great deal depends upon this decision; the definition that is settled upon will, if followed consistently, profoundly affect the nature of the program. Specifically, it will determine the type of child that will be labeled "gifted." Children will—or will not—be placed in this program according to how closely they resemble the profile delineated in the definition. In addition, the identification process, which is probably the most controversial aspect of the program, will be established so that it follows from this definition. The decision of whether or not to use certain tests and other devices will depend on how well these instruments assess the traits described in the definition. Moreover, the curriculum of the program will be developed in direct response to the needs of the target population, again as specified in the definition. This list of the consequences of the definition could go on and on. However, the essential point is that each component of the projected program will be shaped by the definition that the beleaguered administrator finally produces.

Finally, our administrator realizes that what he had hoped to discover through research (i.e., which children in his schools are gifted) must instead be resolved by administrative action. The complexity and contradiction inherent in the welter of definitions available to him have forced him into a situation where he must choose or fashion a working definition from among the many alternatives. In other words, on behalf of his school district, he must make a policy statement that specifies which children in his district's schools will be deemed gifted for purposes of special education. In a very real sense, he has come to realize that the school district will not be discovering giftedness; rather, it will be conferring it on those children it designates as recipients of special services in the program known as the "gifted program."

One can easily sympathize with this fictional administrator and his real-life counterparts who must, on the basis of conflicting and contradictory information, make decisions that affect the education of children in their charge. Of course, this task is considerably easier if a needs assessment is undertaken, as described in Chapters 3 and 4; but the information gleaned from that needs assessment must be integrated with what has been learned from investigating the available options and the state of the art. And therein, as the above example was designed to show, lies a significant problem.

It may be useful, then, to take a brief look at some of the definitions that one might encounter at this point in the program-planning process. I will highlight only a few of the many available to the assiduous researcher, concentrating on those that are potentially useful, well-known, or exemplary of major trends in the field. Then, I will discuss some of the issues central to evaluating the competing claims of these definitions, stressing the need to clarify basic questions of rationale and intent. Finally, I will propose a working definition of the gifted student that will be broad enough to serve as a guide for those planning special programs for the gifted. Although general by design, this definition is predicated upon some definite beliefs about why such programs are needed and what they should be like.

THE LAY OF THE LAND: SOME DEFINITIONS OF GIFTEDNESS

One can make a useful distinction between formal and informal definitions of such constructs as intelligence, creativity, and giftedness. The reader is probably more familiar with formal definitions, conceptual frameworks, usually proposed by academics or other professionals, that serve as a guide for or a summary of research, theory, or practice in a given field. Formal definitions employ the jargon of the discipline in question, and they are carefully structured, and thus convey their authors' particular point of view with regard to the construct and the field itself. We will look at some formal definitions of giftedness below, and I will propose my own.

Informal definitions are less cerebral, more visceral conceptions of a given construct. They are often intuitive notions shaped more by experience and attitudes than by a comprehensive, scientific investigation of a topic. Informal definitions draw upon feelings and dispositions that most scientists would be reluctant to incorporate into formal definitions. This is not meant to compare informal definitions invidiously with formal ones; often the two are not far removed from each other. Sometimes popular, informal definitions derive from formal definitions that have been superseded by newer research or thinking but still maintain their hold on the beliefs of the public at large. Moreover, professionals as well as laypersons have informal definitions of the constructs with which they work, and these affect their thinking. Thus, knowing that an informal definition of a construct like giftedness is widely held can help one deal with the expectations of parents, administrators, teachers, and children.

It is likely that most individuals in our society would informally define giftedness in children in terms of abilities that relate to the intellect and, at least tangentially, to success in school. Aside from reading about the occasional child prodigy, most of us first encounter the term *gifted child* in connection with an existing or proposed school program. Moreover, some of the earliest definitions of giftedness employed in this country (e.g., Terman's, 1925) were based on studies of schoolchildren and were operationalized using tests of academic aptitude. These have had considerable time to exert their influence. Thus, it would not be surprising to hear a layperson define a gifted child as one who "has a high IQ," "is a brilliant thinker," "does well in school," or something of that nature.

If this is the case, it must be difficult for most people to understand why there is so much confusion over defining gifted children. For them it would seem to be a simple matter of going into a school, identifying the best students or those with the highest IQs, and getting on with it. However, for better or worse, as the fictitious school administrator portrayed above discovered, the field of the education of the gifted has produced a multiplicity of formal definitions. Nearly all of these go well beyond the simple equating of giftedness with scholastic aptitude or IQ that constitutes the informal definition of many individuals.

So, in order to get a sense of the dimensions of the problem and to see what is available to help us in our practical task of defining the target population of a program for the gifted, let us examine a few formal definitions of giftedness. What follows is a discussion of four definitions, representing a small fraction of the conceptions of giftedness currently competing for our attention (see Sternberg & Davidson, 1986, for a more thorough review). These definitions were chosen not to be broadly representative of the range of current thinking in the field but as examples of modern multitrait definitions of giftedness and of a trend toward greater sophistication in the quest for an explanation of giftedness in children. I will begin by discussing the definition that emerged from a document that was the harbinger of, and a major factor in creating, the recent wave of interest in the education of gifted children, the Marland Report (1972) of the U.S. Office of Education (USOE).

The USOE Definition

Dissatisfaction with simple IQ-based definitions of giftedness arose concurrently with dissatisfaction with IQ tests themselves, that is, almost immediately upon the tests' publication (see, for example, the Lippmann-Terman debates of 1922, reprinted in Block & Dworkin, 1976). While Lewis M. Terman (1925), the father of the gifted child movement in this country (and, not coincidentally, the developer of the Stanford-Binet Intelligence Scale), was perfectly satisfied with defining giftedness as the possession of a very high IQ, there were those who disagreed.

Signs of this soon began to appear in the literature. There was, for example, the increased use of the phrase "gifted and talented," implying a broadened perspective incorporating areas of ability not assessed by IQ tests or even addressed by the school curriculum. The midcentury boom in the study of creativity as a human faculty, as exemplified by the scientifically flawed but historically important work of Guilford (e.g., 1950, 1967), Getzels and Jackson (1958, 1962), and Torrance (e.g., 1962), added another dimension to the issue. In reviewing the literature, one can discern a clear trend toward a broadening of the definition of giftedness, which paralleled the growing disillusionment with such instruments as IQ tests. This trend culminated in the promulgation of a definition by the U.S. Office of Education in the highly influential report to Congress known as the Marland Report (1972), named after the then-Commissioner of Education, Sidney P. Marland. This definition, which has acquired quasi-official status, gave the government's imprimatur to the idea that giftedness is a multifaceted construct. It read, in part,

> Gifted and talented children are those identified by professionally qualified persons who by virtue of outstanding abilities, are capable of high performance. . . .
> Children capable of high performance include those with demonstrated achievement and/or potential ability in any of the following areas, singly or in combination:
> 1. general intellectual ability
> 2. specific academic aptitude
> 3. creative or productive thinking
> 4. leadership ability
> 5. visual and performing arts
> 6. psychomotor ability.
> It can be assumed that utilization of these criteria for identification of the gifted and talented will encompass a minimum of 3 to 5 percent of the school population. (p. 2)

This definition was one of the most significant and lasting contributions of the Marland Report, even if its significance derived more from what it suggested than from what it actually said. For by specifying six areas of achievement and ability, the report asserted that giftedness could take many forms, that it was not one thing but many things. It did not take long for this message to reach practitioners in the schools. In the years following the publication of the report, the USOE definition, paraphrased or verbatim, found its way into the program plans of school districts across the nation. Thus, according to their written plans, a large number of schools were designing and implementing programs for a very diverse group of gifted learners.

In reality, of course, most were doing nothing of the kind. Whatever virtues it might possess, the USOE definition is not one that is easily operationalized. In other words, using this definition as a guide to practice is a problematical, if not impossible, proposition. As many writers (e.g., Renzulli, 1978) have pointed out, the six areas cited above are nonparallel, overlapping, inexhaustive of the domain, and often confusing (for example, the last area, psychomotor ability, engendered so much befuddlement that it was dropped from subsequent federal guidelines). In attempting to suggest the range of abilities and performance areas that might be encompassed by the term *gift-edness*, the writers of the USOE definition also managed to open the door to greater imprecision in defining the group of students requiring special programs for the gifted. As Howley, Howley, and Pendarvis (1986) write, referring to this definition and to multitrait definitions in general:

> [They] are so lacking in specificity as to be inapplicable except as a post-hoc justification of intention and sentiment . . . such definitions place unwarranted demands on schools for flexibility and expertise. . . . They provide . . . too contradictory a basis for program development in the context of universal schooling. (p. 376)

To be fair, there is no reason to think that this definition was intended to serve any purpose other than a heuristic one. It was offered as a guide to practice, not as a substitute for it. Quite rightly, it made the point that by the early 1970s the concept of giftedness had undergone an evolution resulting in a multitude of definitions, most of which posited multiple domains of aptitude and performance. By that time, single-trait definitions (those that defined giftedness in terms of one trait, ability, or test score) were an endangered species. Multitrait definitions were (and are) the norm, and the USOE definition reflected this.

What made the federal definition problematic in practice, however, was not its multitrait character but rather its structure. This is an example of what I refer to as *disjunctive* multitrait definitions. The operational word in disjunctive definitions is *or*: One is gifted by virtue of *x* or by virtue of *y* or by virtue of *z*, and so forth. By citing a number of areas in which students can demonstrate potential or achievement "singly or in combination," disjunctive definitions state that giftedness can assume one or another of a variety of forms. Disjunctive definitions invariably are difficult to operationalize because they result in the designation of a number of diverse groups as gifted. One need only imagine the complexity of the identification and programming plan that would have to be put into effect in a school district that adhered faithfully to the USOE definition to realize how unwieldy most disjunctive definitions are.

Thus, most definitions encountered today tend to be *conjunctive* in nature. This type of definition enumerates a number of traits connected by the word *and* (literally or by implication), all of which must be present for giftedness to exist. Conjunctive definitions, like disjunctive ones, are multitrait definitions; they allow for the delineation of a variety of intrinsic and extrinsic factors that, in conjunction, underlie giftedness. However, they differ in that they imply that gifted children are a single group that is homogeneous with respect to the various factors posited as the determinants of giftedness. This is a much more prescriptive approach, in which giftedness is defined as a particular level, state, or quality of ability or behavior that takes a recognizable form and can be applied to a range of performance areas. Let us look at some of these post-Marland conjunctive definitions.

Renzulli's Three-Ring Definition

Joseph Renzulli has proposed a conjunctive multitrait definition of giftedness (Renzulli, 1978; Renzulli, Reis, & Smith, 1981; Renzulli, 1986a) that has generated quite a bit of discussion and controversy (see, for example, Jarrell & Borland, in press; Kontos, Carter, Ormrod, & Cooney, 1983; Renzulli & Owen, 1983). In explicating this conception of giftedness, Renzulli (1978) writes that research on human productivity has convinced him that "creative/productive people . . . possess a relatively well-defined set of three interlocking clusters of traits" (p. 182). These are (1) above-average, but not necessarily superior, general ability, (2) a motivational construct Renzulli calls "task commitment," and (3) creativity.

Renzulli (1978) stresses that none of these traits in and of itself is sufficient to "make giftedness." Rather, "it is the interaction among the clusters that . . . [is] the necessary ingredient for creative/productive accomplishment" (p. 182), although there has since been some equivocation on this point (see Renzulli & Owen, 1983). Moreover, Renzulli denies that cognitive factors should be given primacy in defining giftedness, since they alone do not explain adult productivity, the ultimate criterion of giftedness in this conception. Each of his three clusters is "an 'equal partner' in contributing to giftedness" (1978, p. 182). Finally, Renzulli offers the intriguing notion that giftedness is better conceived of as a state, possibly a transitory one, than as an enduring trait of the individual.

There are a number of features that make this definition preferable to disjunctive ones, such as the USOE definition. For one thing, the traits proposed by Renzulli are features of the individual that can be brought to bear upon problems in any discipline or field. The confusion of traits, abilities, and performance areas that characterize the federal definition is avoided. In addition, there is a recognition that various factors, cognitive and affective, must interact for an individual to be gifted. This broadening of the range of considerations is necessary if gifted performance is to be explicated fully.

However, a host of inadequacies ultimately make this definition less useful than it might appear at first. There are problems with each of the three components of the definition. The positing of above-average ability rather than very high ability as the major cognitive component of the definition is based, in my opinion, on a misreading of the research. Many of the studies purporting to show little or no relationship between measures of ability and achievement in various fields are flawed by virtue of the fact that the ability range of the subjects is greatly restricted. The studies cited by Renzulli (1978) showing that IQ, grades in college, and so forth do not predict future accomplishment for the most part utilized college students as subjects. Since this is a group that is above-average in intellectual ability to begin with, the ability range is severely attenuated, thus lowering the obtained values of the correlations. This is an artifact of the research, however, and not a reflection of the true relationship between ability and accomplishment. Moreover, in a number of fields in which major intellectual (as opposed to entrepreneurial) advances have been made, high academic standing, and thus very high intellectual ability, is required merely to secure a position. Therefore, it is difficult to accept completely Renzulli's attempt to dismiss very high intellectual ability as a requisite for at least some important kinds of gifted accomplishment.

The trait of task commitment is similarly problematic. One can make a very strong case for the inclusion of nonintellective traits in a definition of giftedness. However, should one decide to do so, there is little warrant for stopping with task commitment. Terman, whose *Genetic Studies of Genius* (1925; Terman & Oden, 1947, 1959) Renzulli leans on heavily for support in elevating task commitment to an exalted position in his definition, found that a cluster of traits that one could call self-esteem loomed as large in the accomplishments of his successful adults as did that which Renzulli calls task commitment. More important, a reading of volumes 4 and 5 of *Genetic Studies of Genius* (Terman & Oden, 1947, 1959) reveals that the educational and socioeconomic standing of the subjects' fathers was probably an even greater factor.

The inclusion of task commitment as a requisite for entry into special programs has been subjected to criticism on other grounds. By posing this requirement, one is saying that only highly motivated children should be placed in programs for the gifted. This would tend to exclude many children who might most require such programs. Children bored by a classroom routine that does not challenge them are very unlikely to impress their teachers as task-committed. The same is true of some students from minority cultures. It is possible that many of these students would not conform to concepts of task commitment held by white, middle-class teachers and administrators and thus would not be referred for special services. Incorporating this construct into the definition is a step in the right direction for definitions of the type that attempt to predict future accomplishment, but the research and logical bases for including only task commitment are weak.

Finally, with the notion of creativity one encounters an even weaker link in the chain. Renzulli himself (1978) admits that creativity is at present an unmeasurable entity. It is likely to remain so because, as researchers such as D. N. Perkins of Harvard's Project Zero suggest, there probably is no such thing as a single trait that could be identified as creativity. In his book, *The Mind's Best Work*, Perkins (1981) lampoons the belief in a "stuff" called creativity that explains the genius of a Beethoven or a Joyce. To try to sum up the many traits, forces, circumstances, and events that lead to creative accomplishment by positing a measurable construct called creativity that is possessed by individuals to varying degrees is so simplistic as to invite derision. Nevertheless, creativity is present as one of the three components of Renzulli's definition.

In summary, although Renzulli's three-ring definition points the way toward definitions that specify more clearly the components of giftedness, it is inadequate for practical purposes. It appears to be based on a questionable reading of the research marshaled in its support (see Jarrell & Borland, in press), and this results in a definition that attempts to carry too much weight on its slender shoulders. Moreover, the consequences of using this definition are such that only those children who already are succeeding in the regular classroom are likely to receive special services. What is needed is a definition that rests on a firmer foundation of scholarship and logic and is better considered in terms of the effects of utilizing it. Happily, definitions of giftedness exist that meet these criteria.

Tannenbaum's Psychosocial Definition

Abraham J. Tannenbaum (1983) has proposed what he calls a "psychosocial" definition of giftedness that, as its name suggests, considers factors both endogenous and exogenous to the individual. Underlying his five-factor conjunctive definition is the premise that gifted children are those with the "potential for becoming critically acclaimed performers or exemplary producers of ideas in spheres of activity that enhance the moral, physical, emotional, social, intellectual, or aesthetic life of humanity" (p. 86). The key phrase in this passage is "producers of ideas," for Tannenbaum believes that the gifted are producers, not merely consumers, of knowledge and ideas.

According to Tannenbaum, the factors that contribute to the production of ideas are general ability, special ability, nonintellective factors, environmental factors, and chance factors.

General Ability. Tannenbaum includes, as does Renzulli, general ability as a factor in his definition. However, Tannenbaum realizes that the threshold levels of ability required for giftedness will vary for different fields of endeavor. For example, a higher level of general intellectual ability would probably be required for a distinguished career in literary criticism than would be required for similar eminence in dance. This is not to denigrate dance or other artistic pursuits. Rather, it is a recognition of the fact that a single level of the aspect of human ability known as general intellectual ability will not suffice as a prerequisite for high levels of achievement in all fields.

Special Ability. Even theorists who assert the primacy of general intelligence in human accomplishment (e.g., Spearman, 1927) recognize the importance of specific ability factors. Thus, Tannenbaum believes that in addition to general intelligence, a specific aptitude for a given field is requisite for gifted performance. There are crucial differences both in the nature of the abilities and in the critical period for their nurturance. Literary talent is usually manifested fully in adulthood, whereas some physical abilities (e.g., swimming), performance skills (e.g., musical performance), and academic strengths (e.g., mathematical precocity) can appear much earlier in life and often demand identification and encouragement during the childhood or even early childhood years (see, for example, Feldman's book *Nature's Gambit*, 1986, on child prodigies).

Nonintellective Factors. Included here would be Renzulli's task commitment along with a number of equally important factors of a noncognitive nature. Among these one could expect to find ego strength, dedication to or even obsession with a particular field, need for achievement, willingness to delay gratification for the sake of long-term accomplishment, and other traits. These, according to Tannenbaum (1983), are "integral to the achieving personality regardless of the areas in which talent manifests itself" (p. 88). It is also probable that there are important personality–discipline field interactions that loom large in the success of certain individuals. Extroversion, for example, would appear to be required for achievement in the political realm, but it is less likely to be requisite for the attainment of excellence as a historian (academic politics aside).

Environmental Factors. By the inclusion of this group of factors, the "psychosocial" label is earned. As in other sophisticated definitions of giftedness (see Sternberg's triarchic theory below and Arieti's, 1976, discussion of the "creativogenic society"), there is a recognition here of the importance of context. Giftedness is not an autistic phenomenon; it must find its expression in a particular place at a particular time. Environment plays a role both in shaping an individual's abilities (through the influence of parents, teachers, peers, the community, the media, the arts, and so forth) and in allowing for its blossoming (there must be a favorable climate for the particular gift to be expressed). Manifestations of giftedness are in great part dependent on the zeitgeist and the current state of development of a culture. The human aptitude for computer programming lay fallow during the Middle Ages, while vast numbers of promising but unheralded stone-ax fabricators probably exist today.

Chance Factors. Curiously unremarked by most other writers in this field (but, again, see Feldman, 1986), the role of chance is given its due in Tannenbaum's formulation. Being in the right place at the right time (or in the wrong place at the wrong time) can be the deciding factor in the realization or frustration of great potential. While it is disquieting to think that mere chance can exercise veto power over the other four factors, reality demands that its pivotal role be acknowledged. "Getting the breaks" can make the difference between the fruition and recognition of great ability and a life spent, in Thomas Gray's phrase, as a "mute, inglorious Milton."

Although considerably more complex in scope and character than Renzulli's three-ring definition, Tannenbaum's psychosocial definition more than makes up in plausibility and face validity what it loses in parsimony. By stipulating internal and external factors that contribute to the realization (or frustration) of an individual's potential, Tannenbaum makes a convincing case for the need to expand our focus beyond the individual. He describes both the end state of giftedness (the production of ideas) and the factors leading to its attainment. He thus takes a major step forward in our progress toward a comprehensive definition of giftedness.

If there is a problem with this conception from the point of view of the educator, it is that it really looks beyond the classroom both in terms of the factors that facilitate or frustrate the realization of potential and in terms of when that potential will be realized. The ultimate criterion for Tannenbaum is "critically acclaimed" performance—almost always an adult accomplishment. Moreover, while nonintellective factors, environmental factors, and chance factors are quite plausible mediators of the expression of early aptitude in later life, they are largely out of the sphere of influence of the school (although, or course, the school itself is an environmental factor).

This does not detract from the validity of Tannenbaum's conception of giftedness; it simply clarifies its focus. The psychosocial definition is intended less as a guide for programming than as an explanation of how psychological and sociological factors interact in the development of adult giftedness. As I will discuss in Chapter 8, Tannenbaum's notion of the gifted as producers of knowledge does provide guidance for developers of curricula for gifted children.

Sternberg's Triarchic Conception of Giftedness

Robert J. Sternberg (1986) has proposed a theory of giftedness that is a special case of his general triarchic theory of human intelligence (e.g., Sternberg, 1984). The term *triarchic* is employed because the theory comprises three subtheories, each with its own character. Sternberg's approach to defining intelligence and giftedness is daring in its breadth and scope, and it has elicited a great deal of comment (see the various responses to Sternberg, 1984, in the journal *The Behavioral and Brain Sciences*, 1984, Volume 7, pp. 287–304).

One of the most interesting features of this conception is the fact that in this, perhaps the most complex definition of giftedness yet offered, giftedness is defined once again in terms of high intelligence. Thus, one can trace the development of theories of giftedness from a simple equating of giftedness with high general intellectual ability (as in the work of Terman), to the search for additional traits needed to account for that which general ability leaves unexplained, to a theory that, although quite elaborate, brings giftedness back into the realm of human intelligence. Let us examine the three subtheories of Sternberg's triarchic conception.

Contextual subtheory. Like Tannenbaum's psychosocial definition, Sternberg's formulation take cognizance of the role of the environment. Thus, he starts with a contextual subtheory that focuses on the individual's control over his or her relationship to the immediate environment. Whereas Tannenbaum conceives of environmental factors as being separate from intelligence, Sternberg emphasizes the process of dealing with the environment as one facet of an individual's intellectual makeup. Briefly, Sternberg asserts that intelligence must operate in *real-world* environments that are *relevant* to the individual's life and aspirations and that intelligence must be *purposive* or goal-oriented. It is expressed at various times by the *adaptation to* an environment, or, when adaptation fails, by the *shaping of* an environment so that the environment is better suited to the realization of one's abilities, or, failing both of those, by the *selection of* a different, more congenial environment. Without championing extreme relativism, Sternberg allows for the inclusion of a number of what Tannenbaum would call environmental and nonintellective factors under the rubric of intelligence as part of his contextual subtheory, since these would be required for adaptation, shaping, and selection.

Two-facet subtheory. As Baron (1984) points out, Sternberg's theory contains both criterial elements (positing what must be explained, in this case adaptation to, shaping of, or selection of environments) and explanatory ones (positing factors that account for success or failure in meeting these criteria, as in the componential subtheory below). Although Baron labels this second, two-facet subtheory as criterial, it seems to bridge the gap between criterial and explanatory statements in that it refers to things that could be construed both as outcomes and processes.

Whereas the contextual subtheory relates intelligence to the external world, the two-factor subtheory relates one's history of experience with certain tasks to two mental processes or skills. These processes or skills (or, perhaps, outcomes) are the *ability to deal with novelty* and the *ability to automatize information processing.*

The ability to deal with novelty, which has a commonsense "rightness" as a facet of intelligence, is, according to Sternberg, largely a matter of facility with "nonentrenched" tasks (those outside one's usual range of experience) and novel situations. A *task* can be nonentrenched with respect to the operations it requires or the concepts it presents. Implicit in this is the possibility that a task can be novel in terms of its comprehension (where the goal is to figure out what to do) or in its execution (where the goal is to figure out how to do it). Similarly, a *situation* can also require one to deal with novelty. Cooking dinner is not a novel task demand in ordinary life, but it becomes so with a few situational modifications (e.g., finding oneself unprovisioned in a wilderness area, or after sustaining a major debilitating injury).

The other of the two facets, the ability to automatize information processing, is, in a sense, a consequent of the first. This refers to a sort of "subcontracting" of intellectual functions to the preconscious mind, where they take place more or less unnoticed and thereby allow the central executive function to operate on other tasks. In other words, certain tasks, once they are no longer novel, start to become entrenched or overlearned and ultimately do not require conscious direction. Fortunately, a great many learned processes are automatized (e.g., reading), allowing them to be executed quickly, smoothly, and without requiring one to think about every step. As with the ability to deal with novelty, the ability to automatize can be applied to both tasks and situations.

Sternberg states that a trade-off exists between the ability to deal with novelty and the ability to automatize. The more efficiently one can deal with novelty, the more resources one has left for automatization and vice versa. Experientially, as one deals successfully with a novel task or situation, the demand shifts to the need to automatize. Thus, these abilities play off of one another with respect to an individual's particular strengths and experiences.

Componential subtheory. The purely explanatory aspect of Sternberg's formulation is his well-known componential theory, which is incorporated here as a subtheory of the triarchic theory. This subtheory specifies the mental processes or mechanisms whereby intelligent performance is effected. The basic unit of intelligent behavior for Sternberg is the *component*, "an elementary information process that operates on internal representations of objects or symbols" (1984, p. 281). According to Sternberg, there are three kinds of components:

1. Those mental processes used in gaining new knowledge are called *knowledge-acquisition components*. Sternberg posits three distinct kinds of knowledge-acquisition components, all of which involve encoding, the basic process of creating representations of information from the environment or memory and bringing them into the conscious mind, where they can be processed. *Selective encoding*, the first of Sternberg's knowledge-acquisition components, involves distinguishing relevant from irrelevant information for encoding, separating the "wheat from the chaff" in Sternberg's phrase. *Selective combination* entails the combination of encoded information in such a way as to produce a knowledge structure or scheme. Simply acquiring information is not enough; it must be integrated into a conceptual whole for it to be of use. *Selective comparison*, the third of the knowledge-acquisition components, involves relating new information to information already stored in memory.

2. The workhorses of the componential subtheory are the *performance components*, the mental processes that actually execute intellectual strategies for task performance. These are the mental activities that can be identified as the components of a circumscribed intellectual task, the things the mind does during purposeful acts of cognition. They organize themselves into three recognizable stages of the execution of a task: *encoding of stimuli, combination or comparison of stimuli, and response*. The first and last of these are performance components in themselves (analogous to input and output functions). The middle stage can consist of various performance components, for example, inferring, mapping, application, and justification (see Sternberg, 1979, for a discussion of specific performance components).

3. Finally, and in many ways most interesting of all, there are the various *metacomponents*. These are higher-order processes, often referred to collectively as the executive. Metacomponents plan, direct, and monitor the execution of the lower-order components, controlling the strategic realization of an intelligent act. Some of the metacomponents identified by Sternberg are: *decision as to what the problem is that must be solved, selection of lower-order components for problem solution, selection of a strategy for combining the selected components, and monitoring the solution*.

Summary and Implications. According to Sternberg, then, intelligence is a tripartite construct that relates to one's environment, one's experience, and one's information-processing capabilities. Thus, giftedness is "extraordinary intelligence" as intelligence is defined by his triarchic theory. Within this context, stating that giftedness is extraordinary intelligence has special and wide-ranging connotations. For example, under the terms of the contextual subtheory, giftedness would be related to the ability to function in a congenial environment for problem solving, broadly defined. This might involve, in D. N. Perkins's (1981) phrase, "knowing the informal rules of the game" (p. 213) within a given discipline, being able to play a professional role in a way that maximizes the impact and benefits of one's work. In terms of the metacomponential aspect of the componential subtheory, Sternberg (1981) has found that gifted individuals allocate more time than the average person to the encoding of information in their overall componential strategies, thus giving the appearance of delaying the actual beginning of the problem-solving process. However, this additional attention to encoding pays off in faster and more effective problem solving in the long run.

Sternberg's is a compelling and scholarly approach to the comprehension of giftedness. It is the most forceful linking of a conception of giftedness to cognitive theory that the field has yet seen, and it bids fair to change our thinking about the underpinnings of observable manifestations of giftedness. Sternberg's theory, in both its general form and the special case that deals with intellectual giftedness, will be debated, elaborated upon, and doubtless superseded, in complexity if not in adequacy, by newer theories. But at this point in the development of the field, it can hardly be ignored.

I have devoted considerable space to Sternberg's theory because it exemplifies the trend toward more rigorous definitions of giftedness. The implications of this trend and of this definition are many; I would like to discuss two of them here.

First, as mentioned above, Sternberg's theory returns the concept of giftedness to the realm of intelligence without being in any way reductive. On the contrary, the breadth of this conception of intelligence is sufficient to convey the richness and variety of this complex phenomenon without resorting to the futile stockpiling of perhaps chimerical traits (creativity, leadership ability, psychomotor ability, and so forth) that characterize most multitrait definitions. Adding such terms to definitions of giftedness does little to increase their explanatory power (for example, stating that Eudora Welty is a gifted writer or that David Byrne is a gifted composer and musician because each has an unusually high amount of "creativity" does not help to explain their giftedness). Moreover, whereas many definitions of the "shopping-list" type appear to be atheoretical (e.g., the USOE definition) or theoretically weak (e.g., the three-ring definition), Sternberg's triarchic definition rests on a firm foundation of theory and research. Thus, this conception tightens the rules by insisting that we locate giftedness in the realm of cognition and by adhering to standards of scholarship rarely encountered in this field in the game of defining giftedness.

The second implication would not have escaped our fictitious school administrator whose travails were described above. Let us assume that he concludes that Sternberg's is the most valid definition of giftedness currently available. The obvious problem that he must face is one of practicality: How can this definition be operationalized? What does this definition give him by way of assistance in the tedious and complicated (but important) task of identifying gifted children in the schools? By and large, given the current state of our knowledge, it gives him very little in the way of practical help. Direct measures of the constituents of Sternberg's subtheories are either nonexistent (measures of automatization), mired in complex laboratory settings (measures of componential resources), or so demanding of time as to resemble biography more than psychometrics (measures of the efficacy of adapting to, shaping, or selecting congenial environments).

Our bewildered administrator might understandably fear that the best theory is moving further and further away from the practical realm; but this may be too dire a conclusion. Theories that are on the cutting edge of any science must run far ahead of their field's current ability to translate them into practice. However, the administrator will probably conclude that, for the moment, the utilization of the triarchic theory in the practical sphere is still more of an ideal than a reality.

What one must hope for, then, is that practice will be informed by, if not strictly guided by, the best theory of the day. One could not expect operationalizations of the triarchic theory, for example, to be found in the program plans of schools and school districts across the country. One could, however, fairly expect to find employed definitions of giftedness that are both reasonably operationalizable and consistent with what the theory teaches us. This is the best translation of theory into practice that is now possible. Let us look at how this might work.

TRANSLATING THEORY INTO PRACTICE

Talents and Gifts

Gagne's dichotomy. In a perceptive and useful paper, Francoys Gagne (1985) examines the distinctions between the terms *giftedness* and *talent* and their use within the field of the education of the gifted. As Gagne demonstrates, the terms have not been employed very precisely in the literature. Most writers appear to regard them as synonymous. Those who do take pains to distinguish between giftedness and talent do so in a variety of ways. Some make a distinction in terms of domain, with giftedness referring to intellectual accomplishments and talent designating ability in the arts and other supposedly noncognitive areas. Others make the difference one of degree, so that talent refers to above-average ability while giftedness points to more rarefied levels of aptitude. Another approach is to reserve the term *gift* for an innate capacity, and *talent* for an acquired one.

Gagne proposes a better dichotomy, one that may help us out of our theory–practice bind with respect to definition. In his formulation, the distinction is made between competence or ability, on the one hand, and performance, on the other. For Gagne, "*Giftedness* corresponds to competence which is distinctly above average in one or more domains of ability," and "*Talent* refers to performance which is distinctly above average in one or more fields of human performance" (p. 108). He proposes a model of giftedness and talent that delineates a number of ability domains (intellectual, socio-emotional, and so forth) that are mediated by various "catalysts" (environment, personality, motivation) in the process of becoming manifest as talents. This model incorporates Renzulli's (1978) three-ring conception and Cohn's (1981) model of giftedness and talent.

An expanded model of giftedness and talent. Gagne's use of the terms *giftedness* and *talent* appears to be the least arbitrary and the most useful of those proposed thus far. The distinction between competence and performance is a real and meaningful one, and it allows for the building of a model that permits the operationalization of the concepts. In fact, using the structure of Gagne's model, it is possible to produce a more elaborate formulation that incorporates features from the most promising of the definitions cited above, Tannenbaum's psychosocial definition and Sternberg's triarchic conception. This model is illustrated in Figure 2.1.

This is a bit complicated, so some explanation is in order. Moving from left to right in Figure 2.1, one generally goes from the level of the internal and the potential to the level of the behavioral and the observable. On the far left are found the componential and metacomponential functions that Sternberg posits as the information processes that underlie intelligent behavior. The two factors that govern automatization and the ability to deal with novelty (shown here for the sake of simplicity as input from the external world) condition the effectiveness and efficiency of these componential processes (which have their own limitations as described by Sternberg, 1984), with the result being identifiable abilities. This is the level Gagne refers to as giftedness.

Abilities, or gifts, do not find automatic expression as talents, however. There are various mediators that qualify the expression of giftedness and that influence each other. Among these are psychological factors (incorporating

Figure 2.1: Graphic representation of an expanded model of giftedness and talent.

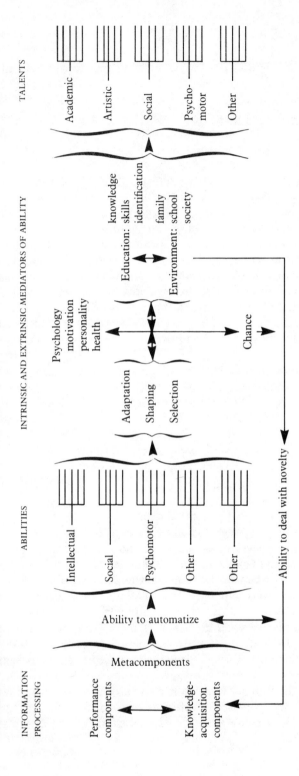

Componential processes, facilitated by automatization and the acquisition of figurative and operative schemes and the developmental increase in M-power, underlie abilities, which are mediated by intrinsic and extrinsic factors (including chance factors), resulting in identifiable talents. Missing in this representation is a domain of knowledge structures or schemes.

Tannenbaum's nonintellective factors and Renzulli's task commitment), chance factors (a likely source of novel stimuli, by the way), formal education (including the acquisition of knowledge and skills as well as the possibility of being identified by the school as gifted), and the environment at large (a grab bag of other extrinsic factors and another fertile source of novel stimuli). The interactions among abilities and intrinsic and extrinsic factors result in the manifestation (or inhibition) of specific talents that, like abilities, are grouped in Figure 2.1 under likely general headings suggested by Cohn (1981).

In addition to all or some of the components of the models of Cohn, Gagne, Renzulli, Sternberg, and Tannenbaum, this model also incorporates the terms of the USOE definition. With respect to this definition, the category of general intellectual ability would be found under the heading of "Abilities" in Figure 2.1, while specific academic aptitudes, leadership ability, and ability in the visual and performing arts would be found under "Talents" (allowing for some argument regarding the placement of specific academic aptitudes).

What is missing is a provision for "creativity," one of Renzulli's trio, or "creative or productive thinking," one of the USOE sextet. If one were to make provision for this construct, it would have to be on the far right-hand side of this model, as a quality of the products of talents in various domains. If Perkins's (1981) well-reasoned argument is correct, creativity is better regarded as a property of the solution of various classes of problems than as an ability or a set of processes. Abilities that some believe underlie creative production (fluency, flexibility, originality, and so forth) are explained as features of information processing, if in fact they exist at all (see Borland, 1986a; Ekstrom, French, & Harman, 1974).

No claim is made for this as the definitive model of giftedness and talent. There are gross oversimplifications here, as there are with most graphic representations of complex phenomena. For example, there is no provision in Figure 2.1 for an individual's knowledge structures (a neglected aspect of most models), and the richness of the potential interactions among the model's components is only hinted at by the few arrows shown in the figure. [A more recent version of this model (unpublished) attempts to deal with these deficiencies by incorporating the ideas of such Neopiagetians as Case, e.g., 1974, and Pascual-Leone, e.g., Pascual-Leone & Smith, 1969. Since the model as shown here may already be too complicated for our purposes, I will leave it as it stands in Figure 2.1.] This model is merely an expansion of Gagne's original concept that makes room for the features of some of the theories and definitions discussed above. It is presented here as an aid in dealing with the issue of defining giftedness for the purpose of developing programs for the gifted. By creating a general structural framework into which the terms of various definitions can be placed, one can begin to look at the problem of giftedness in a manner that clarifies certain questions that affect programming.

Questions Relating to Talents and Gifts

What are some of the questions that one ought to ask in order to focus better on the problem of definition? One basic question concerns whether we should focus on the realm of giftedness or that of talent. Using Gagne's definitions, this boils down to a choice between potential, competence, and ability (giftedness) or performance (talent). One way of thinking about it is in terms of the age or grade of the students being considered.

The younger the children, the more appropriate it is to consider abilities or gifts rather than developed talents (depending, of course, on the nature of the ability and the talent, since some talents manifest themselves earlier than others). Although one could argue that students should demonstrate well-developed talents in order to be selected for certain special programs in high school, one is generally on solid ground focusing upon ability (i.e., giftedness) in the context of most programs for school-age children. By initiating a program for the gifted, we are creating an environmental factor, a mediator of ability or giftedness that we hope will result in the realization of talent. Therefore, with respect to defining and identifying giftedness for educational purposes, we should be looking at the left-hand side of Figure 2.1, that which Gagne labels "Giftedness."

A related question deals with the role of education as a factor in the nurturance of gifts and talents. As one moves from the consideration of abilities or gifts to the consideration of talents, the role of education shifts somewhat. With younger children, education can be viewed as a force that can be brought to bear upon potential or giftedness in the future; its role is speculative. With older students, however, education can be seen as a factor that has already contributed to observable talents, as well as one that can enhance talent further. Thus, the experiences of older students with the educational process could be looked at as part of the identification process; with younger students, it is a much less important factor in terms of definition and identification.

The role of what in Figure 2.1 are labeled "Intrinsic and Extrinsic Mediators of Ability" must be considered as well. Whereas Renzulli makes one of these (his "task commitment") a precondition for being recognized as gifted and for entering a special program, one could instead view them as skills to be developed or as factors with which students should be prepared to deal after they are identified, especially on the younger levels. For example, a very young child who demonstrates giftedness in terms of unusually high intellectual ability should probably receive special training that would facilitate his or her ability (or talent?) to adapt to, shape, or select an appropriate environment; that would inculcate effective strategies for benefiting from the educational process; and that would encourage the development of psychological traits that would lead, in turn, to the development of potential talents. For older students, as I implied above, these could be regarded as factors that underlie or explain the existence of specific identified talents, and they could be expected to be already present as preconditions of identification.

Another area of interest is the particular realm of ability or talent that is deemed appropriate for treatment in an educational setting. One of the problems with the term *gifted child* is that it is reserved for some children—those whose abilities fall within the realms that local educators see as important—whereas it excludes other children, whose abilities fall outside these realms. Now, the hoary cliché to the effect that all children are gifted is probably true; most, if not all, children excel in something. Thus, designating some children in the schools as gifted is really a process of ranking some gifts above others, and this is clearly a value decision. This might not appear to be a very difficult decision when the competing abilities and talents are creative writing and facility with video games. However, given the range of areas incorporated within Paul Witty's (1958) famous phrase "potentially valuable line of human activity" (p. 62), more difficult choices loom. Therefore, educators must take a careful look at what abilities and talents they wish to cultivate in their special programs.

Reference must also be made to the purposes of public education. As this is construed by most people, there is greater support for emphasizing intellectual abilities or talents than social or psychomotor ones (in the formal curriculum at least). Age again plays a role in this consideration. For example, general intellectual ability would be the central factor in the giftedness of younger children, but specific academic talents would loom large for older students.

All of these considerations must be incorporated into the basic question of definition, of who will be served. Underlying this, however, is a larger policy issue, which is the question of why we need to have such programs in the first place. Whatever rationale is derived from the resolution of this question informs the consideration of the various factors shown in Figure 2.1. This rationale is central to the development of a workable definition of the target population for a special program for the gifted. Let us examine two basic rationales for such programs.

National-Resources versus Special-Educational Rationales

The national-resources approach. One way of conceiving of the education of the gifted is to view it as a process of resource development. According to this view, gifted children are a vast untapped resource that should be identified and exploited for the common good. This was the rationale behind the somewhat frantic talent search that followed closely upon the launching of Sputnik I by the Soviet Union in 1957. It also appears to be the unspoken basis for definitions and enrichment models such as Renzulli's (1978, 1986a; Renzulli, Reis, & Smith, 1981) that are derived from the study of productive adults.

For those who adhere to this approach, special programs are justifiable because society as a whole benefits from the cultivation of gifts and talents. The existence of these programs, they argue, is in our collective interest as a nation. A logical extension of this position is that the major goal of programs for the gifted is the generation of eminent and productive adults whose accomplishments will redound to the benefit of us all. Thus, this position dictates that definitions of giftedness revolve around notions of productivity, and the identification process becomes a matter of locating children who possess traits that mark them as future producers. In terms of Figure 2.1, the emphasis is on the realm of talents; everything to the left of that column is seen merely as a potential source of markers and signs that might be used to distinguish the future talented producer from the future untalented nonproducer.

As I mentioned above, this rationale guided the vogue for programs for the gifted during the post-Sputnik panic of the late 1950s and early 1960s. There was a clear emphasis at that time on talent development for the national good (indeed, the major federal educational initiative of that time was entitled the National Defense Education Act), and special programs were justified as means by which valuable talents could be developed. However, as Tannenbaum (1979) points out, there was considerable disaffection on the part of many of the students who were routed through those programs. A number of the students found the programs depersonalizing and concluded that the educational system was interested only in exploiting their brains, not in responding to them as individuals. Moreover, as we soon learned, such mass production of talents can lead to a glut in the future as the talent supply outpaces the demand. Thus, Tannenbaum (1983) labels the sort of skills developed by these programs "quota talents."

In addition to the unfortunate tendency to regard children as mere resources (something perhaps akin to geothermal heat deposits) and the problem of the unpredictability of the demand for talents in the future, there are other difficulties with this approach. For example, the central underlying assumption that productivity or eminence is the best criterion for giftedness is open to question. This is a venerable point of view and can be traced back at least as far as Galton's seminal *Hereditary Genius* (1869). Indeed, it has found support at various times over the past century. But are there no other meaningful criteria for giftedness other than worldly success? Certainly, one could argue, as Terman and Oden do on the last page of volume 5 of *Genetic Studies of Genius* (1959) in discussing their subjects whose adult success was unimpressive, that a failure to attain eminence does not necessarily mean that one is not gifted. Furthermore, success, eminence, and productivity can be judged differently by one's contemporaries and by posterity. By the standards of his day, Mozart was hardly a gifted individual according to the criterion of eminence, if burial in an unmarked pauper's grave is a valid indicator.

Even if one accepts eminence as the ultimate criterion of giftedness, there are problems that appear to be intractable from the point of view of educational practice. For example, those who advocate a national resources approach to the education of the gifted advocate identifying gifted students by seeking out those who possess the traits characteristic of productive adults. However, it seems naive from the point of developmental psychology to believe that the traits demonstrated by gifted adults will necessarily be present in that same form in those children who are destined for future greatness. Children are not homunculi or miniature adults whose development is a simple matter of physical and psychological accretion. As Piaget and others have demonstrated, children undergo qualitative developmental changes that frustrate the simple mapping of the traits of gifted adults onto those of gifted children. Just as one would not expect children with the potential for the gift of leadership to have beards because Abraham Lincoln had a beard, one should not produce a list of the traits of talented adults and assert that these are what we should seek in our gifted children.

Then, too, there are enough case histories of gifted adults whose childhoods seemed to hold little promise for future accomplishment to prevent our taking very seriously the claim that any identifiable cluster of childhood traits presages adult giftedness. We are all familiar with the early life histories of Churchill, Edison, and others who as children were neither task committed nor academically able but went on to great things. There might have been signs of giftedness in the early lives of these individuals that could have been perceptible to the very sensitive observer, but there was no clear-cut cluster of traits of the sort that many insist on as precursors of adult success.

The ineffectuality of the national-resources approach is highlighted in a paper by Barry Bull (1985). His critique of programs for the gifted focuses in particular on the problem of talent identification. Bull writes, "It is not at all clear that those who as adults significantly shape our culture share any especially salient characteristics as children." Moreover, he asserts that "we do not currently have any especially well founded techniques for identifying the eminent while they are still children" (p. 4). With respect to identification and programming models that stress student productivity, Bull states, "It is patently not the case that these [eminent adult] individuals are all notably productive before they turn seventeen" (p. 4). Yet, it is on just these premises that Bull finds invalid that the national-resources approach is based.

Bull despairs of our ever being able to fashion a workable model of talent identification based on what I call the national-resources approach. This is because "eminence arises from the coincidence of cultural opportunities and individuals with the specific abilities to take advantage of them and *not*, as our current conceptions of giftedness seem to imply, from certain general and timeless forms of individual genius" (p. 7). Because of this,

> Our conception of giftedness must be far more precisely attuned to the partic-
> ularities of the opportunities for revolutionary cultural change than is currently
> the case if it is to serve as a workable predictor of eminence. This requirement,
> however, is impossible to fulfill. (p. 7)

The improbability, if not the impossibility, of predicting future gifted-ness is the major practical liability of the national-resources approach. In addition to its lack of practicability, however, there are some negative policy implications of this approach. For one, the emphasis on productivity tends to reduce the search for gifted children to a search for those who, at an early age, appear to be among the most likely to succeed. Thus, it is up to the child, regardless of his or her background, to show that he or she is motivated, creative, productive, and so forth, and not up to the program to identify and encourage the development of these traits in those who have the potential to acquire them. This effectively serves as a barrier for the able child who is underachieving or whose antipathy for formal education interferes with the expression of certain characteristics, such as "task commitment." Further-more, since the traits of successful adults in any culture will invariably reflect the values of the dominant group within that society, clusters of traits derived from the study of eminent adults will discriminate against children from cultures outside the mainstream. The end result of the application of this approach is the exclusion from programs for the gifted of significant numbers of able children who are not achieving in the regular classroom, not happy with school, and not the products of middle-class white families. In many cases, though, these are the children whose needs are the greatest owing to the discrepancy between their potential and the services they are receiving in the regular classroom.

The final problem with the national-resources approach is that its preoc-cupation with future achievement takes us away from our proper object of concern, that is, the student in the classroom of today. This is perhaps what is most wrong with this approach. By trying to predict Nobel Prize winners three and four decades hence, it loses sight of the fact that there are children in our schools with clear and present needs. Rather than chase a magical formula that will enable us to predict future eminence from childhood char-acteristics, we should instead look at what certain children require now if the schools are to meet their special needs successfully (see also, in this context, Borland, 1986b, 1986c). An alternative to the national-resources approach is necessary. The one I am offering is called the special-educational approach.

The special-educational approach. The basis of this rationale for special programs for the gifted is the same as that for special programs for the handicapped, namely, the conviction that there are children in our schools who, because of exceptionalities that affect their ability to acquire and process information, are ill served by the regular core curriculum. We readily accept (with a little boost from the courts and the federal government) the fact that various characteristics known as handicapping conditions mandate the provision of modified curricula if certain children are to teach their educational potential. Without such modifications, these students will not receive appropriate educations, if the word *appropriate* is defined with reference to the needs of individual children.

Similarly, there are other characteristics that can render children exceptional so that they, too, require curricular modifications. For these children, the exceptionality is the result not of handicap or disability but of potential or ability. Some children have such a markedly enhanced potential or ability to acquire, process, and produce knowledge that the all-purpose core curriculum scarcely begins to meet their educational needs. These are the exceptional children known as the gifted.

The central concept of the special-educational model is that of educational need. Students are given special services not because they promise to be productive adults or because they fit an expert's profile of the gifted child, but because they demonstrate pronounced educational needs that can only be met by the provision of a special or modified curriculum. As is the case with other special-educational populations, these children are in danger of suffering developmental deficits if left to fend for themselves in the regular classroom, although these deficits may be apparent only in comparison with the students' own potential for accomplishment.

There are a number of implications of this approach that I want to address here. The first of these is nominal. "Gifted education" is special education, although there are those in the field who shy away from this identification. Unfortunately, in some cases this derives from an elitist desire not to be associated with traditional special-educational populations. Perhaps the less that is said about this the better. Others claim that what we are doing with gifted children is different from what special educators are doing with handicapped children and thus should not be designated special education. Educators of the gifted, however, spend their time identifying children who are educationally different from the rest and providing these children with curricular modifications predicated upon what it is that makes them different. This, in essence, is special education.

The second implication of this approach is that the classrooms of today, and not the boardrooms, laboratories, and studios of tomorrow, should be the focus of our concern. I hope that the preceding discussion of the perils attendant upon trying to predict the future of schoolchildren is sufficient to convince the reader of the folly of treating children only as potential adults. Of course, they *are* potential adults, but they are also actual children with pressing needs in the real world of today's schools. This should be our primary concern.

The third implication is that the child's need, not society's need, should be paramount for educators. Now, it is true that as a country we certainly ought to try to assess our collective need for talent now and, to the extent possible, in the future. Moreover, we owe it to ourselves and to our children to encourage in them a sense of civic responsibility as an antidote to both narcissism and excessive materialism. As educators, though, our prime responsibility is to secure every child's right to an appropriate education, and this places children's needs in the forefront. Our obligation is to them individually and not to ourselves as a society, even though, in reality, this is less of a conflict than it may first appear. The overreaching goal of special education is to strive to make our educational system responsive to the needs of every student, regardless of the nature and degree of his or her exceptionality. To the extent that this goal is met, society, as well as the individual child, will be enriched.

Finally, the special-educational model implies something central to the question of definition, bringing us back to our original focus. What is implied in the preceding paragraphs is that the gifted children in any school or school district are those with the greatest educational needs resulting from exceptional potential or ability. This is the essence of the conception of giftedness and of the approach to the education of the gifted that informs this book. It also serves as a general definition of the gifted student that, with some elaboration and explanation can, I believe, serve as a guide for practice in the real world of the schools. This definition, as it is spelled out below, is sufficiently general to accommodate various resolutions of the questions posed above about talents and gifts, abilities and potentials, and so forth. It allows for the incorporation of constructs and variables from whatever explicit definitions one finds congenial as long as they relate to the assessed needs of the school and its students. Let us look, therefore, at this general definition and what it implies for educators, such as the poor soul portrayed at the beginning of the chapter, who must define the target population of a program for gifted children in a school or school district.

A GENERAL DEFINITION OF THE GIFTED CHILD IN THE SCHOOLS

My definition of the gifted child, derived from the special-educational rationale described above, reads as follows: For the purposes of education, gifted children are those students in a given school or school district who are exceptional by virtue of markedly greater than average potential or ability in some area of human activity generally considered to be the province of the educational system and whose exceptionality engenders special-educational needs that are not being met adequately by the regular core curriculum. This definition has a number of components that require explanation and justification. I will discuss each of them in some detail.

The Specific School as the Frame of Reference

The phrase "in a given school or school district" refers to the conviction stated above that the child's present classroom situation is of greater special-educational import than his or her situation, whatever that may be, a few decades hence. This has, I trust, been given sufficient elaboration above. It also implies that the definition is a relative one, that it is specific to a given context. According to this definition, a child is gifted if he or she stands out in comparison to other children in his or her school. The frame of reference is local and relative rather than general and absolute; one could almost say that a child is "locally gifted."

One might object that this means that a child who is considered to be gifted in one school district may not be so-considered in another. This is, indeed, a likely consequence of the application of the definition. It is also something that frequently happens in practice in programs for the gifted today, but in most cases without a good explanation. However, there is no reason why this should not be the case. Children do not, of course, become any less able as they cross school-district borders, but their needs for special provisions may change significantly. Thus, although it is unfortunate that a child's label might change as he or she moves from one school to another, it is only right that his or her placement should change if the new circumstances indicate that it be necessary. For example, a child who has been receiving special instruction in science from a mentor in his or her old school may find that the regular science program in the new school, with its honors and advanced-placement courses, is sufficient to meet his or her needs. Similarly, a child who was only an above-average student in one school may be one of the very brightest in another, thereby creating the need for special enrichment or acceleration. When the needs of the individual child are made central to the question of his or her giftedness (for educational purposes), context must play a crucial role.

It is, therefore, undesirable for a body such as a state education department to promulgate a strict definition to which local school districts must adhere, especially one that specifies operational standards such as minimum test scores. Such a definition cannot apply fairly to all districts. It cannot, for example, take into account the various strengths of the curricula in the different schools or guard against the danger that a student who is already well served by the rich core curriculum in his or her school may be singled out for special services.

Nor can centrally promulgated definitions allow for demographic differences, especially socio-economic ones, that affect the relative levels of student achievement in different school districts. The most pernicious effect of centrally imposed standards, such as statewide IQ cutoffs for admission to programs for the gifted, is that the rich get richer and the poor get poorer. The more affluent districts, which already have more resources owing to a stronger tax base, will have a greater number of students designated as gifted. In the less affluent districts, where able students may be in greater danger of not receiving adequate educational stimulation, few students may qualify for special programs. This basic inequity can only be avoided if giftedness is defined in relation to a given school or school district.

Exceptionality and Giftedness

The central meaning of the phrase "exceptional by virtue of markedly greater than average potential or ability" has been discussed at length above in the section on the special-educational approach to the education of the gifted. However, some clarification of "markedly greater than average" is required. This is meant to bring the definition more into line with the USOE definition (Marland, 1972), which identifies some 3 to 5 percent of the population as gifted, than with Renzulli's definition (1978), which, in the context of his revolving-door model (Renzulli, Reis, & Smith, 1981), allows for the identification of a talent pool of 15 to 20 percent (or more) of the student body.

Special education, in order to be special, must deal with a small percentage of students. This is required if the term *exceptional child* is to have any meaning. The branch of special education that deals with the gifted should be no different. If one-quarter of the student body of a school is receiving special services in the "gifted program," it would appear that the regular curriculum is not doing its job. Certainly, most or all students in a school or school district could benefit from and should receive some enrichment, but this should be distinguished from the program for the gifted, which ought to respond to the needs of an exceptional minority. Unfortunately, some schools, in a misguided if understandable concern over elitism, have opened the doors of their programs of the gifted to a large number of students. This results in the creation of an upper track of students who receive some form of special instruction or opportunity; but the truly exceptional child is not likely to have his or her needs met by such a program, which has to accommodate itself to such a large number of children. It is probable that this child will still be quite different from the students in the "special" program, who will, in most cases, be working with a less extensive knowledge base at a significantly lower cognitive level.

The goal is not to identify an elite. This is a false issue; an elite can be constituted by 20 percent as well as 3 percent. Nor is it the goal to hurt more children by excluding them from the program. There will be children who will not be chosen whether the program includes one child in four or one child in 50. Moreover, it is probably more painful to be left out of a less exclusive program than a more exclusive one. The true goal is to provide special services for those children who really require them because of their exceptionality. The meaning of the word *exceptional* is strained to the breaking point when programs swell to the extent they have in some schools.

Activities Relevant to the Educational Enterprise

In many respects, it is unfortunate that we use the term *gifted* (and especially the term *not gifted*) in the way that we do, because, as I assert above, most or all children are gifted in some way and to some extent. However, *gifted* is the well-established generic term for the group of children with whom this book deals, and it would do little good to try to change that usage now. Nonetheless, educators should keep in mind that the process of grouping some children for special instruction in a "gifted program" has falsely invidious connotations for other children in the school. It suggests that they are "not gifted," when it may only be the case that their strengths are in areas outside those emphasized in their school's program for the gifted.

Inevitably, programs for the gifted must make distinctions between those areas of potential and ability they wish to address and those they do not. Trying to accommodate all "potentially valuable line[s] of human activity" (Witty, 1958, p. 62) would be an impossible and unprofitable exercise. Even attempting to devise a program or programs to provide for all the children who could be considered gifted under the terms of the USOE definition (Marland, 1972) would tax the resources of a school district and the patience of its personnel. Educators must make clear and careful decisions about what aspects of human ability they will incorporate into their definitions of the gifted child if their programs are to have any chance of succeeding. Let me stress once again that this is a policy decision and a value decision. The literature dealing with the education of the gifted will be of little help, since there are too many differing points of view over what activities and abilities should be subsumed under the meaning of the term.

The phrase "some area of human activity generally considered to be the province of the educational system" in my definition indicates how I think that value decision should be made. My concern throughout has been with the needs of children as they relate to their right to an appropriate education. Although there is considerable disagreement on this point, I believe that the essential purpose of education is to transmit our cultural and intellectual heritage to our children by increasing their knowledge, encouraging in them an interest in knowledge for its own sake as well as for "practical" purposes, enhancing their ability to acquire additional knowledge on their own, and helping them develop their abilities to interpret and to produce knowledge. As educators, we live by the myth that this purpose can be accomplished by exposing fairly large groups of children, grouped roughly according to the dates of their births, to a uniform common-core curriculum. The kind of exceptionality I would like to see serve as the basis for special education in programs for the gifted is the kind that makes certain children singularly ill-served by this common-core curriculum. Specifically, these would be students whose ability to learn and to think about what they learn is most compromised by this lockstep group approach.

To put this in other terms, I believe that to be true to the purposes of education, our programs for the gifted should primarily serve students with very high cognitive and academic potential and ability. We should be encouraging our brightest students to develop their intellectual capacities and affinities. We should urge them to dedicate themselves to the life of the mind or at least to hold it in special esteem. Stated simply, we ought to be concerned with the nurturing of intellectuals. Other concerns are, in my opinion, peripheral to the essential goals of education, and they have less of a claim on us in our capacities as educators of the gifted.

This is by no means a call for a "return to basics" as that phrase has evolved into an educational and political slogan. I am not advocating that gifted children spend all of their time in endless drill and meaningless rote memorization, nor am I calling for an end to efforts to teach children to think critically and creatively. Critical thinking and creative thinking, in spite of the debasement of these terms by purveyors of educational trivia, are basic to the intellectual life. What I am calling for is a response on our part to those students in our schools who are crying out for more intellectual stimulation, for more knowledge and higher-level knowledge, for exposure to more challenging and more complex content. If education is all about teaching and learning, these are the children who have the greatest educational need; we could be teaching them more, and they could be learning much more.

I do not deny that other areas of human activity and accomplishment are important, or even equal in importance to the intellectual, but I do assert that they should be less central to our curricular concerns as educators. Referring to the USOE definition (Marland, 1972), I am championing "general intellectual ability" and "specific academic aptitude" over the other four areas, and I believe that there is justification for doing this. "Psychomotor ability," for example, is well addressed in those highly competitive programs for the talented known as interscholastic sports. Intramural athletics also provide stimulation for the development of these abilities, as do such activities as cheerleading, baton twirling, marching band, and so forth.

"Leadership ability" is also stimulated through extracurricular activities, as students are encouraged to run for class and student government offices and to join and lead clubs. Even more vigorous exercising of leadership talent is found in the day-to-day realities of school life as students try to manage the social demands of being children and adolescents in twentieth-century America. "Creative and productive thinking," another category of the USOE definition, is a hallmark of effective problem solving in any domain: intellectual, social, psychomotor, or whatever. We should encourage creativity in everything our students do, but there is no reason to think that there are students who are "creatively gifted" outside of the context of a specific sphere of activity.

Finally, "ability in the visual and performing arts" presents a more equivocal picture. One could argue that school activities such as band and orchestra, chorus, art classes and clubs, and so forth bring the creative and performing arts into the curriculum of all children. To the extent that this is not the case, a strong warrant for providing special services for children exceptional in these areas exists. However, rightly or wrongly, these are mostly elective areas that, at least at the upper levels, serve those with demonstrated talent. Some educators argue that these are already programs for the gifted, although I suspect that many educators in the visual arts, music, and dance would disagree.

The role of the arts in the education of the gifted is a confused one. We offer lip service to the idea that the arts are important by our frequent use of *gifted and talented* (in the vernacular, not Gagne's, 1985, sense). Nevertheless, programs for the gifted overwhelmingly cater to the needs of students whose gifts and talents lie in the intellectual and academic spheres, not the artistic. Where does this leave the arts in the education of the gifted?

One answer is that the arts should be central to the curriculum of all students, gifted and nongifted, and that the study of esthetics, art history, music, and the like should be inextricable components of the common core. This would mean that differentiating the curriculum for the intellectually and academically gifted requires the differentiation of these subjects as well.

However, in terms of defining who is gifted, the real question is whether students gifted and talented in the creative and performing arts should be given the same opportunities that should be extended to students who are intellectually and academically gifted and talented. I would argue that they should be, but I realize that this is generally not the case. Therefore, for the purposes of this book, I am somewhat arbitrarily focusing on students who are gifted or talented in terms of intellectual aptitude and academic ability. This is not meant to imply a denigration of the arts; it is simply a restriction of the scope of the book.

The notion of concentrating our efforts on behalf of the gifted in the areas of intellectual and academic abilities would not seem unusual to the founders of the gifted-child movement in this country (e.g., Hollingworth, 1942; Terman, 1925) nor, I suspect, to the interested layperson. It is only fairly recently that the concept of the gifted child as future intellectual has become suspect in this field. To some extent, no doubt, this is due to the influence of the national-resources approach to the education of the gifted and a misreading of the research literature that shows low correlations between IQ and job performance. I also suspect that our national distrust of and antipathy toward intellectualism (see Hofstadter's classic *Anti-intellectualism in American Life*, 1963) play a role, however small. There are enough disparaging references to "lesson learners" and "test takers" in the recent literature dealing with the education of the gifted, references of the sort that remind one of the playground taunts of "teacher's pet" and "bookworm" directed at able students, to convince me that as a field we are not free of this unfortunate tendency. For whatever reason, except for those rare instances when we attempt to bring the arts into the classroom, I feel that we stray too far from what we ought to be about when we attempt to expand our conceptions of giftedness in the schools beyond the realm of the intellectual and the academic. When we do this, we lose sight of the true purpose of formal education.

Educational Need

The final part of my definition refers to special needs that are not being met by the common-core curriculum. As I state above, the concept of educational need is central to the special-educational approach to the education of the gifted. We can justify the expense and bother of special programs only if there is a demonstrable need for them, and we can justify the placement of a given child in such a program only if this placement is made in response to his or her educational needs. The issue of the need for special programs for the gifted is one that I do not wish to address in detail here—this book is intended to serve as a guide for educators who have already decided to implement such programs.

The issue of an *individual* student's educational need, however, is basic to the question of definition. I want to be careful to distinguish the notion of need from that of reward, for I suspect that these are confused by many people. For example, a teacher may resent the placement of a student in the program for the gifted because he or she is doing less-than-adequate work in the regular classroom. Why, the teacher may ask, is this uncooperative, seemingly unmotivated child in the program while students who are more task-committed, better mannered, and clearly "superior students" are left out?

In cases like this, there is often a confusion between need and reward in the teacher's mind. The "better" students may seem more deserving of a special program, but they may not *need* one. They may be working up to the level of their potential in the regular classroom, and the core curriculum may be meeting their educational needs. The other child, who seems to be the far-from-ideal student, may be foundering in the regular classroom because the work assigned there is too easy, too slowly paced, and not responsive to his or her need to grow intellectually. From the point of view of special education, it is this child who needs the special program. Whether or not he or she appears to be deserving of the program is irrelevant.

From the special-educational point of view, there is only one justification for making a significant change in a child's educational life: an educational need of sufficient magnitude to make the change necessary for the child's curriculum to be appropriate. If such a need does not exist, if the only reason for placing a child in the program for the gifted is that he or she "deserves" the placement, it is better not to make the change. In other words, "If it ain't broke, don't fix it."

CONCLUSION

The definition I proposed may not find favor with all educators, especially those who believe that gifted children should be defined in terms of their probability of becoming eminent adults. It is, however, consistent with and exemplary of the special-educational approach to educating the gifted delineated above. It makes the statement that we should define giftedness for educational purposes as the need for curricular modification created by highly exceptional academic or intellectual aptitude in relation to that possessed by other children in a given school or school district.

The definition is broad enough to allow one to incorporate aspects of other, more psychological, definitions, such as Tannenbaum's (1983) or Sternberg's (1984), although these are clearly geared toward the identification of future genius. However, it is less compatible with definitions such as Renzulli's (1978) for reasons stated above. This definition also allows for considerable latitude with respect to the issues of talent and gifts as raised by Gagne (1985) and elaborated above.

It could be argued that his definition is too broad, and that while it is specific with respect to policy it is vague with respect to the actual characteristics of gifted children, leaving too much still unclear. What abilities, one might ask, really make a child gifted? Is there a profile of specific intellectual factors or abilities that can help one recognize giftedness? Which areas of potential or ability should be the focus of concern in a given school district? How should the school administrator portrayed at the beginning of this chapter, who by now must be even more confused, write a definition that will work in his district? These and other questions must be answered before this definition can be used as a guide for planning and implementing a program for the gifted. How, then, are the specifics of a definition to be filled in? How does one go about writing a definition that can be integrated into a program that meets the needs of students in a given school district?

The following chapters will address these and other questions relating to programs for the gifted in real settings. The issue of definition will be treated in the context of a system approach to planning and implementing programs. Other components of programs for the gifted will be placed in this framework as well, and most of them will receive extended treatment in subsequent chapters. In every case, however, the question of definition will loom large, for it is the definition that specifies which students will be in the program. And it is for these students that the programs ought to exist.

CHAPTER 3

A System Approach to Planning Programs for the Gifted

"Let the jury consider the verdict," the King said, for about
the twentieth time that day.

"No, no!" said the Queen. "Sentence first—verdict
afterwards."

"Stuff and nonsense!" said Alice loudly. "The idea of
having the sentence first!"

Carroll, Alice's Adventures in Wonderland

A foolish consistency is the hobgoblin of little minds.
Emerson, "Self-Reliance"

The speaker, a teacher, was the chairwoman of the District-Wide Committee for the Education of the Gifted in a prosperous and progressive suburban school district. Her committee had recently engaged the services of consultants from a nearby school of education; this was the first meeting between the consultants and the committee members. The chairwoman began by relating the unhappy history of the committee's efforts to plan and implement a program for the gifted in this district.

"I honestly don't know how or where we went wrong," she said. "We did everything by the book. We read every text and every journal we could get our hands on so we would know what was going on in the field today. We attended every conference and workshop we could. We talked with the experts and with teachers from programs in other districts. We visited schools across the state and compared notes, discussing what we liked and what we didn't like. We did all our homework, every bit. We really made an effort to gather the latest information and to be familiar with the best thinking before we even thought about actually planning a program. We didn't take a step until we researched this thing inside and out.

"After all this research, we put together a plan that we thought, and still think, was the best possible one for us. We adopted the strongest features of the models that seemed to make sense for our district. We did everything the

41

books and the experts said we should do. We had, in all honesty, what we thought was a state-of-the-art program plan. We were rather proud of ourselves.

"Anyway," she continued, "the board voted to accept the plan last May, and we started to work on actual implementation near the end of the school year. The district hired a teacher, and we began identifying kids late in the summer. Everything looked great for the fall, when the program was supposed to begin.

"But over the summer, things began to happen. You won't believe this, but what really killed us was a group of parents who belong to a local beach club. These people all had children they thought should be in the program, and in some cases they were actually right. But without even knowing what the program was going to be like, they started worrying that their kids wouldn't be chosen or that the program wouldn't be what they wanted. Since they didn't have any real information about the program, they spread rumors. This is a small town, and soon it seemed that everybody was talking about the gifted program and what it was going to be like. You wouldn't believe what some people thought we were going to do with these kids.

"By the time the school year began again in September, the program was a major issue, and it hadn't even gotten off the ground. We didn't have a chance. We tried to explain to parents and our colleagues what we were trying to do and how we were trying to do it, but everyone thought he knew what was 'really' going on. Some parents wouldn't let their children join the program, and others complained to the superintendent and board members when their kids weren't identified.

"But the most discouraging thing was that, once the program began, some teachers put terrible pressure on kids who were in it. This was a resource-room program, and the kids had to be pulled out of their regular classes. Some teachers didn't like that at all. This really threw us for a loop. Our research had convinced us that this was the best approach and that gifted students could easily make up the work they missed. But a lot of teachers were fed up with having kids pulled out for this program and that program, and they just rebelled. They made it very hard for a lot of kids to go to the resource room when their time came. And this just made the parents angrier.

"Things quickly went from bad to worse. The parents circulated a petition saying that they had lost faith in the program and that the school board should do something about it. They did. They canceled the program and told us to start again. That's when we called you.

"Maybe you can figure it out; we sure can't. I still think we did everything right, but it blew up in our faces. I honestly don't know what we could have done differently."

This scenario was reconstructed from a consultancy undertaken by the Center for the Study and Education of the Gifted at Teachers College, Columbia University. It illustrates graphically the most difficult task facing educators charged with the responsibility of planning a program for gifted students: the development of an effective plan for a program that will best serve the needs of gifted students and is also acceptable to the various groups that will be affected by it.

Educators undertaking the task of program planning are faced with what must appear to be a bewildering variety of choices. There are theories and models of nearly every conceivable type. There are slickly packaged plans for complete programs as well as piecemeal approaches to developing such specific program components as identification procedures or curricular provisions. There are "revolving doors," "talent totem poles," and "complete creativity programs." The range is staggering.

Faced with this array of options, few know where to begin. Some hire consultants and defer to their judgment. Others fasten onto a particular approach, convinced by what they have read or have heard at a conference that this approach is the correct response to the needs of gifted students in their school or their district. The most ambitious among them, like the members of the committee described above, take the time to do some research and to look carefully at the problem before leaping to a solution. In some instances, these efforts are successful. In others, as we have seen, even the most assiduous efforts come to nought.

In this chapter, I will examine the complex issue of planning programs for the gifted, the central topic of this book. I will turn first to the question of what constitutes a program for the gifted. This will be followed by a comparison of two general approaches to program planning. One of these, the system approach, will be advocated as the more logical and effective one for educators to follow. We will then examine this model in some detail, focusing on its applicability in a range of situations. This examination will include an overview of the components of a program for the gifted and a discussion of the decisions that must be made in dealing with each component. Particular attention will be paid to the subject of the previous chapter— defining the target population—since that issue was left with a rather general resolution and the questions it raises illustrate nicely the utility of the system approach.

PROGRAMS VERSUS PROVISIONS

Tannenbaum (1983) draws a useful distinction between *provisions* for the gifted and *programs* for the gifted. Since the subject of this chapter is the planning of *programs*, his distinction has relevance to our discussion here.

According to Tannenbaum, provisions are "fragmentary, . . . ad hoc offering[s], relatively brief in duration, . . . and supplemental to the [district's] major offerings, not integral with them" (p. 515). A situation typical of those that give rise to provisions for the gifted is one in which a teacher, realizing that there is a gifted student or two in need of curricular modifications in his or her class, decides to provide special activities in an attempt to meet the students' special needs. Usually, the content of the special activities reflects the teacher's particular interests and skills; sometimes it is developed in response to student interests. In any case, the provisions represent a unilateral response on the part of the teacher to demonstrated educational needs of gifted students that are not being addressed by the school or school district.

There is nothing at all wrong with provisions for the gifted. These special opportunities may be among the most valuable offered to students in their school careers. However, provisions of this sort have one major drawback: they are not programmatic. Since they have been implemented by a single teacher with the vision and energy to go beyond the regular curriculum, there is no guarantee that all gifted students in the system will be exposed to them. Moreover, there is no commitment on the part of the school or school district to maintain the provisions. If the teacher receives a new assignment, retires, or is "excessed," the provisions are likely to disappear.

Most critical of all, provisions are not really curricular in the true sense. They do not represent a mandated, systemwide modification of the curriculum that is designed to meet the special needs of all of the district's gifted students. Instead, they stand alone as an adjunct to the core curriculum and often bear very little relationship to it. No matter how good the provisions are or how many there might be, there is still no curricular plan for the special education of gifted learners in a school or school district unless there is a true program, not merely provisions.

What, then, is a *program* for the gifted? In many respects, programs are everything provisions are not. Whereas provisions are often temporary expedients, programs are designed to be permanent features of school districts' educational offerings. Whereas provisions are fragmentary, programs have well-articulated sequences of goals, skills, and content. Whereas provisions are extracurricular, programs consist of activities that constitute a prescribed part of the course of study of identified gifted students. Whereas provisions are optional, programs are required for all gifted students who move through the system.

Programs, in other words, are part and parcel of the curricular offerings of a school or school system. Unlike provisions, they are not add-ons, options, or frills. They represent an acknowledgment by a school or school district that there are gifted students in the system, that these students have special educational needs, and that educators have an obligation to address these needs within the curriculum.

This, of course, is a list of the specifications of an ideal program. Even if these specifications are met, there is no assurance that the program will be a good one (and it is worth repeating that provisions can be of very high educational quality). However, it is important, given the lack of standards in this field, that some sensible guidelines be followed in determining what is and what is not a program. Tannenbaum's guidelines fit that requirement nicely.

Given some standards for which to aim, one needs a method of planning a program that will be, in the sense defined by Tannenbaum, truly programmatic. Let us now discuss two approaches to this problem.

APPROACHES TO PLANNING PROGRAMS FOR THE GIFTED

The Packaged-Program Approach

Given the confusing array of options available to program planners, it may seem sensible to school personnel either to adopt a packaged approach or to try to replicate locally a program that is working well in another setting. There are a number of reasons why these may be attractive alternatives for the perplexed educator, and together they appear to make a compelling argument.

The allure of a packaged program is twofold. First, such a package has been put together by a professional, an expert who ought to know his or her business. It often seems to make sense, given the daunting nature of the task, to defer to the judgment and experience of an authority on the education of the gifted. The second attractive feature of this approach is its comprehensiveness. A packaged program is often the educational equivalent of the Swiss Army knife; it includes everything deemed necessary by its developer to institute a program for the gifted. It is not unusual for such a package to include a definition of the target population, identification procedures, a curricular framework, an evaluation plan, forms to be filled out, and arguments to be used in response to those who have misgivings about the particular approach.

Similarly, one can make a persuasive case for replicating a model that has been successful elsewhere. One could argue that by adopting a program plan developed by another school system, one avoids the risk of repeating the mistakes of others and the wasted effort of reinventing the wheel. After all, nothing succeeds like success. Why not borrow the successful result of another's efforts and save both time and money in the process?

In light of the various economies promised by these methods, there would seem to be much to recommend buying or borrowing a program. This is, in part, what was done by the school district planning committee, the tale of whose plight opened this chapter. It seemed only sensible for this group to learn what the experts advocated and to try to isolate and then adopt the best features of successful programs operating in other districts. The fact that the program born of all these efforts came to grief, though, illustrates the unreliability of this approach.

Why do I believe that this seemingly sensible strategy is fraught with danger? The answer lies in the rather commonplace fact that all schools and school districts are different in important ways. This being the case, there is no guarantee that a packaged approach, no matter how persuasively it is sold, is right for all of them. The demographic characteristics, levels of pupil achievement, provisions within the core curriculum, personnel, tax bases, local resources, systems of governance, and many other features of school systems vary greatly from locality to locality. No single model can hope to meet the needs of school districts that differ along so many lines.

By the same token, this variability among school districts makes it difficult to replicate in one system a program that is successful in another. Just as some plants will grow only in certain soils, some programs will flourish only in certain localities. A successful program works because it effectively addresses the needs of gifted students in a specific school or school district, and these needs generally vary from school to school, district to district. When a replication is attempted, the surface features of a successful response to a particular problem are copied, but the replication may be the right answer to the wrong problem.

The case history related at the beginning of this chapter is an example of what can go wrong with this approach. The committee in that district did everything by the book, but the book did not contain a chapter dealing with the rumor mill at the local beach club; nor did the book take into account the past experiences of the district with programs for the gifted or the idiosyncratic nature of the community. Although it is true that the district in question was an unusual one, it is also true that, in one way or another, all districts are unique. Each has its own set of characteristics and needs that must be taken into account when planning a program for the gifted.

Does this mean that a packaged program can never work or that there is no reason for a planning committee to familiarize itself with the literature and with what other districts are doing? Obviously it does not. It does mean, however, that in planning a program for the gifted one must take into account the unique needs of the school or school district in which the program will be implemented before the plan is developed. An assessment of these needs must be an integral component of the development.

I am arguing here for a diagnostic–prescriptive approach to program planning, one in which educators look before they leap. To borrow an analogy from the medical profession, packaged programs are somewhat like patent medicines that promise to cure "anything that ails you." Such nostrums may, indeed, soothe indigestion or help one sleep, but they are never the panaceas their proponents make them out to be. To continue with this analogy, replicating the program of another school district is like taking medicine prescribed for another person whose symptoms appear to be similar to one's own. Again, the medicine may have the desired effect; however, the result could also be far from what was desired and could even be quite harmful. The best course is to have one's condition diagnosed by a competent practitioner who can prescribe the medicine or regimen that is appropriate for the specific malady and system. The same holds true in planning programs for the gifted in the schools. It makes sense to examine carefully the needs of the local school or school district before prescribing a program. This is the essence of the system approach that we will now examine.

The System Approach

By the phrase "system approach to planning programs for the gifted," I am referring to an approach that conceives of a program as a deliberate response to the assessed needs of a school or school district. This approach has as its syntax a diagnostic phase (needs assessment), followed by a prescriptive phase (program development and implementation), which is in turn followed by an evaluation phase (program evaluation).

What I am here calling the system approach, which is outlined below and elaborated in the chapters to follow, may not meet the rigorous standards of a serious student of system theory, but I think the designation is valid nonetheless. It is valid because the approach envisions the program being planned as an integrated system subserving a larger system (the school or school district), not as a portmanteau accretion of haphazard parts that may (or may not) complement the larger system. Let me discuss these two elements, the relationship between the smaller system and the larger system and the program as an integrated system.

System and subsystem. Looking at a program for the gifted as a system that serves the needs of the school or school district is a way of trying to avoid the pitfalls I feel are inherent in buying or borrowing a program. This goes back to the diagnostic–prescriptive model cited above. A program for the gifted is instituted for a reason. In some cases the reason is a political one, but in most cases there are more valid educational rationales. These vary, but in general a school or school district will undertake the planning of a program of this type because there is a perceived deficiency in the way it serves a significant number of its students, that is, those it labels gifted. Thus, the program for the gifted is, in a sense, remedial for the system, since it addresses needs within the system.

This can be summed up in the phrase "meeting the needs of our gifted students," but this can mean different things in different schools and school districts. In one district, for example, it may mean offering extremely capable students the opportunity for acceleration in their areas of specific interest and competence. In another district, it may mean instituting a series of regular seminars to challenge and motivate bright underachieving students and to encourage them to stay in school.

In any case, the new subsystem (the program for the gifted) must serve the greater educational purposes of the larger system (the school or school district) by addressing educational needs that the larger system is not meeting. Moreover, as Kaplan (1974) states, "a program for the gifted and talented should reinforce and be compatible with other programs within the same institution" (p. 7). For this to be the case, the needs of the students and the range of existing services must be known, and this requires a thorough diagnosis of local educational conditions. Without this necessary step, educators who create programs for the gifted have no way of knowing whether they are responding to their responsibility to their students or merely to the current vogue for programs for the gifted. This is why it is important first to determine what is needed and then to plan a program. Otherwise, one is in the position of rushing to a solution and hoping it is the right one for whatever the problem might be.

Although there is no shortage of speakers and writers who claim to have *the* single program model that is right for "the gifted child," their claims must be evaluated in light of common sense. Variety is not merely a luxury in our society; it is in many cases a necessity. For example, residents of Minnesota and residents of Florida dress differently in February, and not only for reasons of fashion. Mrs. Jones drives a pickup truck while Mr. Smith drives a station wagon, and there are reasons for this that go beyond what each can afford. Mr. Brown pours salt on his food; Mrs. White avoids sodium in any form because of her hypertension. These everyday examples illustrate the point that the varying needs of different people dictate a multitude of approaches to nearly every feature of modern life. Why should programs of the gifted be excluded from this general law?

In fact, they should not be. There is no single approach that will serve the needs of every school or school district, no matter how attractively packaged and aggressively marketed that approach may be. If a program is to meet the needs of a particular school, it must be designed with those needs in mind. This requires a thorough knowledge of the particularities of that school, something that cannot be found in a packaged program. In terms of the system model, the subsystem (the program for the gifted) can enhance the effectiveness of the larger system (the school or school district) only if it articulates well with the larger system and fills a recognized gap in it.

The program as a system. With respect to the program for the gifted being thought of as a system (or as a subsystem within the larger educational system) in and of itself, one must hearken back to Tannenbaum's (1983) definition of a program. The reader will recall that a program, as distinct from a provision, is an integrated, permanent curricular response to the needs of gifted students that articulates with the basic core curriculum. In order to meet these requirements, the program planner must carefully consider the various elements of the proposed program in order to insure that they will work together as a unit and that this system will be integrated into the larger one. This is more easily accomplished if the program is conceived of in advance as its own system.

Figure 3.1 contains a flowchart depicting the components of a program for the gifted. Each component is viewed here as an element of a system consisting of the various components and their interrelationships. Each element is conditioned and shaped by other elements in important and characteristic ways. For example, the component labeled "Identification Procedures" is developed in response to the characteristics set forth in the component labeled "Definition of Target Population."

Figure 3.1 suggests graphically that the program be conceived of as a well-integrated system rather than as a piecemeal agglomeration of random parts. The integrity of the system is important. Each component should play a purposeful role in meeting the overall goals of the program; each one should be a "team player." The choice of a particular option for any given program component (e.g., the choice of a self-contained program over a pull-out program or provisions within the regular classroom with respect to program format) should be dictated by considerations relating to the purposes of the program and the relationships between and among the other components.

This means that program planning must be done as systematically as possible, with full consideration of the entire program. Only thus can there be a high probability that a program, rather than a patchwork series of provisions, will emerge from the planning process. Figure 3.1 can be used as a reminder that program planners must focus on the entire program in advance and not merely try to deal with things as they come.

By conceiving of a program for the gifted as a unified system whose parts work together toward a common goal, one increases the chance that the program will be effective. This is the objective of the whole enterprise: to design a program that will successfully address the issues that created a need for it

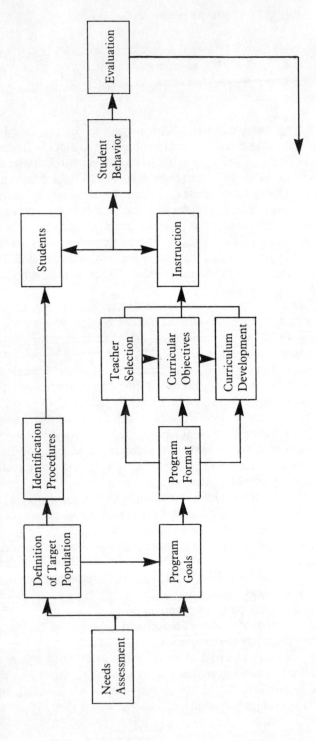

Figure 3.1: Flowchart representing the program–planning process.

in the first place. The best way to do so is to determine what those needs are (needs assessment), to determine how the new program can address those needs in the school or school district (relationship of the subsystem to the larger system), and to design a program that is a unified realization of the required response to the system's deficiencies (a systematic program).

A COMPONENT-BY-COMPONENT OVERVIEW OF THE SYSTEM

In an effort to flesh out the method of program planning I am advocating, let us look at the various components of a program for the gifted as set forth in Figure 3.1. These discussions will be general ones; more detailed examinations of, and recommendations for implementing, program components will be found in the appropriate chapters of this book. The intention here is to look at the programmatic function of each component within the program system. The exception will be the component labeled "Definition of Target Population." This was the topic of Chapter 2, where it was discussed at some length. The discussion of that component in this chapter will complete some unfinished business from the previous one.

Needs Assessment

The subject of the following chapter, the needs assessment, is what makes the system approach systematic. This is the diagnostic aspect of the diagnostic–prescriptive model advocated in this chapter. An effective needs assessment enables educators to gather information about the particular school or school district in question, thus allowing them to develop a program that is tailored to the needs of that setting.

A competent needs assessment removes much of the risk from program planning. It reveals what is optimal and, equally important, what is workable in a given school or school district. It takes program planning out of the realms of chance and commerce and returns it to the realm of education where it belongs.

Chapter 4 will deal with the mechanics of conducting a needs assessment, on both a formal and an informal basis. The issue of using the data gathered through needs assessment in the process of program planning will also be addressed.

Definition of the Target Population

The single most important result of a needs assessment is a clear definition of the proposed program's target population. This definition serves as the foundation of the program; every other component should be designed to serve the group designated by the definition. There can be no persuasive rationale for the choice of a program component other than the belief that it works best with the other program components to meet the needs of the target population.

In the previous chapter, I discussed at length the problem of defining giftedness and especially the elusive being known as the gifted child. After examining some definitions proposed by various writers, I proposed a special-educational definition that read as follows: For the purposes of education, gifted children are those students in a given school or school district who are exceptional by virtue of markedly greater-than-average potential or ability in some area of human activity generally considered to be the province of the educational system and whose exceptionality engenders special-educational needs that are not being met adequately by the regular core curriculum. The problem posed by this definition for program planners is one of generality; it is so broad as to offer insufficient practical guidance in such matters as identifying students for actual programs. Clearly, more specificity is needed in order to fashion a definition that can be made operational.

This is where the needs assessment enters the picture. The above formulation places some limitations on the emerging definition. It specifies a local frame of reference, a well-above-average level of potential or ability, a focus on intellectual and academic traits, and, most crucial here, the centrality of the concept of educational need. The needs assessment can supply the data required to make the definition sufficiently specific for use in a given locality in the following manner.

First, a survey of the system's needs can identify the existence in that system of appreciable numbers of students with potential or ability in areas delineated by various definitions and descriptions of the gifted. In other words, one goal of a needs assessment is to identify groups of students who are arguably gifted under the terms of the standard definitions. These students should also meet the requirements of the special-educational definition proposed above. This is the starting point: a list of areas of giftedness and talent represented by significant numbers of students in a given school or school district.

Second, the needs assessment can also examine current offerings within the common-core curriculum and, perhaps, provisions available through extracurricular and out-of-school programs. The goal here is to determine which, if any, of the groups listed above are currently having their needs met by available offerings. For example, a needs assessment may reveal the existence of a significant group of students academically gifted in the area of science, a specific academic aptitude according to the USOE definition (Marland, 1972). The same needs assessment may also reveal, however, a strong hands-on science program in the elementary grades; a variety of course options, including honors and advanced-placement courses, on the secondary level; various science clubs that meet after school; and a science enrichment program for school-age children on weekends at a local college.

The needs assessment thus reveals a group of students who "deserve" to be called gifted children. However, it also reveals that this group's profile of abilities has not engendered any unaddressed educational needs. The current system is responding quite well to their requirement for advanced study in this area. It does not make any sense, therefore, to create a program for them. Although they have the ability, they do not have the need.

Instead, the definition of the target population for the proposed program should describe those students who have both the ability or the potential and the educational need for a special program. One should look for groups of students identified in the first step of the needs assessment who are "falling through the cracks" of the curriculum. This is the population for whom a program should be planned.

This is a rather pragmatic, empirical approach to defining giftedness in a school or school district, but it is no more atheoretical than any other of which I am aware. Keep in mind that of the multitude of definitions of giftedness currently being bruited by various psychologists and educators, none has received the unanimous blessing of the field at large. Thus, practitioners must choose from among them. A basis is needed for choosing a definition—which I earlier identified as a policy decision—and pragmatism based on need provides a sound basis.

The essence of the pragmatic approach is the greatest good for the greatest number; that is the goal of this method. By defining the target population in this manner, one is taking steps to address as many unmet needs created by exceptional potential or ability as possible. The object is to strengthen the system by enhancing its ability to respond to student needs. The desirability of that object is difficult to deny.

Not only is such an approach conducive to greater effectiveness as a result of its diagnostic character, but it also minimizes concerns about elitism in that students are not singled out for any reason other than their educational need. There is no question of reward or favor; students are not designated for special services unless there is evidence that they will suffer educationally without those services. This is contrary to much current practice, in which, unfortunately, children are often placed in programs for the gifted merely as a reward for previous educational success or high test scores, or for demonstrating pleasant traits or good work habits.

To summarize, defining the target population within the system approach is a process of determining which groups of students, among those who could plausibly be designated as gifted according to the special-educational definition, have the greatest educational needs that are not being met by the core curriculum or other provisions. This requires a needs assessment of some kind if the delivery of services to the students whose need is the most acute is to take place.

Identification Procedures

Of all the components of a program for the gifted, the identification of gifted students arouses the most controversy and creates the greatest problems for local educators. It is here that students are either chosen or passed over for placement in the program, and this is a sensitive matter. It is made even more sensitive if it is approached as an issue of labeling *the* gifted, instead of one of placing some gifted students who have unanswered needs in programs designed to address those needs.

In terms of the system model as represented in Figure 3.1, the arrow extending from the "Definition of the Target Population" box to the "Identification Procedures" box is an important one. It is meant to suggest that a functional relationship obtains between these two components. The identification procedures must work on behalf of the definition if control of the system is to be maintained. Unless the identification plan is designed to be the best possible method for locating exactly those students described by the definition, the definition becomes superfluous. If there is a discrepancy between these components—if the definition specifies one group and the identification procedures select another group—the written definition is supplanted by the operational one, the identification scheme. This means that the school policy inherent in the definition has been superseded, probably without good reason, by a collection of tests and other devices. When this happens, control of the most central aspect of the program, the specification of the students who need services, has been lost or abdicated.

I will examine in detail a number of issues and concerns related to identification in Chapter 5. Among the topics of that chapter will be screening and placement, the use of matrices, effectiveness and efficiency of screening methods, and the validity of various tests and referrals.

The goal of identification is, of course, to constitute a class or classes of gifted students as represented by the box labeled "Students" in Figure 3.1. These students, by definition (my definition, at least), require a program. The lower portion of the figure contains boxes representing components of that program.

Program Goals

The formulation of a definition of the target population establishes an implicit rationale for the nascent special program for the gifted. The fact that there are within the school district students with special needs, along with the district's knowledge of this fact, creates the need for the program. The program ought to be viewed, then, as an opportunity for a rational educational response to the district's awareness of the needs of a group of exceptional students. Program goals set forth the desired results of this response.

Therefore, the goals of the program should be written as clear statements of what the district will have the program do to respond to the needs of the target population. Program goals should be stated in terms of outcomes; they are the desired consequences of the program under development. These goals have functions at both temporal ends of the planning and implementation sequence. In planning, they serve to guide educators in their efforts to provide a programmatic response to the needs of the targeted population. Then, once the program is implemented, the program goals serve as a basis for evaluation; the program can be deemed successful to the extent that it has attained the program goals. I will return to this in Chapter 9.

The program goals are, in one sense, a series of answers to a general but important question about the entire planning enterprise. Once a population is defined, program planners should ask themselves, "Given what we know about the needs of the defined population, what changes in the system and what educational outcomes would we like to bring about by instituting a program for the gifted?" The answers generated by this question should be the basis of the program goals.

Program goals can refer both to the school system and to the students who will be served by the program. In examining the goals of programs for the gifted, one often reads statements about what the school or school district will do (e.g., "To provide opportunities for advanced interdisciplinary inquiry") and statements about the benefits to be derived by the students (e.g., "To develop the students' independent research skills"). I will make a point of distinguishing between the former and the latter types of goals in Chapter 9. In fact, I will argue that the former are enabling or instrumental goals, that is, means to the desired program ends, whereas the latter are true program goals. Now, during the process of planning a program for the gifted, means must obviously be considered, so I will be less scrupulous here. However, it is never too soon to focus one's thinking on the ultimate goals of the program, the benefits that should accrue to its students, and it makes sense to maintain the distinction between these crucial goals and those activities that are designed to accomplish them.

The program goals can, and probably should, be printed prominently in the preface to a written program plan, which can be made available to parents, teachers, and other interested parties. This will tell the reader why the school or school district has created the program and what it is designed to accomplish. The importance of communication in programs for the gifted can hardly be overstated, and communication of the program's major goals is central to that effort. I will return to the issue of communication at the end of this chapter, and I will discuss the tendency to overstate these published goals in Chapter 9.

To summarize, the program goals should consist of clear and unambiguous statements of the desired outcomes of the program, and these outcomes should reflect the needs of the students described in the definition of the target population. Program goals serve both as a guide for planning and as a basis for evaluation of the program. The goals can be stated in terms of the effects on the system (describing, for the most part, modifications of or additions to the services available) and, more important, in terms of the effects on the students (describing the knowledge, skills, and products gained or produced by the students), although only the latter are true program goals. Finally, these goals should be prominently featured in any written or oral communication about the program.

Program Format

In Chapter 6, I will look at various options relating to program format and discuss the merits and demerits of each option. Here, I will try to fit this component into the overall program system under discussion.

By *program format*, I am referring to the form that the delivery of special services to the gifted will take within the school system. Specifically, this involves decisions about how students will be grouped for instruction, where the instruction will take place, how often special instruction will be offered, and a range of administrative considerations of varying degrees of importance and annoyance.

The most central consideration found under the heading of program format is that of the grouping of students. How homogeneously should students be grouped? Should they be in self-contained classes, or should they receive special instruction on a part-time basis in a resource room or "pull-out" class? Should they be removed from the regular classroom at all? Other considerations are subordinate to this one. Questions regarding the location and duration of special instruction, for example, can only be made after it has been determined how the students will be grouped.

The discussion of the alternatives for grouping in Chapter 6 will be organized so that the options are on a continuum ranging from completely homogeneous and segregated programs at the one pole to completely heterogeneous and integrated programs at the other. Many readers will regard one of the poles of this continuum, a priori, as the more desirable one. For example, some educators view anything other than homogeneous grouping for the gifted as a compromise in educational quality; others see such grouping as something strictly to be avoided.

However one feels about this issue in the abstract, one thing should be kept in mind when we come to Chapter 6, especially the discussion of the pluses and minuses associated with each option. That is the central theme of the present chapter and, indeed, of this book: While it may be interesting and even enlightening to discuss the pros and cons of various program alternatives in general, these issues take on new meaning within the context of a developing or existing program. Thus, whether one initially favors special schools for the gifted, complete integration into the heterogeneous mainstream, or something in between should make little difference in planning an actual program. What should matter is resolving the issue of which format will best serve the needs of the defined special population within the school system in which the program will be operating. In other words, a format should be chosen only on the basis of whether or not it will work for the target population, given the goals of the program.

Certainly, questions of an instructional nature loom large here. If, to take one example, the target population is, or includes, underachieving adolescents with high general intellectual ability, one must ask whether it is wise or is counterproductive to take such students out of the regular heterogeneous classroom. However, questions that are less lofty but equally important to the success of the program, must also be addressed. For instance, program planners contemplating a program that requires that students be removed from their regular classrooms for significant periods of time should ask how classroom teachers will react to this arrangement. This was neglected in the district whose experiences with its program for the gifted were described at the beginning of this chapter, and the results were predictably unfortunate.

The choice of a program format involves a number of decisions, some of obvious import, some seemingly trivial. But each of these will have an effect upon certain individuals within the system, and they will not be minor from their point of view. Bitter battles have been fought and the instructional quality of special programs has been significantly affected by matters relating to space allocation, busing, pulling children out of classrooms, lunch provisions, and so forth. All these matters can be included in the untidy category of program format, and they must all be resolved if they are not to return to haunt one later.

Staff Selection

It hardly needs to be stated that the choice of a staff, especially classroom teachers, is crucial to the success or failure of a program for the gifted. The finest program plan in existence will do little to compensate for ineffective instructional personnel, and inspired teachers can compensate considerably for inadequacies in the planning and implementation of a program. Chapter 7 will deal with the problems and issues of putting together a staff of educators for a program for the gifted.

A basic problem, however, confronts us here: our continued failure as a field to isolate the qualities of an effective teacher of the gifted. We can, of course, specify some desirable characteristics that collectively constitute the sine qua non of good teaching with gifted learners; but human beings perversely refuse to be pigeonholed, and excellent teachers of the gifted persist in manifesting significant differences with respect to a variety of characteristics. Thus, while some space in Chapter 7 will be devoted to a discussion of teacher behaviors that facilitate success with the gifted, no definitive profile of the ideal teacher of the gifted will emerge. It may be some consolation to know that our colleagues in other branches of education face similar problems. The standardization of the human race fortunately still has quite a way to go.

The chapter will also include a discussion of supervisory staff, since all the professional work involved in the operation of a program for the gifted does not take place in the classroom. The program must fit into the system's overall organizational framework, and how it does so has a decided effect on its effectiveness.

As before, it will be important to see this component within the framework of the total program, and once again the characteristics of the target population take center stage. For example, a program designed to meet the special needs of secondary students gifted with the ability to carry on independent research in the sciences will require an instructional staff with considerable knowledge of the various scientific disciplines and the scientific method. Moreover, the other components of the program, such as program format, affect this decision. If students are transported to a central location for enrichment activities, a teacher with a regular class load is a poor choice as teacher of the special class.

In fact, all of the components begin to affect each other at this point. The flowchart in Figure 3.1 and our sequential examination of the various program components should not be taken to imply that one should march steadfastly through the program-planning process, one component at a time, in an invariable sequence. The needs assessment and the definition of the target population are logical and imperative first steps, and the formulation of program goals should follow shortly. Thereafter, however, there is no inflexible order that one must follow in the course of program planning. For example, there is no need to have identification procedures completely worked out before attending to questions of program format. Although some components have a natural sequence (for example, teacher selection should precede curriculum development if teachers are to play a role in curriculum development, as they should), the rest is catch-as-catch-can as far as order is concerned.

Curricular Objectives and Curriculum Development

Chapter 8 will focus on an issue that could be, and has been (see, for example, Maker, 1982a), the topic of a number of books: the proper curriculum for a program for the gifted. This discussion will be limited by the framework of this book. Curriculum will be treated in the general sense as it fits into the program-planning process. We will happily sidestep issues relating to specific models and instructional methods unless they bear upon the topic at hand. Instead, we will explore the role the curriculum should play in a program for the gifted and how this relates specifically to the systematic planning of a program as advocated here.

Two boxes in the flowchart of Figure 3.1 refer to the issue of curriculum. The one labeled "Curricular Objectives" refers to a more specific group of goals than those included under the heading of "Program Goals." The former are the specific objectives, usually set by the instructional staff, that outline the instructional activities and desired educational outcomes for a given year. The curricular objectives are subordinate to the program goals and represent ways of moving toward the accomplishment of the larger goals. They are the specific strategies for working toward the enduring systemwide goals delineated in the program goals.

For example, a program goal might read as follows: "To encourage the development and expression of creativity on the part of students in the program for the gifted." This establishes one of the reasons for the existence of the program and reflects a need revealed in the needs assessment. As part of their ongoing efforts toward the achievement of this program objective, the instructional staff, probably with some assistance from the administrative staff, will decide on one or more instructional objectives for the coming year. One of these might read: "Students will design and, if possible, produce one original invention as part of our 'Inventions' unit."

The program goals represent policy. They indicate what the program is designed to do and reflect why the program must exist in the first place. Instructional objectives represent means of effecting established policy over the short term. They indicate what will be done for or by students in an attempt to achieve the larger program goals. Program goals are more or less permanent. Instructional objectives may change from year to year, but they will always subserve the larger program goals.

The second box on the flowchart that refers to curriculum is labeled "Curriculum Development." The key word here is *development*, implying that an effective curriculum for gifted learners in a specific setting is developed locally. Depending on how rigorously one defines the term *curriculum*, one could argue that a curriculum for the gifted cannot be bought or adopted, only developed. In many programs for the gifted, especially those that present enrichment activities supplemental to the regular curriculum, purchased materials substitute for a curriculum. Unfortunately, given the low quality of most commercial materials for the gifted, the result is difficult to defend. Even if so many of these commercial materials were not educationally unsound, the manner in which they are often used, in a hodgepodge with no scope or sequence, would preclude the use of the designation *curriculum*. The result has been a black eye for the field of the education of the gifted and a collective reputation as purveyors of trivia and "fun and games."

The various "models" and "paradigms" developed by educators that have gained currency in the field (for an overview see Maker, 1982b, and Renzulli, 1986b) are, in many cases, also difficult to defend as curricula. Some, like the Enrichment Triad (Renzulli, 1977), are little more than management plans for various curricular options, such as independent study. They do not address the basic but difficult curricular issues of content, process, and articulation with the core curriculum. Others, like the SOI materials developed by Meeker (as described by Maker, 1982b), are trivial in the extreme and require the use of instructional time in an attempt to develop atomized cognitive abilities whose importance—and even existence (e.g., Carroll, 1968; Horn & Knapp, 1973)—has been questioned.

Even if the program for the gifted is a self-contained one in which the curriculum is largely built upon the prescribed core curriculum, the purchasing of textbook series does not answer the curriculum question. At the very least, one needs to develop a curricular framework into which the texts must fit. There must be some conception of how gifted students will approach the core material in a manner that differs from that of other students. Moreover, it is necessary to go beyond the use of basic texts where gifted students are involved. To deal with content at the level appropriate for the gifted, watered-down text material must be supplemented by other sources. Appropriate measures for telescoping, compacting, or condensing the common core, or better yet for acceleration, must be incorporated into the curricular scheme as well. Opportunities for productive work will also be required.

In short, there is no way to buy, literally or figuratively, a curriculum for the gifted. Like the rest of the program, the curriculum must be developed locally with the conscious intent of meeting the needs of the target population by educators who know what those needs are. This is best done by the persons who will be responsible for carrying out the program for the gifted, namely, the instructional and administrative staff of the program.

Instruction and Student Behavior

These terms need little, if any, explanation. Instruction, formal instruction at least, is what occurs when teachers and students interact in a curricular context or when students engage with material or take advantage of opportunities provided by teachers. Student behavior, construed in the broadest possible sense, is the result. Student behavior can include test scores, attitudes, productive activity, and any other planned or serendipitous outcome of the instructional process. It is included here for completeness and as a basis for evaluation.

Evaluation

The component that makes the system self-correcting is the evaluation component. By assessing the efficiency and effectiveness of the various program components, one can take steps to facilitate the accomplishment of the program goals and thus to meet the needs revealed in the needs assessment. Evaluation involves both pupil evaluation (which addresses placement issues; see Chapter 5) and program evaluation (which addresses issues of program effectiveness; see Chapter 9). It can, and should, be both formative (in-progress) and summative (dealing with final outcomes).

Evaluation is one of the most important issues facing the field of education of the gifted, since it bears directly on the basic question of whether or not the programs we are advocating are doing what we want them to do. It is also, as we will see in Chapter 9, one of the most difficult. At present, the development of satisfactory methods for evaluating programs for the gifted is more of a goal than a reality.

Summary

This overview of the components of a program for the gifted is intended to serve three purposes. The first is to familiarize readers with the various parts of a program of the sort with which this book deals, or at least with one way of cataloging those program parts. Second, it was meant to demonstrate the manner in which the individual components interact within and subserve the program. Since the components are interactive, and their interrelationships are planned rather than aleatory, the program can be legitimately regarded as a system. Third, this overview was meant to reinforce the points that a program for the gifted should be planned in response to the identified needs of a specific, known group of students and that every component of the program should represent the best choice, from among the many options available, for those particular students.

These themes have been developed at some length, and they will be played out with minor variations in subsequent chapters, as indicated above. Before turning to those chapters, however, let us take a quick look at some necessary program-planning preliminaries. By this I mean those practical issues to which one must attend at this initial stage of the planning process.

These are, for the most part, commonsense, nuts-and-bolts considerations that do not fit neatly into any of the boxes of Figure 3.1 but are important, even crucial, nonetheless.

PROGRAM-PLANNING PRELIMINARIES

There are a number of small but important details that must be seen to as the planning of the program gets under way. Limitations of space and of omniscience preclude a comprehensive delineation of them here. The following, however, should not be overlooked.

Naming the Program

There is only one reason to think of a name for the program this early in the game, and this is to discourage people from calling it the "Gifted Program." Although this unfortunate designation will be used by more than a few people, the school or school district should not give it its imprimatur. As I endeavored to make clear in Chapter 2, we should not conceive of this enterprise as a process of defining and identifying *the* gifted. We are not, or ought not to be, in the business of conducting an existential triage, separating the "gifted" from the merely "average" or "nongifted." We are, instead, planning and instituting programs for those gifted students whose needs are not being met by existing curricular provisions. These programs may not be appropriate placements for some gifted students, and placement in the programs should not be seen as the sole criterion of giftedness.

It is never too early to begin to refer to the program as something other than the "Gifted Program." Cute acronyms appear to be almost de rigueur in this field, and while they may seem frivolous, they are preferable to the "Gifted Program" (except, of course, acronyms such as the almost ubiquitous TAG, standing for "Talented and Gifted," that incorporate the word *gifted*). Even better is a title that is descriptive of the program's curriculum or intent. The "Critical-Thinking Program" or the "Interdisciplinary-Studies Program" are far superior to the ungainly label of "Gifted Program." What we are trying to avoid here is the labeling of students, an issue to which we will return in Chapter 5, which deals with identification.

On the basis of good usage alone, such constructions as *gifted program* should be avoided. We rarely or never encounter the term *retarded program*, and for good reason: Not only is the term offensive, it is ludicrous. Educational programs are not, despite what some students claim, retarded, nor are they gifted. Special programs may serve and be staffed by gifted people, but that is a different matter. Similarly, the phrase "gifted education," used by many to refer to the field at large, is both bad English and (as many familiar with the field admit) inaccurate. The field of the education of the gifted gives rise to efforts to create special programs for gifted students who require differentiated curricular opportunities. But "gifted education" is not the sum total of "gifted programs" across the country. These terms do little good (although some years ago, according to the school district in which I taught, I was transformed from a "retarded teacher" into a "gifted teacher" over the course of a summer). They are sloppy phrases that reflect sloppy thinking, the kind of thinking that results in much negative regard for the field.

Developing a Program Philosophy

It is a good idea at this point to spend some time thinking about and fashioning a statement of program philosophy (see Kaplan, 1974, for some elaboration on this point). Why is the program necessary? How is the proposed program consistent with the mission of the school or school district? How committed is the school or district to this type of special education? These and other questions should be answered in a statement of program philosophy.

This should take the form of a written document that at some point (the sooner the better) receives the blessing of the administration and the board of education. This statement can serve as a guide for program planning and as a statement of commitment on the part of the school or district. This latter function is important, since some will greet the news of an impending program for the gifted with skepticism.

The statement will prove to be useful in talking with parents and teachers, especially in answering those difficult "why" questions. Ultimately, it should be featured prominently in the booklet, pamphlet, or information sheet that describes the working program.

Fundamentally, it is important that those involved in the program-planning process ask themselves why they are doing what they are doing and how they ought to be doing it. One should reflect for a while on the whole enterprise, even if one has been a longtime advocate of special programs for the gifted—perhaps even more so in that case. It is necessary to translate those gut-level beliefs into clear, articulate statements of educational philosophy that will be comprehensible and, one hopes, persuasive to any parent, teacher, student, administrator, taxpayer, or school board member who reads them.

Forming a Planning Committee

Usually, the planning of a program for the gifted is the responsibility of an administrator or a teacher who has been designated as coordinator (a slippery title that I will discuss in Chapter 7). In other cases, a consultant is brought in for this purpose. Although one person may have the ultimate responsibility for the planning of the program, it is a wise practice to establish a schoolwide or districtwide planning committee for a variety of reasons.

First, a planning committee that is broadly representative of the school or school district can afford program planners a wide range of knowledge and perspectives. Classroom teachers can make suggestions that will make the final product more palatable to their colleagues. Building administrators can share information that is necessary in making decisions about where the program should be housed and other related issues to that. School psychologists can offer advice about testing. In other words, a committee that represents each constituency within the school or district can bring more knowledge to upon the program-planning process than can a single individual.

Second, a committee can serve as a sounding board for evaluating the practicality of proposed program components. Planners cannot be familiar with every aspect of the functioning of a school district, and some of their proposals may well be unrealistic. Educators who are in the classrooms and buildings on a day-to-day basis can be reality testers for the planners, suggesting modifications to bring the developing program more into the realm of reality.

A third reason for establishing a committee is for the purpose of communication. This is a crucial matter, and I will discuss it a bit more below. Simply by virtue of having teachers, administrators, and others from various buildings actively involved in the planning of the program, one takes a major step toward improving communication. Various people will want to know about the proposed program. The greater the number of people who are working on the planning, the more likely it is that accurate, firsthand information will be passed along.

A fourth reason to have a committee is a practical one. Planning a program for the gifted is a challenging task involving a great deal of hard work. With a committee, one can share the work load. The extensive reading and the visits to conferences and to other programs that were described by the teacher at the beginning of this chapter were worthwhile undertakings, although the final result in that district was less than satisfactory. They could not have been undertaken without a committee. There are other tasks, such as tallying the responses to needs-assessment questionnaires, that are much less onerous if they are shared. Anybody who has single-handedly taken on the job of planning a program for the gifted would second the idea of forming a planning committee.

Who should serve on such a committee? The answer to this question will vary somewhat from district to district and school to school, but some generalizations can be made. First and foremost, the committee should be made up of willing participants, individuals who want the program to succeed and are amenable to working, probably without compensation, to that end. These people must volunteer; they should not "be volunteered." This point is essential.

To be more specific, the following should definitely be members of a districtwide planning committee:

- As committee chairman or chairwoman, the program coordinator or administrator or whoever is responsible for the planning of the program.
- At least one classroom teacher from each building in the district
- Special-class teachers if appropriate (e.g., art, music, bilingual, resource room, physical education)
- One or more building administrators
- A representative of central administration
- A representative of the board of education
- In large districts, one or more department chairmen or chairwomen or curriculum coordinators in various disciplines
- A school psychologist or guidance counselor

In addition, some districts include one or more students or parents on this committee. This can present some difficulties as well as advantages. The inclusion of parents may cause a public-relations problem if not a more substantive one, especially if the participating parents have children who may be candidates for the program.

However the committee is constituted, its value should be obvious. Unless there are compelling reasons for planning the program in complete secrecy, a planning committee is essential. It is also compatible with the system approach advocated in this book. As Kaplan (1974) states, "A program that is simply imposed upon a system is less likely to fulfill the needs of students or achieve the commitment of the system than is a program which emerges from a well-chosen, instructed, and communicative planning team" (p. 13).

Doing One's Homework

There is a hoary cliché to the effect that it is not very productive of one's time and energy to reinvent the wheel. This is a lesson that program planners should heed. Thus, this is a good time to put the committee to work doing its research. Before a choice can be made from among the available program-component options, it is necessary to know what they are. First and most important, one should read. Books about gifted children and their education are proliferating, as are journals devoted to this population. One will have to separate the wheat from a considerable amount of chaff, but this homework is necessary to obtain an orientation to the field and a knowledge of the range of available options.

More and more colleges are adding courses and degree programs in the education of the gifted to their offerings in education. Enrolling in one or more courses is a good way of learning more about the field and doing so in a systematic manner under the guidance of an individual who should have extensive knowledge of the topic.

One also could, and probably should, attend conferences, workshops, or in-service presentations dealing with the gifted. It would be best to attend generic rather than brand-name workshops, that is, to avoid sales meetings for particular approaches disguised as educational conferences.

There is also value in visiting programs in other schools and districts. Here one can see in reality what is described in theory in the books, journals, and presentations. It is important to keep in mind, however, that one is seeing a particular program model at work in a specific setting. What works at the site visited may or may not work in one's home district.

Whatever opportunities arise for learning more about the psychology and education of the gifted should, if possible, be taken. One should keep in mind, however, that one will read and hear a lot that is confusing, contradictory, and downright silly. Nevertheless, by thinking critically—as we would have our gifted students think—a great deal of useful information can be gathered.

Communicating Promptly, Effectively, and Honestly

The teacher whose sad tale opened this chapter would have a great deal to say about the value of timely and, above all, accurate communication. The need for this is paramount. If program planners were required to have a few key words inscribed on their walls, one of these would be *communicate*.

When a school or school district announces that it is planning a program for gifted students, people take notice. Teachers, administrators, board members, students, parents, taxpayers, local politicians, reporters, and individuals one would not expect to care in the least suddenly become very curious. This curiosity, which is often tinged with fear or suspicion, usually revolves around the question of how the program will affect the individuals' classes, sons and daughters, buildings and schedules, tax rates, budgets, prospects for promotion, and, in the case of students, class placements.

Since this curiosity about the program is compounded by perceived personal involvement, if no information is forthcoming to satisfy the curiosity, speculation begins and rumors fly. The rumors can, in many cases, extend far beyond the seeming bounds of credibility. People will believe them nonetheless. Teachers will grow resentful over imagined disruptions of their class-rooms, additions to their work loads, or slights to their professionalism. Parents will be up in arms over elitist provisions and unfair selection procedures. Students will regard the prospect of more work with scant enthusiasm. Taxpayers will fire off indignant letters to the newspaper editor complaining about expected tax increases. Politicians and political activists will fulminate over "this liberal threat to our traditional American way of life" or "this reactionary conspiracy to aid the already privileged" (both of these may happen simultaneously).

Much of this (obviously, but not extremely) exaggerated panic can be avoided, or at least minimized, by communicating promptly and truthfully to the various interested parties. One should take an active, not a reactive, role here and give out information before people begin to clamor for it. If people know what is happening, they will not have to speculate about what *might* be happening. If the truth is known, rumors have a harder time spreading unchecked. The importance of this cannot be overstated; thus the anecdote that began the chapter.

With whom should one meet? Two groups come to mind immediately. The first of these is parents. As soon as the program is approved and a planning strategy is developed (preferably the system model described here), a meeting should be scheduled for any parents interested in hearing what is being done by the school or school district. The program planner or planners should then explain in direct and honest language why the program is needed and how it will be developed. The flowchart in Figure 3.1 has proven to be a useful visual aid in my experience. Parents will ask many questions (such as, "How will you choose students for the program?") that cannot be answered at the time of the first meeting. By explaining that the program is being developed systematically and diagnostically for local students, beginning with a needs assessment, one can demonstrate why such questions are premature and how they will be answered by the school or district in due course.

I have found that parents in school districts in which I served as a consultant were very accepting of this approach. They understood that we were starting with more questions than answers and why one should be skeptical of schemes that purport to have all of the answers. They understood why the district needed a special program and how the planning process would work. They also understood that the district will, or should, or had better, have some more specific answers for them in the future.

Thus, the reason for the first meeting with parents is to tell them why and how: why a program is necessary and how it will be developed. Another reason is to tell them when the "whats" can be presented: what type of student, what manner of identification, what kind of program, and so forth.

Then, of course, one must follow up on this promise and meet with them later with more specific information. One practical note related to seating: estimate reasonably the number of chairs you will need for the meeting and then double that number. Any meeting that has the words "program for the gifted" associated with it will draw a crowd.

The second group with whom it is imperative that one meet is the faculty of the school or school district. These people will want to know what is being planned and how it will affect them; in fact, they deserve to have this information. Again, if they do not know the truth, they will have only rumors and speculation on which to base their opinions. By meeting with faculty early on and by being completely straightforward with them, one maintains more control over the situation than if one allows the rumor mill to operate at full capacity.

In a large or even fairly large district, it makes sense to have a meeting in each building, with the principal present. It is important once again to explain the present status of the planning process and that, at this early stage, there are more questions than answers (assuming that one is using the model advocated here). It is also essential to convince the teachers and building administrators (and the parents, when they are seen) that they will have their say and that they will be important sources of information in the needs assessment. This should not be an empty promise, as we will see in Chapter 4, where I discuss needs assessment.

Both of these early meetings, that is, the one with parents and the one with building personnel, have dual functions. The function of supplying accurate information to these interested parties has been mentioned. In addition, one should also be there to listen. These meetings can and should be part of the needs assessment. The alert program planner can learn things about the school or school district by listening to the questions, responses, and suggestions of parents and teachers. Moreover, one should also try to read between the lines in an attempt to divine the attitudes, preconceptions, misconceptions, prejudices, and expectations of those attending the meetings. The sensitive listener can glean quite a bit of helpful information that can alert him or her to possible pitfalls or opportunities. Thus, it is as important to listen well as it is to speak well at these meetings.

Additionally, one should try, and one will probably be expected, to meet with the central administration and the board of education. Although one would not be planning a program in this manner without the blessing of these parties, the blessing may not be unanimous. It is good to know where one stands and where the program stands with the powers that be. Moreover, it should not be assumed that these persons know or understand the process being employed, especially if it is the system method described here. One or more administrators or board members may want to know why the district did not "buy" so-and-so's program or program model. This is the time to answer that question and any others that may be asked, for these individuals in turn will have to answer many questions put to them about the program that is being planned. It is essential that they be able to answer them accurately.

In conclusion, it is a good idea to convene as many informational meetings as can be tolerated. Although these meetings may be tedious and even trying, they pay off in the long run. It is difficult to conceive of a situation in which there is too much accurate information; it is easy to conceive of a situation in which there is too little.

Dealing with Objections to Programs for the Gifted

No matter how strong the mandate for starting a program for the gifted might be, no matter how unanimous the board of education or how enthusiastic the administration, there will always be naysayers. Skeptics, doubters, and individuals bitterly opposed to programs of this sort will be encountered from time to time. They will object to the notion of a program for gifted students for reasons both frivolous and serious. Some will react reflexively out of perhaps unconscious anti-intellectualism; others will be opposed because of carefully considered fears of elitism. Their objections will be many and varied, and program planners should try to anticipate as many of them as possible.

One will never be able to convince everybody of the desirability of special education for the gifted. Nevertheless, for a variety of reasons it is still important to be able to respond to arguments against special programs. First, it is important not to be in a position of being unable to respond cogently and knowledgeably to objections to the program one is planning. One does not have to win every debate, but one must be able to demonstrate that serious consideration and awareness of possible pitfalls underlie one's actions. Above all, one must show oneself to be an intelligent, reflective educational professional.

Too many times, educators give the public the impression that they act without thinking, jumping on and off bandwagons with dizzying frequency. As interest in the education of the gifted increases across the country, suspicion that this is just another educational fad increases as well. Unfortunately, some of the less substantial schemes for educating the gifted have served to reinforce in the minds of some the sense that "gifted education" is not serious education. The alert program planner will be aware of this and keep in mind the need to present himself or herself as a competent, serious professional. The less we talk about "McTalent burgers," "creativity kits," and "the psychically gifted," and the more we deal with substantive educational issues, the more credibility we will have as professionals. Thus, one must be able to respond to arguments against special programs for the gifted not with canned, memorized counterarguments but with thoughtful comments that demonstrate that the critic's point of view is understood, that the possible dangers have been considered, and that steps are being taken to avoid them.

Second, while one need not agree with one's critics, one also need not alienate them and encourage them to redouble their opposition by suggesting that their concerns do not deserve serious consideration. Proponents and opponents of special education for the gifted can agree to disagree amicably and supportively, or they can be at each others' throats. The difference often relates to how much respect is given to a critic's right to disagree. It is not necessary to agree with opposing points of view, but it is necessary to take these views seriously enough to give them the thought they deserve. It has been our experience that some of the most intransigent opponents of special programs will cooperate, however grudgingly, if there is an atmosphere of mutual respect for irreconcilable points of view.

Third, one must be convinced oneself that programs of this type are educationally defensible and necessary. This does not mean the adoption of the stance of the "true believer" who will not listen to arguments counter to his or her beliefs. Rather, it implies a full awareness of alternative points of view and a belief that, despite their persuasiveness, another course is the better one. It is necessary, therefore, to be aware of every conceivable objection to programs for the gifted so that one can be clear in one's own mind that such programs are of real educational value. A belief that cannot admit of the possibility of other points of view is a weak belief. Blind faith is a poor model for the educator advocating the encouragement of critical thinking for the gifted.

There is not room enough in this or any other book to cite all of the possible objections to programs for the gifted. Rather than attempting an exhaustive list, I will cite some of the arguments I have encountered in the course of my work with school districts. There have been quite a few of them; the following are among the most frequently encountered:

- This program will be a waste of money! These kids don't need a special program. If they are so smart, they'll learn on their own.
- Programs for the gifted encourage elitist attitudes. Gifted kids are obnoxious enough already; this will only make them more stuck-up.
- We should be concentrating on the handicapped and disadvantaged. These so-called gifted programs are nothing more than fun-and-games for a few privileged upper-middle-class students who already get more than their fair share.

- What about the average child? When is somebody going to do something for him?
- Not again! These are my best students, and I never get to see them. They are pulled out for every conceivable program already. When are they going to do their classwork?
- What about Churchill and Edison? They did all right without these programs for the gifted. If they could make it, so can these kids.
- Programs for the gifted are undemocratic.
- We don't have any gifted students in our district.
- All of the students in our district are gifted.

Since responding to these arguments is beyond the scope of this book, I will leave it to the reader to produce his or her replies (the truly perplexed might want to consult sources such as Marland, 1972, and Tannenbaum, 1983, for guidance). I urge the reader to think carefully about each of these objections and to try to anticipate others. It would also be a good idea to realize that each of these arguments has at least the potential for truth. In other words, some of these charges are true with respect to some programs for the gifted. Some programs *do* encourage elitism; some consist of little more than fun-and-games activities; some pull children out of their classrooms with no regard for the regular classroom teachers. Thus, it is necessary to listen to one's critics, not only the better to understand and counter their arguments but also to be able to anticipate pitfalls lurking in the future. Finally, it is quite likely that some of the critics are speaking from experience.

Summary

There are probably many other program-planning preliminaries that spring to the reader's mind. I have attempted to mention only those that seem to me to be the most critical. What is important at this point is to try to anticipate the needs, questions, and objections of others and to establish a modus operandi for oneself that will make the task of planning a successful program a practicable one. Not every contingency can be anticipated, but it is worthwhile to try—an ounce of anticipation is worth a pound of extemporaneous rationalizing.

CONCLUSION

The message of this chapter can be summed up in the trite admonition, "Look before you leap." I have tried to make a strong case for a systematic, diagnostic–prescriptive approach to planning programs for the gifted as opposed to an impulsive, let's-try-it-and-hope-it-works approach. I trust the logic of the method I am advocating is apparent.

To this point, we have explored the problems and possibilities inherent in defining gifted children; we have looked at one way of resolving that problem within the context of a system approach to program planning; and we have discussed the merits and components of that approach. In the chapters that follow, the system approach will be delineated further in the context of the specific program components that were briefly outlined above. Our starting point will be the needs assessment, that component of a program for the gifted that does the most to make the program truly programmatic.

CHAPTER 4

Conducting a Needs Assessment

The notion of "need" as an outcome gap is of critical
importance, for it will allow us to design and plan for success,
and it will keep us from jumping into solutions before we
know the problems. . . .

The concepts are basically simple—to determine and
validate what should be accomplished before collecting and
mobilizing the means for education. It is so simple that it is
easy to write it off as being what we already do or have done.
In most cases it is not.

Kaufman & English, *Needs Assessment: A Guide to
Improve School District Management*

The development and implementation of a program for
the gifted and talented is contingent upon assessing and
integrating the factors which are EXISTENT within the
institution with those which are IDEAL for students.

Kaplan, *Providing Programs for the Gifted and Talented*

In the previous chapter, I argued that an effective program for gifted
students is more likely to emerge from a systematic, diagnostic–prescriptive
approach to program planning, one that takes into account the particularities
of a specific school or school district, than from an impulsive, wholesale
adoption of a program model that appears to be working elsewhere or that is
aggressively marketed as the *one* approach that is appropriate for all settings.
I advocated what I referred to as a system approach, which has as its starting
point a thorough knowledge of the local setting, as a basis for actual program
planning. At the heart of this system approach is the needs assessment (refer
to Figure 3.1), the tool that enables educators to gather the data upon which
the planning process depends.

The importance of needs assessment in the planning of programs for the gifted cannot be overstated. Fine's (1969) assertion that "assessing the quality of our educational institutions is an essential activity if we are going to meet the needs of youth and of society" (p. 30) is especially of relevance in the case of programs for the gifted. He goes on to state that "we can no longer afford to pursue an educational program based primarily on historical precedent, for this offers little assurance that what is being achieved is appropriate, relevant, or even desirable" (p. 30). Given the questions raised about the efficacy and soundness of many of the existing precedents for programming in the field of education of the gifted (e.g., Cox, Daniel, & Boston, 1985), this admonition is worth heeding.

This chapter will treat the issue of needs assessment in some detail. In the sections that follow, I will define a needs assessment within the context of the system approach advocated in this book; I will list some of the questions that a needs assessment should answer; and I will present some ways, formal and informal, to conduct a needs assessment. I will then discuss the interpretation of the data generated by the needs assessment and how they can be incorporated into the planning of a program for gifted students.

WHAT IS A NEEDS ASSESSMENT?

Kaufman and English (1976) define needs assessment as "a series of empirical steps to define organizational purposes and/or bring valid and compatible means for their realization" (p. 7). This is a serviceable definition for our purposes, because embedded within it are some concepts that are central to the system approach that I am advocating.

The word *empirical*, for example, implies that one begins by going into the schools and the community to seek information, that one's experience in the local setting is paramount. This does not necessarily dictate an atheoretical approach. It does, however, indicate that the immediate reality of the school or school district in question should shape the application of one's theory and that a priori conceptions and predispositions should bow to the specifics of the situation. In other words, one should be guided by what one learns from one's experience rather than trying to impose a particular paradigm upon a reality that may be resistant to a given theoretical perspective.

The phrase "organizational purposes" is also freighted with meaning. It may seem that one of the givens of a situation in which there is a desire to institute a program for gifted students is that the organizational purpose of the school or school district is clear: to create a "gifted program." There is more to it than that, however. As I hope I made clear in the two previous chapters, this bare-bones statement of purpose leaves a number of fundamental questions unanswered (and, more to the point of this chapter, unasked). Among these questions are, "Who are the gifted?" "What are our goals for these gifted students?" "How should we accomplish these goals?" and so forth. The desire to institute a program for the gifted, therefore, is more a vague intention than a clear statement of purpose. Specific organizational purposes are yet to be defined.

Finally, the phrase "valid and compatible means for their realization" suggests that the one goal of a needs assessment is the determination of means to the specific ends inherent in the delineation of organizational purposes. Kaufman and English and other writers on the topic of needs assessment often take pains to separate means from ends and to stress that the latter are the true goal of needs assessment. I will be somewhat more permissive, as Kaufman and English uncharacteristically are in the definition of needs assessment cited above, and include a focus on means as one desired outcome of a needs assessment.

The modifiers *valid* and *compatible* are important in the above definition, for they underscore the adaptive nature of a good needs assessment working within the context of a system approach. Means are *valid* to the extent that they work toward the realization of the explicit goals of the school or school district and operate in the service of considered and stated policy. The more that methods deviate from intentions, the less valid they become. This can cause us to apply the wrong solution to a given problem and sometimes to misidentify the problem altogether. This is a danger inherent in buying or adopting a program and hoping it will work well in one's school or school district.

Similarly, means are *compatible* to the extent that they are feasible and consistent with available resources. A lack of compatibility implies that a school or school district is attempting to undertake a solution that is beyond or inconsistent with its means; i.e., it is not utilizing that which it actually has in order to work toward the realization of its goals. As Barclay (1974) indicates, in conducting a needs assessment, "the . . . policy-making group must allocate limited resources to maximize educational effects" (p. 47). It can do so only if it proposes means that are compatible with both the desired ends and the available resources.

Thus, a needs assessment forces a school or school district to examine carefully its intentions, motivations, goals, and resources rather than just rush into the process of creating a program. This establishes a reflective rather than an impulsive manner of doing things that, although sometimes difficult to maintain under the strain of inevitable pressures for immediate action, should result in a more effective program in the long run. As Kaplan (1974) asserts, "The level of acceptance, integration, and workability of a plan within an institution is directly related to the involvement of the planners and the amount of time spent in program planning" (p. 13). It can also, somewhat paradoxically, be the fastest route to a successful program, since it can save the additional time required to scrap an unsuccessful program and replace it with a new one.

Kaufman and English tell us that "educational managers too often assume the functions and results of the school system are known and accepted. While many people may think they are known, there is most likely a great deal of confusion over what should be the directions of the enterprise and what should be its products" (pp. 8–9). It is this state of affairs that a needs assessment is designed to prevent. A good needs assessment compels a school or school district to confront the possibility of its ignorance with respect to its goals and resources as they relate to the creation of a program for gifted students. While this may be uncomfortable in the short run, in the long run it is a salubrious exercise that should work toward the common good.

HOW DOES ONE CONDUCT A NEEDS ASSESSMENT?

Conducting a needs assessment can be an extensive, time-consuming process, or it can be a more informal undertaking of shorter duration. How involved the process will be is determined by certain characteristics of the school or school district, such as size, degree of heterogeneity in the school population, mean level of achievement of the student body, attitudes toward programs for the gifted, and available resources.

There is no set formula for determining how detailed a needs assessment should be. Common sense is often the best guide. For example, in a small school district with two or three buildings and a few hundred students, it would probably be neither necessary nor desirable to undertake an in-depth survey utilizing questionnaires, interviews, round upon round of meetings, and so forth. Existing channels of communication can be used, and one can take advantage of the fact that "everybody knows everybody else." I do not mean to suggest that administrators should fall prey to the complacency and false sense of omniscience that Kaufman and English warn against in the passage quoted above. However, I do mean to suggest that different methods of needs assessment are appropriate for different settings.

Information to Be Sought

However grand one's plans for a needs assessment are, there is certain basic information that should be gathered. This is perhaps easiest to summarize in the form of questions for which one should seek answers. Although it is not possible to produce a complete list of questions that should be asked in every school or school district (this, like everything else in program planning, is conditioned by the setting), the following should figure prominently in such a list.

What special abilities do appreciable numbers of students in the school or school district exhibit? This is one of the questions whose answer(s) determine that most basic component of the program: the definition of the target population. I have discussed this issue at length in the two previous chapters, and so I will merely restate here my conviction that the program should take shape as a means to serve those students defined as needing special services because their educational needs, engendered by their special abilities or potential, are not being met by the regular core curriculum.

Moreover, since communities, schools, and their curricula vary widely, this group of students must be defined with reference to the local setting in which their needs are expressed. It will not do, therefore, blithely to adopt a definition of the gifted child from a textbook or a workshop presentation. There is no guarantee that the group of students defined by an "expert's" research or theorizing will correspond to the group or groups of students needing special services in a real school or school district. Determining who will receive special services is a policy decision that should be made by responsible local administrators who know (through needs assessment) what is needed in the school or school district. They should not be willing to turn over this decision-making responsibility to someone who has never set foot in their schools.

What special abilities are currently being addressed by the regular core curriculum? This is the second important question that allows one to define the target population of a program for gifted students. Since educational need is the linchpin of the definition of gifted students proposed in this book, identifying need is central to defining the target population. As I stated in the previous chapter, it makes little sense to prescribe special education for students whose educational needs are already being met, no matter how "gifted" they may be. One should instead look for students whose needs are being ignored, those who are left over when students who are well served by the core curriculum are subtracted from all of those with a strong claim to giftedness. Thus, one must examine existing curricular offerings in order to learn what areas of ability and potential are currently being stressed and slighted.

What extracurricular and community-based programs exist to meet the needs of gifted students? This question is an adjunct to the one directly above. In the process of triage that constitutes defining the target population, one often must reduce the pool of students who could benefit from special services to a smaller number than one would wish to be able to serve in ideal circumstances. The question of who is already being served thus becomes an extremely important one. This is why extracurricular and community programs should be examined carefully. Perhaps a science club is meeting the needs of students with unusual potential in that area. An enrichment course in computer programming offered by a local college might serve the same function for talented "hackers." Similar provisions could be available for creative writers or actors.

This is not to say that clubs always meet the needs of gifted students or that special programs are unnecessary if there are enough extracurricular activities available. Nor does it mean that meeting the educational needs of gifted students is not the curricular responsibility of the school or school district. What *is* meant is that, lacking an ideal situation in which every plausibly gifted student could receive special services, one must seek to learn whatever one can about existing services so that limited resources can be distributed as fairly as possible.

These first three questions relate directly to the idea advanced by Kaufman and English that a needs assessment is primarily concerned with defining organizational principles or "necessary and specific ends" (p. 8). "To create a program for gifted students" is not a specific end, necessary as we might think it to be. "To create a program for the following able students who have critical educational needs . . . ," where the ellipses are replaced by a clear delineation of the target population, *is* a specific end. It is also one whose means are more readily identified.

What information can be found in existing records? Students have histories, as developmental psychologists are constantly reminding those of us concerned with individual differences. A typical sixth-grade student has spent between six and eight years and some months in a formal educational setting. This experience leaves a trail of documentation of varying degrees of specificity that can be found in the student's permanent record. An examination of accumulated student records can tell an educator conducting a needs assessment quite a bit about the student body as a whole.

For example, test data are generally available for various groups of students. Many school districts screen incoming kindergarten students for handicapping conditions and for signs of potential giftedness. Some schools administer aptitude tests to all students at certain grade levels, and nearly all schools subject their students to yearly achievement testing beginning at some point in the primary grades.

What one is looking for here is not necessarily information about individual students, but a sense of the level of achievement or ability of the entire student body. The fact that the mean IQ in a given school or school district is 115, for example has implications for defining the target population, even if IQs will not figure prominently in the definition. Such a datum would tell one that a child with above-average ability as defined by national IQ norms is decidedly average in this setting. By the same token, pronounced peaks and valleys with respect to subscores on achievement tests can be revealing. A high local mean score on mathematics subtests might suggest that there are few students with superior mathematical potential whose needs are not being met (ignoring for the moment the likelihood that there is more to mathematical ability than what is measured by achievement tests). Conversely, a low local mean score in knowledge of scientific concepts might suggest that there is considerable wasted potential in this area and that one should look for indications of scientific ability somewhere other than in achievement test scores.

Existing test data can also be examined selectively to look for patterns that could lead to unfair representation in the program for the gifted. If the mean IQ for minority students is significantly below that for students in the mainstream, a cautious use of IQs for purposes of identification is dictated. In such a case, one should be unwilling to exclude students on the basis of IQ and should use additional sources of information for purposes of inclusion. The same sort of analysis should be carried out by sex, especially since different patterns of ability and achievement are demonstrated by boys and girls at different points along the sequence of grades (see, for example, Silverman, 1986a).

Teachers' and administrators' anecdotal comments are also of potential use here. Even records of disciplinary actions can reveal that bright students are bored and unchallenged in the regular classroom or that considerable creativity is being exercised in ways that school personnel do not appreciate.

The point I am making is that there is a rich vein of information valuable for purposes of needs assessment already existing in the schools. It should be mined extensively before trouble is taken obtaining the same data through more expensive and time-consuming procedures.

What attitudes toward gifted students and programs for gifted students are held by teachers, administrators, parents, and students? Kaufman and English (1976) stress the need to involve "the partners of education: the learners, the implementers and the society (or community)" (pp. 20–21) in the process of needs assessment. The reasons for this are many, and they have to do in part with shifting the perception of "the educational system . . . from 'theirs' to 'ours'" (p. 21). The educational partners are valuable sources of information who can help answer the questions posed above and below, and their knowledge and perceptions should be sought out. This involves them in the needs-assessment process and in the overall process of program planning, thus fostering better communication and encouraging support for the school's or the school district's efforts. Moreover, knowing the attitudes held by these groups toward the gifted and special programs for the gifted sheds light on the nature and reliability of the information they provide.

These attitudes are also useful data in their own right. For instance, the importance of knowing that teachers are hostile to the idea of a program for gifted students or that the vast majority of parents are supportive of the idea should be obvious. Forewarned is, indeed, forearmed. Or, more optimistically, it is valuable to know where one's support lies.

More basically, in planning a program for the gifted, one ought to know as much as possible about the environment in which the program will be operating. As Barclay (1974) reminds us, "Learning is influenced by student, teacher, curriculum, parental, and other environmental factors" (p. 47). The attitudes of the educational partners are some of the most powerful environmental factors one will encounter. They should be known to the individual charged with planning the program for gifted students.

What is the estimated incidence of giftedness according to parents, teachers, and administrators? At some point, a decision will have to be made with respect to the percentage of the student body that will be served in the program for gifted students. While I am not suggesting that the matter be put to a vote, it is often useful and interesting to know how prevalent various groups believe giftedness to be.

Why is this information potentially useful? First, it sheds light on the way people view giftedness. If it turns out that a significant number of individuals in any group thinks giftedness is either a rare or a commonplace phenomenon, that is a clue to the nature of their informal definitions of giftedness.

Second, these estimates add some more to what is known about the school or school district. If teachers, for example, think that 20 percent of the student body is gifted, this could reflect a high mean level of achievement, aptitude, or special ability in the school population. This should be checked against school records.

Third, this information reflects the attitudes of certain groups. It is not unusual to find teachers who state that they see gifted children in their classes infrequently, and some will claim never to have encountered one. This may indicate that some in-service education is necessary to correct misconceptions, probably deriving from the use of the unfortunate and misleading term *gifted child*, regarding the nature of giftedness in the schools, or it may indicate that some teachers are less than enthusiastic about the prospect of a program for gifted students. It is also not unusual to find that many parents will have a high estimate of the number of gifted students in the school or school district. This again might reflect a need to clarify what is meant by the term *gifted child*, or it may simply be the result of parents' wanting the school or school district to cast a wide enough net to increase the chance of their child's inclusion in the program.

What do certain groups (e.g., parents, teachers, and administrators) believe other groups think and feel about programs for gifted students? This is a somewhat convoluted question that requires some explanation. It is important in planning a program for the gifted to secure the amicable cooperation of the various groups who will be affected by it, the groups Kaufman and English (1976) refer to as the "educational partners." To the extent that these groups mistrust each other, obtaining their cooperation is problematic at best. Quite often, in my experience, mistrust is based on mistaken assumptions about the attitudes and opinions of others.

It is not at all unusual for parents who support the creation of a program for the gifted to assume that teachers or administrators are opposed to the idea. If there is such opposition, it must be addressed. If, however, there is general agreement with regard to this aspect of the educational enterprise, it should be known. Thus, it can be very enlightening to compare the stated attitudes of the different educational partners with the attitudes these groups are assumed by others to hold. If there is suspicion of opposition where none exists, sharing needs assessment data regarding attitudes can eliminate a great deal of needless animosity.

What should be the focus of the program for the gifted? Given the range of possibilities, it is necessary to begin to think about program goals and a program focus. This, of course, depends largely upon the needs of the target population. The program should strive to deal with content and skills that will remedy deficiencies in the curriculum for these students. Yet, even with the target population well in focus, there are still a number of choices with respect to program goals, curricular objectives, curriculum development, and so forth. There should be a conscious effort during the needs assessment to gather data that will help define a focus for the program so that it will be more likely to meet the needs of the children for whom it is being designed.

What are the geographical and demographic features of the school or school district? Geography may not be destiny when it comes to planning a program for the gifted, but neither is it irrelevant. Knowing that many students are concentrated in a small geographical area or that a few students are scattered over vast expanses of land affects basic decisions relating to delivery of services. To take a specific example, one is not very likely to recommend transporting gifted students to a central location if the bus ride from the most distant point of the school district will consume one-and-one-half hours each way. Decentralized classes, probably with multigrade grouping, would be a more reasonable alternative.

Similarly, there is much that can be learned about the school population that will be valuable later. It is useful to know how many students are enrolled at each grade level, how the student population is constituted with respect to ethnicity and socioeconomic status, and other facts about the student body from which the students who will receive special services will be drawn.

What facilities are available? Are there any space limitations? The practical considerations implied by these two questions greatly affect the nature of the program for the gifted. It will be difficult to run an experimental science program if laboratories are unavailable. Likewise, a computer center is a distinct advantage if a program stressing computer programming is envisioned. Although it is not necessary to tailor the program exclusively to what happens to be currently available (the program, after all, should be tailored to the needs of the target population), the availability of resources and facilities cannot be dismissed as an irrelevancy.

Similarly, scarcity or availability of space is a factor to be considered. If the student population is increasing and sufficient funding to build new classrooms or a new school has not been forthcoming from the taxpayers, space will be at a premium. It may be impractical, then, to propose a program that requires a separate resource room in each building. The reader can imagine other such situations. Again, it is not true that the availability of facilities and space should dictate important features of the program for the gifted. However, these factors are realities that have to be considered and, in some situations, overcome.

How do the educational partners feel about various program formats? A specific example should suffice to reveal the importance of this question. Suppose an educational planner is contemplating a program for gifted students that requires removing, or pulling out, children from the regular classroom for significant periods of time once or twice a week. Suppose further that students, especially able students, are already pulled out for numerous activities ranging from band to speech therapy during the school day. Imagine, then, the spirit of hearty cooperation with which these teachers are likely to greet the announcement that they will be losing their "best" students even more frequently. This touches upon issues of fairness and educational effectiveness. We want to be fair to all of those affected by the program for the gifted, and we need their support for the program to be effective.

Is the issue of elitism a major concern? For some people, the phrase "program for the gifted" reflexively connotes unfair advantage and a retreat from egalitarianism. As John Gardner (1961) and Richard Hofstadter (1963) have written, the linking of excellence and elitism is an ingrained national tendency, an enduring facet of our national character, and it is something of which educators working with gifted students should be aware. However, this association need not exist, although, sadly, there are programs for the gifted that fully deserve the label "elitist."

There are numerous reasons why special-educational programs for gifted students do not have to be characterized by unfairness and elitism. I refer the reader to Marland (1972), Newland (1976), and Tannenbaum (1983; see especially his "Bill of Rights for the Gifted," pp. 462–466), who are among those who have argued persuasively that it is the absence, not the presence, of special programs for the gifted that constitutes an injustice. This, however, is not the major concern of this chapter; I am more concerned here with this issue in the context of needs assessment.

If many people view programs for gifted students as elitist enterprises, it is important to know that this is the case. This perception can be the foundation for powerful and well-intentioned opposition to the program. It is crucial that fears of elitism be laid to rest as soon as possible; otherwise, one must contend with people who oppose the program on moral grounds. Central to countering the fear of elitism, of course, is a willingness to communicate that one is aware that this is a valid concern, a potential pitfall for programs for the gifted, and something that will be avoided in the program being planned.

It is insufficient to dismiss fears of elitism as unfounded or benighted. The history of our movement has not earned us that luxury. Instead, we need to become aware of whatever misgivings others have about what we are doing and try to allay their fears by speaking to them directly. To the extent that our critics are basing their objections on valid concerns about elitism and not using the issue to mask other objections, we should have some success in reassuring them or at least earning the chance to be judged on our performance.

Who might be qualified to teach in the program for the gifted? One of the most important components of a program for gifted students, in some respects *the* most important one, is the teaching staff. Recruiting and selecting the right people for the job is a task of the greatest importance. Early on, during the needs assessment, is a good time to begin.

As I will discuss in Chapter 7, it is not easy to specify with a great deal of confidence the traits that characterize an effective teacher of the gifted.

Moreover, the absence of categorical certification for teachers of the gifted in most states (Mitchell, 1988) leaves the field wide open with respect to choosing candidates. At this point in the planning process, people should be made aware of the fact that one or more positions will need to be filled, and the planners should in turn be alert for overt or covert recommendations or expressions of interest. Since the needs assessment takes place well before the position will be advertised, one is free to pursue things informally and even to encourage or discourage certain applicants.

It is also possible that the prospect of hiring teachers for a program for the gifted could cause some concern among the faculty and their elected representatives. If school enrollment is declining and teachers are being "excessed," there could very well be considerable resentment if teachers believe that outsiders will be brought in to teach in the new program while experienced teachers with valid contracts with the school or school district are being laid off. It is important, therefore, during one of the meetings advocated in the previous chapter, to make the policy regarding the hiring of teachers for the new program very clear. One should reassure the faculty that established and negotiated hiring procedures will be followed. This is not the time to earn the animosity of the teachers' organization or to prompt the filing of a grievance. If one contemplates circumventing this contractual agreement, one should stop and consider the cost such chicanery might incur in terms of ill will toward the program.

What strengths, weaknesses, or special characteristics of the school or school district should be taken into consideration in program planning? A central theme of this book is that every school and school district is unique in ways that should matter to those planning a program for the gifted. The specifics of this uniqueness should be sought out in the needs assessment. Thus, it is necessary to try to pinpoint both the district's strengths and its weaknesses with respect to its ability to house a program for the gifted. What resources and abilities are present that should be known to program planners? What limitations or dangers exist? In what ways is this school or school district special? The answers to these questions will be very useful later in the game; one cannot assume that they are known from the beginning.

One would not need to ask all of these questions in every needs assessment effort, and there are additional questions that would have to be pursued in certain situations. What *is* necessary in every case is that the planners generate and discuss as many questions as possible and then decide which ones need to be answered. The goal is sufficient information—rarely is sufficient information obtained in response to an unasked question.

Sources of Information

The section above dealing with questions to be asked logically suggests the sources of many of the answers. For example, I stated that existing student records should be examined for the wealth of information they may hold. Human sources were also mentioned in passing. I will elaborate on these in this section.

Human sources of information. The "educational partners" referred to by Kaufman and English (1976, p. 21)—teachers, administrators, students, and the community—constitute the human sources of information for needs assessment. Justifying their role in the process is hardly necessary. They are the ones who will be affected by the program, and some of them will be responsible for its implementation.

It would be inconceivable to undertake any educational program without some input from the administrative and teaching staff. It should be equally inconceivable to do so without soliciting ideas and information from parents and students. Keep in mind that a needs assessment is not a plebiscite or a popularity contest, but a way of generating data that should make one's job easier. Incidentally, it is also a means of communicating with important groups concerned about the program for the gifted. This being the case, one should not hesitate to ask parents and students questions whose answers could be quite valuable.

Organized groups within the community probably should also be canvassed. Parent–teacher organizations may want to have their say in the needs assessment. If, as is the case in more and more communities, there is a local advocacy group concerned with the needs of the gifted, one should take advantage of the tendency of these groups to do their homework thoroughly. Again, one is not merely asking them what should be done (although knowing what they would like to have done is worth knowing). Rather, one is seeking information, a commodity over which no group has a monopoly.

Other sources of information. I have already discussed the advisability of perusing student records. Another potentially valuable source of information is printed curriculum guides. These will need to be examined in order to answer the second question posed in the section above, what the regular curriculum is doing for gifted students. Further, any documentation left over from previous programs for the gifted or attempts to create programs should be scrutinized. There might be opportunities to learn from the successes or mistakes of others, evidence of which may be scattered throughout such documents.

Other likely places to look may suggest themselves to the reader depending on his or her situation. Bus schedules, business records, tax records, and other more arcane sources may be appropriate in different cases. I cannot begin to enumerate every source here. What is important to keep in mind is that one should look wherever necessary to find answers to the questions that need answers. Although the search for answers may lead one to places off the beaten educational track, the goal of gathering as many relevant data as possible should justify whatever side trips are necessary.

How to Get the Information

I can only list some ways of generating the information that a good needs assessment should produce. Moreover, I will not deal with some of the more specialized methods, such as Delphi techniques, that are unlikely to be employed in the typical school or school district. Readers interested in pursuing the topic in greater detail should consult, among others, Barclay (1974), Fine (1969), Kaufman (1971), and Kaufman and English (1976). However, the following methods should always be considered.

Questionnaires. This is what first comes to mind for most people when a needs assessment is being considered. In many situations, the distribution of questionnaires and the interpretation of questionnaire data will play a major role in needs assessment. This will be so especially in populous schools or school districts, where face-to-face interviews and small-group meetings would not be a practicable means of collecting sufficient information from enough individuals.

The questions posed above, with necessary deletions and additions, should be the basis of the needs-assessment questionnaire. However, they must be written in a manner that is appropriate to the situation. For example, once one determines which groups will receive the questionnaires (e.g., teachers, parents, students), one must try to anticipate how each of the items will be read and interpreted. Words and phrases that are perfectly clear to teachers and administrators might be ambiguous or have little meaning for parents who are unfamiliar with educational jargon. An item that asks teachers how they feel about "self-contained classes for the gifted," therefore, might need to be rewritten for parents so that it asks how they feel about "a program where gifted students spend all of their class time with other gifted students."

Moreover, while one can assume that a certain level of literacy and vocabulary obtains among educators, one must realize that parents, as a group, are much more variable in this respect. Thus, while one might ask teachers if "programs for the gifted are elitist," one would probably want to ask parents whether they agreed that "programs for the gifted give some students an unfair advantage." I do not mean to imply that parents are on the average less intelligent or less literate than educators. I am simply suggesting that one should recognize that educational levels among the population at large vary greatly, and thus one should write items so that all parents will have the opportunity to read and understand them and then contribute information to an educational enterprise that is likely to affect them in some manner.

It is important, therefore, to write questionnaire items so that they will be understood by all readers while striving not to give the impression that they were taken from a Dick-and-Jane primer. This is not always easy to do; the writing of questionnaire items is more of an art than a science. However, common sense (and a good book dealing with research methods, such as Kerlinger's, 1973) can go a long way toward making one's needs-assessment questionnaire successful.

One should also make it clear to the groups receiving the questionnaires that they are being distributed to collect information, not to put certain options and policies to a popular vote. This is not decision making; it is data gathering in preparation for decision making. This should be known to all parties in advance.

It is also a good idea to keep the questionnaire as short as possible without omitting essential items. There is a trade-off that operates here. While a longer questionnaire will supply more information from each respondent, it will also result in fewer returned questionnaires and some cursory responses to items. Generally, the length of the questionnaire is inversely proportional to the percentage of response. The potential loss of information resulting from the omission of a given item must be weighed against the gain resulting from more returned questionnaires and a more representative sampling on the retained items.

It will probably be necessary to sample some groups instead of distributing questionnaires to every individual. For example, whereas one can probably distribute questionnaires to every teacher in most schools and school districts, one might find this to be an overwhelming task when it comes to parents and students. It would make sense, then, to distribute the questionnaires to a smaller number of individuals within these populations. There are numerous means of sampling large populations in order to increase the chances of obtaining a representative group (see, for example, Cochran, 1977). However, it is probably not necessary in most cases to go to elaborate lengths to insure the adequacy of the sampling. A simple stratified sample that surveys each significant group within the school or school district boundaries will probably suffice.

I mentioned above the well-known fact that one never achieves a total return of one's questionnaires. In fact, in a mail survey, one very rarely gets back as many as half of the questionnaires distributed. (With "captive audiences" such as teachers and students a higher return can be expected.) Moreover, I suspect that in the case of questionnaires dealing with proposed programs for the gifted, one not only gets a less-than-total return but one that is unrepresentative as well. It is quite likely that those who expend the time and effort to complete and return a questionnaire are those who feel strongly about the issue one way or another. Those who are indifferent have less motivation to respond. Therefore, if the returns from one's survey suggest that the population is strongly polarized with respect to programs for the gifted, one might suspect that there is a "silent majority" that did not bother to respond to a questionnaire dealing with a topic about which they have no strong opinions.

Questionnaires can be difficult to construct, expensive to print and distribute, and laborious to interpret. However, they are a useful and fairly efficient means of collecting a considerable amount of information from a large group of individuals (as well as a way of communicating with relevant groups within the population). Their use in a given school or school district will be determined by the availability of resources and the suitability of less burdensome methods of data collection. They should, however, be considered in most settings, even if one finally decides against their use.

Interviews. A more direct way of gathering information is the face-to-face interview. It makes sense to sit down to talk with certain persons who possess valuable information or whose opinions will figure prominently in future decisions about the program for the gifted.

The extent to which interviews will play a major role in the needs assessment depends, as I stated above, on such factors as the size of the school or school district. In a small district, interviews might suffice as a means of data collection. In a larger one, they can be used to augment questionnaire surveys. In the latter case, one must determine who should be interviewed in person according to certain criteria.

For example, one would most definitely wish to interview those who were involved with any previous programs for the gifted in the school or school district in order to learn from their experience and to avoid repeating their mistakes. People who function as representatives of significant groups within the educational community—department chairpersons, teacher association officers, officers of parent groups, school board members—should also be seen in person. And, for reasons of protocol as well as to try to divine a sense of how much support might be forthcoming for certain proposals, important decision makers, such as the superintendent of schools, should be interviewed. I do not mean to imply by the last sentence that one should try to develop a program plan only to please one's superintendent, but merely to suggest that it helps to know the thinking and opinions of influential leaders within the school or school district.

Like questionnaires, interviews require planning and structure. It is not enough to make an appointment and then to drop in for an informal chat. An interview schedule should be prepared in advance so that one can be certain of covering all essential items with every interviewee, thus making possible a broader and more comprehensive sampling of ideas and feelings. Certainly, one should be alert for unexpected bits of information, and one need not be inflexibly bound by the interview schedule. It is permissible and desirable to pursue any leads that crop up. However, without a plan for one's interviews, one is likely to miss essential information.

Interview data can also be compared with questionnaire data in an interesting and enlightening manner. If the ideas, opinions, and attitudes revealed through anonymous questionnaires differ significantly from those expressed face-to-face by a representative sample of interviewees, one can safely assume that a number of individuals feel compelled to parrot a party line in public with which they privately disagree. The implications of such a finding will vary from setting to setting. If, for example, questionnaires reveal less favorable attitudes toward programs for the gifted than do interviews, a possible interpretation might be that support for the program, although it may appear to be broad, is not very deep.

However extensively they are conducted and however revealing the results, interviews should be a part of any serious needs assessment. There is no substitute for direct questioning of individuals who have information that will assist in the program-planning process. Questionnaires, while usually quite useful, do not always give people a chance to say all they want to say. Interviews, by virtue of their more open-ended nature, can do just that.

Other ways of obtaining information. In the section above dealing with sources of information, I suggested that various organized groups within the community—parent–teacher organizations, parent advocacy groups, taxpayer committees, and so forth—might have information to supply. One way of obtaining this information, in addition to distributing questionnaires and interviewing the group leaders, is to ask them to submit position papers. This serves to commit these organizations to putting in writing their ideas, opinions, and attitudes toward programs for the gifted and the efforts of the local school or school district. It also reassures them that their input is being considered, even if it is not relied upon exclusively for ultimate decision making.

Finally, one should do some digging in order to uncover whatever information might be waiting to be discovered in various handy or out-of-the-way places. The gold mine of information available in student records has been mentioned above, as has the value of examining curriculum guides and documents remaining from any previous attempts to serve gifted students. In some communities, a trip to the public library to browse through back editions of the local newspaper can be worth the effort. Schools and school districts have histories, and concern for gifted students has probably played at least a small role in the history of most. A knowledge of past events could well shed some light on the present and offer some suggestions for the future.

To bring the major theme of this book to bear on the issue under discussion here, appropriate and effective means of gathering information will be suggested and shaped by the conditions in each individual school or school district. I could not hope to provide in this chapter a comprehensive listing of ways to uncover information that would serve as a guide for all individuals. The important thing to keep in mind is that the more information collected the better, within reason and the limits of one's resources. One should strive to ask the right questions of the right people in the right manner and to pursue the gathering of data in a dedicated and energetic fashion. Data gathering is the essence of needs assessment, and, in the context of the system approach I am presenting in this book, needs assessment is the essence of program planning.

How to Interpret the Information

The heading of this section is a bit ambitious and even misleading, for I cannot really state definitively how to interpret the mass of data that usually results from a comprehensive needs assessment. Certainly, one could summarize the data according to standard descriptive–statistical procedures, but the construction of narratives, graphs, and tables is data presentation, not data interpretation. More is needed, but what this "more" is will vary from situation to situation.

The interpretation of data involves the process of ferreting out answers to important questions, and these questions provide a good starting point. Specifically, the questions should revolve around decisions concerning the various program components discussed in Chapter 3 and displayed in Figure 3.1. I discussed in the last chapter how one might try to answer the question, "What is a gifted child in this school or school district?" Similar questions about program components should guide one in the interpretation of information gathered through needs assessment. Examples of such questions are: "What sources of information will help us identify gifted students?" "What program format will work to the best advantage of our target population?" and "What are the curricular needs of gifted students in this school or school district?" Knowing that these and others are the questions to be answered assists one greatly in the process of interpreting the information gathered. This provides a framework for one's data interpretation and an organizing structure for the task of confronting a sometimes confusing mass of information.

In addition, one should try to reach some general conclusions about attitudes, past experiences with programs for the gifted, administrative priorities, and the like. These should be kept in mind throughout the program-planning process; they will be factors that affect the implementation of proposed program components.

Different individuals can look at the same collection of data and see in it different things. Kurosawa's classic film *Rashomon* and the story of the blind men and the elephant come to mind here. In the case of interpreting needs assessment data, where one person sees a potential problem, for example, another might see an opportunity. It makes sense, therefore, to bring the committee whose formation was suggested in the previous chapter into this step of the process. It makes little sense to seek information from a broad and representative array of individuals and then to trust the interpretation of this information to a single person.

As was the case with the designing of questionnaire items, data interpretation, despite the protestations of some psychometricians, is often as much an art as a science. The only true guidelines are that one should be guided by the fact that needs assessment is what makes a program for the gifted truly appropriate for a given school or school district; that one should seek answers to questions that relate to major program components; and that one should make every effort to interpret honestly and accurately the information that the individuals canvassed have labored to provide.

CONCLUSION

Conducting a needs assessment may seem like a daunting task, and I will not suggest that it is either quick or easy. However, my attempt to touch as many bases as possible in outlining what a needs assessment might try to accomplish and include should not be taken to suggest that it is necessary to invest an amount of effort, time, and rigor equal to that required to complete a doctoral dissertation. A needs assessment can be a major undertaking, or it can be a less involved and more informal activity. Again, it all depends on what is needed in the particular school or school district.

However extensive the effort, I would like to insist that a needs assessment, rather than being an expensive and time-consuming luxury, is a necessary component in the planning of an effective program. A program for the gifted is—or should be—a response to the educational needs of identified gifted students. If those planning a program do not know what these needs are in the local setting, they are not in a good position to address them; that is a prescription for ineffective program planning.

CHAPTER 5

Identifying Gifted Children In The Schools

Oh, how hard it is to find
The one just suited to our mind.

Campbell, "Song"

. . . choose if you dare

Corneille, *Heraclitus*

Mr. and Mrs. Wilson were visibly upset when they arrived for their appointment with Mrs. Carter, the director of the program for the gifted in their daughter's school district. The source of their anger soon became clear. "Julie was in a gifted program in her old school, but we were not very happy with it," they said. "One of the reasons we moved to this town was the reputation of your program. Now we find out that, according to you, our daughter is no longer gifted. How can she be gifted in one school district but not in another?"

Ms. Hernandez burst into the faculty room and collapsed into a chair. "Agreeing to serve on the gifted program selection committee was one of the major mistakes of my life," she moaned to no one in particular. "It was bad enough when parents started calling me at home to lobby for their kids' admission to the program. Now they've talked school board members into trying to twist my arm. I've got plenty of aggravation already. What do I need this for?"

"I give up," sighed Dr. Strawberry, the school psychologist. "I was giving a second grader the Stanford-Binet as part of the screening for the program for the gifted. Before I could begin the test, he asked if he could play with the car. When I asked him what car he meant, he said, 'The car that comes with the game. Daddy always lets me play with the car when we play this game.' The boy knows the test materials! The parents have been practicing the test with him at home!"

"That so-called gifted program is a joke," sniffed Mr. Gooden. "Do you think it's just a coincidence that the kids of three board members are in it? It's the same old story: It's not what you know; it's whom you know."

THE PROBLEM OF IDENTIFICATION

The incidents related above will sound all too familiar to anyone who has been involved in the selection of children for a program for the gifted. As I suggested in Chapter 3, of all the tasks related to developing and implementing such programs, the identification of students is the most difficult, the most controversial, and certainly the most thankless. Those charged with this responsibility can expect to encounter considerable politicking and more than a few disgruntled children and adults. Inevitably, they make many temporary friends and some permanent enemies. And lurking in the back of their minds will be the knowledge that mistakes will be made, feelings will be hurt, and some children will be ill served.

Why is the seemingly straightforward act of placing children in appropriate educational settings the cause of so much anxiety, even hostility? The basic answer is that few of the affected parties—parents, teachers, and children—see the matter in such straightforward terms. For many of them, there is much more than an educational placement at stake.

Parental Concerns

Although few would admit it, I suspect that many parents view the issue as one of family (or individual) honor. To a certain extent, this is neither unusual nor alarming. A child who is recognized for his or her academic ability is, and probably ought to be, a source of family pride. However, parents can take this to extremes, sometimes obnoxious extremes, lording it over other parents and ostentatiously basking in the glory reflected from their gifted offspring. Like the overinvolved Little League parent whose self-esteem rises and falls with his or her child's batting average, the "professional gifted parent" is one whose paternal or maternal pride has crossed the boundary that separates healthy from unhealthy behavior.

It is not only pride that motivates some parents to become overly concerned about the identification process. In some cases an understandable, if misguided, concern for the child's future is the root of the problem. Parents may conclude that the welfare of their child depends upon his or her admission to a program for the gifted, reasoning that such a placement is the first step on the fast track to success.

This concern can begin quite early in a child's life. I used to see this with some frequency among parents of applicants for admission to the Hollingworth Preschool at Teachers College. However, the most extreme case involved a father who stopped by my office a few years ago. This man told me that for the past two months he had been using flashcards in an attempt to teach his son to read. Not being particularly enamored of flashcards as a pedagogical device, I wanted to suggest more creative ways for the two of them to explore the written word, so I asked the father how old his son was. He told me that the boy was four months old. Upon regaining my senses, I endeavored to persuade this man, that, while his motives were doubtless noble, his methods were doomed to failure and could even have consequences quite contrary to his intentions. Unfortunately, my insistence that a child of such tender age lacked the cognitive structures requisite for reading and my suggestion that this man could better spend his time simply being the boy's father fell on deaf ears.

Although as educators we may shake our heads sadly and knowingly when we hear of cases like this one, we also should acknowledge that to a certain extent we are culpable in these situations. We often speak glibly about gifted children as "the leaders of tomorrow," implying that children not in programs of the gifted will be their followers. We issue dire warnings about the harm that results from our failure to identify and provide for the special needs of gifted children early in their school careers, perhaps exacerbating parents' anxieties over "the crucial years." And by selecting some children and passing over others for programs for the gifted (children as young as three years old in the case of the Hollingworth School), we establish competitive situations in which, whether we want to view it this way or not, there are winners and losers.

Perhaps this is unavoidable. Places in programs for the gifted are limited, and placement in such programs is not in the best interest of every child, despite some parents' protestations to the contrary. However, it is incumbent upon us as educators to be careful when we describe (and even more so when we design) programs for the gifted not to give the impression that we are creating classes for an elite or that we are providing opportunities for a chosen few to prepare for their ascendency to favored status in our society.

Teachers' Misconceptions

Parents are not the only ones who can misunderstand the intent and purpose of identification. Teachers, too, are bemused by the process at times. As I mentioned in Chapter 2, a classroom teacher may view placement in a class for the gifted as a reward for success or appropriate behavior in the regular classroom. It can be difficult for a teacher to understand why the polite, well-behaved child who always turns in his or her homework on time and earns straight A's has been passed over in favor of the less respectful, more erratic underachiever who refuses to play by the rules of the game. It needs to be stressed, therefore, that placement in a program for the gifted is not, or at least should not be, a reward but a response to an educational need. Just as we do not "reward" the healthy with unnecessary medical treatment, we should not necessarily "reward" the child who is functioning well in the regular classroom with a modified curriculum. Such a modification should be prescribed only if it is warranted in light of a proper educational diagnosis.

Even when they understand the reasons for placement in programs for the gifted, teachers will, on occasion, hinder the process. The reasons for this are often quite understandable, and it is not difficult to sympathize with the teachers. Programs for the gifted are more frequently than not pull-out programs, in which the children are periodically taken out of their regular classrooms for special instruction. Teachers sometimes resent this, especially when they feel they are losing their best students. Resentment is even more likely when it is implied that the students are too bright for the classroom teacher to deal with. The problem is often compounded by the fact that the children who are pulled out for the program for the gifted are active in other such activities such as chorus, band, sports teams, and various clubs. The situation is so critical that in some schools there is a part of the school day that is "protected," during which time no child may be taken from his or her classroom.

Frustrated by the continual disruption of their classes and angered by the implication that their classrooms are of secondary importance, some teachers respond by refusing to recommend children for admission to the program for the gifted. Since teacher recommendation is the most frequently used source of information for making such placements (Butler & Borland, 1980; Marland, 1972), this presents serious difficulties for those who are responsible for identifying gifted children.

Student Resistance

Finally, students themselves, the putative beneficiaries of programs for the gifted, can complicate the situation. Not only do they refuse to fit neatly into the "gifted" and "not gifted" pigeonholes into which some educators would like to place them, they also have their own feelings about the selection process. In some cases they react competitively to the announcement of the existence of a program for the gifted. Those placed in the program sometimes gloat, and those not placed in it may feel hurt. Others may resist placement out of fear that they will be separated from or resented by their friends. Acceptance of a place in the program may result in one's being branded a "grind" or a "nerd." It may also bring on added pressures for achievement and an additional work load.

Thus, educators should not be surprised when some students reject the offer of placement in a class for the gifted. It is the duty of the conscientious educator to try to convince the students of the advantages of the placement if it seems to be in their best interest. However, it is also important that the students' best interest be carefully and objectively defined and that all factors, social and emotional as well as academic, be taken into consideration.

It should be clear by now that the identification process is interpreted differently by the various parties affected by it. Therefore, it is important that we understand the purpose of identification in order to provide a rationale for effective practice. In the following section of this chapter, therefore, I will examine the purposes of this complicated and controversial undertaking. I will then discuss the process itself in some detail, describing an approach to the problem that, in my work with schools and school districts, I have found to be both effective and flexible. I will comment upon and in some instances warn against common practices that I believe are harmful. It is important, however, that the reader keep in mind that there are many approaches to dealing with this program component and that what follows is not *the* approach but *an* approach. It, and any others one encounters, should be interpreted in that light.

THE PURPOSE OF IDENTIFICATION

The purpose of identification is to locate for placement into a program for the gifted those students in a given school or school district who are described in the program's definition of the target population (see Chapter 2). This might seem simplistic or tautologous. However, an aura of mystery and a plethora of misconceptions have arisen with respect to the identification process, and some demystification and clarity are in order.

As I asserted in Chapter 2, by defining the target population, a school or school district is setting policy; that is, it is specifying the type or types of children for whom the program is being established. The identification process is one way in which this policy is implemented. If the definition describes children with characteristics x, y, and z, the identification procedures should consist of the best and most practicable methods available for assessing those characteristics.

This is a straightforward concept; identification is simply a matter of placement. Why, then, are there so many misconceptions and so much confusion? I suspect that part of the problem derives from the fact that many view identification as an exercise in labeling children. For them it is a process of triage whereby the gifted are sorted out from the merely average and are duly labeled. Indeed, special education in general has the reputation of being obsessed with affixing to children labels such as "mentally retarded," "learning-disabled," and "gifted."

Along with many special educators (e.g., Brophy & Good, 1974; Jones, 1972, 1974; Meyerowitz, 1962), I have reservations about labeling children. Although I realize that it is a practice that will probably never be eradicated, and that the distinctions between labeling and placement are often fine ones, I think that it is important to insist that the process of identification in programs for the gifted be conceived of as a matter of placing students in appropriate programs, not one of labeling them. Making decisions about a child's educational placement is a task well within the capability of educators. Deciding if a child is or will become a gifted human being is a much more difficult and speculative proposition.

Labels are too often the result of sloppy thinking or too little thinking. The term *gifted child* itself encourages the tendency to label children, and we might be better off if we could expunge the phrase from our collective vocabulary. This, however, is unlikely to happen. We can, nonetheless, try to avoid labeling children, even if it only seems to be a semantic distinction. By consistently doing so, we can make our job as educators of the gifted quite a bit easier.

IDENTIFICATION AND THE SYSTEM APPROACH

Identification as Part of Program Planning

Viewing identification as a process of placement rather than one of labeling renders the problem merely difficult instead of nearly impossible. How, then, can one resolve this difficulty? The system approach described in Chapter 3 provides some clues.

As Figure 3.1 indicates, identification is one component of the larger program-planning system, and as such it is integrated into that system. The flowchart also shows that identification follows the definition of the target population. Moreover, identification must *logically derive from* the definition; it is the means for locating the group of children the definition describes.

Consistency is crucial here. There must be a direct correspondence between the characteristics specified in the definition and the procedures and devices used for identifying children with those characteristics. Unfortunately, this consistency is often lacking in practice. It is not uncommon to read in a school district's program plan a definition of gifted children that refers to a broad range of human traits and abilities and then to read a few pages further on that children are placed in the program for the gifted solely on the basis of achievement test scores or IQ. What I am criticizing is not the use of achievement test scores or IQ per se but the inconsistency between the definition and the identification procedures.

When the definition and the identification procedures are at variance, the latter *become* the definition. Operational definitions always supplant constitutive ones in practice. The problem is not a lack of pleasing consistency for its own sake; rather, the real problem has to do with a loss of control over the procedure. A school or school district decides to implement a program for the gifted for certain reasons and in an attempt to accomplish certain objectives, foremost among which ought to be the modification of the core curriculum for a group of children whose needs have been revealed through a needs assessment. The definition of the target population is thus a clear statement of policy indicating for whom the entire enterprise is being undertaken. If, through carelessness or thoughtlessness, the school or school district uses an identification plan that results in the selection of students other than those specified in its definition, it has lost control of the process.

Therefore, it is very important that those responsible for the program ask themselves from time to time if they are implementing a program that is both internally consistent with respect to the interrelationships among the program components and externally consistent with respect to the goals of the school or school district. With regard to identification, they should ask whether they are using the best procedures available, given their resources, for revealing the characteristics set forth in the definition. If they can honestly answer affirmatively, they, and not the tests, are in control.

The Identification Process as Its Own System

We can profitably regard identification as a subsystem embedded in the larger program-planning system. Figure 5.1 illustrates this by expanding the "Identification Procedures" box of the flowchart in Figure 3.1 into a flowchart of its own. This illustrates that the identification process has its own flow of processes and should be internally consistent.

The identification subsystem is divided into two major phases, screening and placement. I will discuss these in turn, since each has its own goals, components, and pitfalls.

THE FIRST PHASE: SCREENING

The purpose of screening

At the beginning of the identification process, one must deal with the entire student body of the school or school district, in principle if not in actuality. Somewhere in that mass is a small percentage (3 to 5 percent being the usual rule of thumb) that requires placement in the program for the gifted.

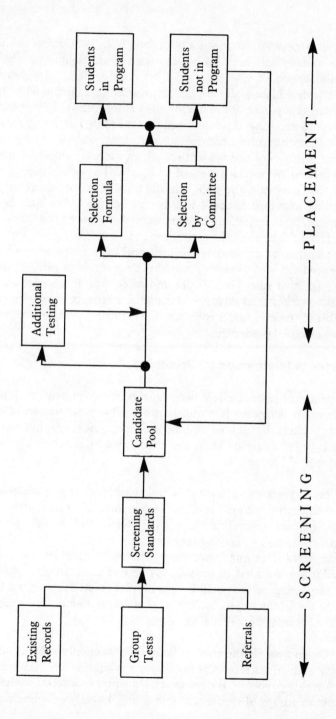

Figure 5.1: Flowchart representing the identification process.

Screening tries to make the task of moving from 100 percent to 3 to 5 percent of the students less daunting by setting an intermediate goal, the creation of a candidate pool.

The candidate pool should comprise those students who are plausible candidates for placement in the program at some time. I emphasize the word *plausible* to stress that this is not the time for fine distinctions between students or for agonizing placement decisions. Instead, one should be concerned to include in the pool any student for whom there is some evidence of special need created by special potential or ability. The percentage of the student body that goes into the pool can and should vary from setting to setting according to priorities that I will discuss below. A reasonable goal in most situations, however, would be somewhere between 10 and 20 percent.

This halfway step, the constituting of a candidate pool, allows educators to concentrate on a reasonably realistic goal and eliminate from consideration those students who obviously would not benefit from placement in the program. In most cases, it is easier and more desirable to err on the side of inclusion rather than exclusion during the screening phase. Later, when the number of students under consideration is smaller, one can deal with the finer points of actual placement.

Sources of Information for Screening

Since the entire student body must be screened, cost- and time-effective methods are desirable. It is usually not feasible to administer individual tests to every child in a school or school district; thus, one must turn to other sources of information. These are represented by the three boxes on the left-hand side of Figure 5.1.

Existing records. Students' cumulative files contain grade-point averages, achievement test scores, teachers' comments, and other things deemed by school personnel significant enough to belong in a student's record. Some school districts routinely administer aptitude tests, such as IQ tests or pre-kindergarten screening instruments, the results of which can also usually be found in student files. In general, any item of information in existing records that may reflect on the possible need for placement in a program for the gifted can be useful for screening. It is logical and economical of time and money to take advantage of what already exists.

Group tests. If the student body is conveniently small or if the school's or school district's resources permit, group-administered tests can be part of the screening process. By group tests, I simply mean those that are administered to groups of students at one sitting, usually by a teacher rather than a psychologist. Some IQ tests are administered in this manner, as are such measures as achievement and "creativity" tests (although I do not recommend that the last-mentioned of these be used for this or any other purpose, for reasons on which I will elaborate below). Group tests, whether they are administered specifically to screen students for a program for the gifted or are administered for other reasons and looked at later for screening purposes, produce scores that must be examined and used with care. In practical terms, this means that if one wishes to establish a cutoff score on a group test for admission to the candidate pool, it should not be too high.

The reasons for using relatively low (e.g., one standard deviation above the mean) cutoff scores on group tests for purposes of screening include the following. First, as I stated above, one wants to screen a relatively large number of students into the candidate pool. One can worry about final decisions later.

A second reason for setting low cutoffs relates to the nature of group measures. Group tests are not suitable for making fine distinctions among students, especially at the upper end of the distribution. They tend to compress scores, pushing them toward the mean, attenuating the tails of the distribution curve. More specifically for our purposes, group tests usually lack sufficient "ceiling." That is, the selection of items and the norming data are such that very able students cannot achieve scores high enough to demonstrate their true abilities; there is simply not enough room on the test for these students to show what they can do. This is a concern to which I will return in Chapter 9 in my discussion of program evaluation.

Third, group tests are less reliable than individually administered tests. The random error component of group-test scores is too large to allow one to treat anything but sizable differences in group-test scores as indicators of true differences in ability. In some cases, because of the exigencies of group-test construction, guessing wrong on one item at a given age level can result in a significant reduction in a student's score. Thus, by setting low cut-off scores on such tests, one avoids making false distinctions among students based upon the often considerable error variance built into group-test scores.

It should go without saying, therefore, that final placement decisions should never be made on the basis of group-test scores. Unfortunately, this dictum is often violated in practice. I have observed programs for the gifted in which a strict cutoff score is used to place students in the special class. This is a bad idea in any case, but it is especially indefensible when group tests are involved. Programs that accept a student with a group IQ of 130 but reject a student with a group IQ of 129 are merely playing a guessing game disguised as psychology. Group IQ tests do not provide information that is sufficiently reliable to provide a basis for such decisions. They are ready and efficient sources of data for screening, but that is where their utility ends.

Referrals and recommendations. These constitute a third source of information for screening. Whereas tests are attempts to reveal the existence and extent of certain abilities in response to questions and problems posed at a single sitting, referrals and recommendations represent judgments based on observations of behavior over time in more naturalistic settings. Therein lies both their strength and their weakness. The fact that referrals and recommendations focus on actual behavior in real educational settings constitutes a strength. The fact that judgment is involved constitutes a potential weakness.

The single most widely used source of information for identification purposes is *teacher recommendation* (Butler & Borland, 1980; Cox, Daniel, & Boston, 1985; Marland, 1972). This is true despite the reservations that many (e.g., Hagen, 1980) have regarding their validity. In fact, the traditional view—and one of many legacies of Lewis Terman's monumental study of gifted children (e.g., 1925)—is that teachers are exceedingly unreliable sources of information for identifying gifted students. This belief derives from a number of studies that asked teachers to list their gifted students or to rank their students from "the most to the least gifted." These nominations or rankings were then compared with the results of individual IQ test scores, the inevitable result being that the tests were better predictors of IQ than were the teachers.

Later studies (e.g., Borland, 1978; Gear, 1978; Gordon & Thomas, 1967; Keogh & Smith, 1970) have shown teachers in a more favorable light in terms of their ability to recognize signs of giftedness. The difference between these studies and earlier ones has to do with the nature of the instruments used. In the cases where the teachers have fared well, behavioral checklists, rather than simple nominations, were used. Teachers were asked to indicate the presence or absence and the frequency of certain classroom behaviors thought to be indicative of giftedness. This is a fair and feasible task, and it is not surprising that teachers are quite good at it. A sensitive and capable educator who spends upward of 180 days per year with a group of children is in a very good position to observe behaviors of interest to those responsible for identifying the gifted. This is information that is too important to ignore.

It is crucial that teacher referral forms or questionnaires pose the right questions so that the proper information can be gathered. The basic considerations are that the teachers be asked to describe behaviors they are in a position to observe in the classroom and that these behaviors relate directly to the characteristics of the students being sought for the program. The scale developed by Renzulli and Hartman (1981) shown in part in Figure 5.2 is a good example of the form that such questionnaires could assume.

This particular form is available commercially, but I present it here for exemplary purposes only. It is very unlikely that this or any other scale will fit the needs of every program. In the schools in which it is being used, it has been my experience that it is usually modified to be more appropriate for the specific setting. School personnel should feel free to examine this and other rating scales and then to develop their own instruments that are more attuned to the needs of the local target population. These are not precisely calibrated or empirically tested instruments, and modifications intended to make them more attuned to the needs of the local target population can only enhance their validity.

Since it is widely assumed that every parent believes that his or her child is gifted, the notion of seeking referrals from parents usually causes quite a few raised eyebrows. However, when carried out properly, *parent referral* can be a useful source of information for screening purposes. There is also some evidence to indicate that parent recommendation fares rather well in comparison to such sources of information as teacher recommendation (Jacobs, 1971; Richert, Alvino, & McDonnel, 1982). Obviously, one does not simply ask a parent if his or her child is gifted. Rather, one asks questions about the child's interests, hobbies, after-school and weekend activities, developmental history, and so forth. Parents know their children better than anybody else, and they have useful information, which they can make available to school personnel. Once again, it is difficult to justify not using otherwise unattainable information that can be gathered with relatively little effort.

Interpreting parent-referral forms poses some unique problems. One must frequently remind oneself that it is the child, not the parent, who is being considered. Since the information about the child must be gleaned from what the parent writes, this is often difficult. Some parents will submit page after page of typewritten documentation, complete with appendixes, footnotes, and references to Piaget's developmental stages. Others will offer minimal responses to the questions in imperfect English. Although it is difficult not to be swayed by a parent's facility with the language or lack thereof, this tendency should be resisted. Try to read between the lines, looking for evidence of the child's ability, not that of the parents. Parent recommendations can be valuable sources of screening data if treated properly. To be on the safe side, however, it is probably better to use such data to screen children into, rather than out of, the candidate pool.

Finally, *students* themselves can be important sources of screening information about each other. Once again, one does not ask children and adolescents directly whether one of their peers is gifted. Instead, a series of indirect questions can be employed to gather the requisite data. Since children tend to be privy to information about each other to which adults do not have access, asking such questions as "If you were asked to do a science project, which of your classmates would you want to have help you?" or "During recess, which of your classmates has the most ideas for new games?" can be quite revealing.

Figure 5.2: Scale for rating the behavioral characteristics of superior students (Renzulli & Hartman, 1981).

Joseph S. Renzulli
Robert K. Hartman

SCALE FOR RATING BEHAVIORAL
CHARACTERISTICS OF SUPERIOR STUDENTS

Name _____ Date _____

School _____ Grade _____ Age _____
                                                  Years   Months

Teacher or person completing this form _____

How long have you known this child? _____ Months.

Directions. These scales are designed to obtain teacher estimates of a student's characteristics in the areas of learning, motivation, creativity, and leadership. The items are derived from the research literature dealing with characteristics of gifted and creative persons. It should be pointed out that a considerable amount of individual differences can be found within this population; and therefore, the profiles are likely to vary a great deal. Each item in the scales should be considered separately and should reflect the degree to which you have observed the presence or absence of each characteristic. Since the four dimensions of the instrument represent relatively different sets of behaviors, the scores obtained from the separate scales should not be summed to yield a total score. Please read the statements carefully and place an X in the appropriate place according to the following scale of values:

- If you have *seldom* or *never* observed this characteristic.
- If you have observed this characteristic *occasionally.*
- If you have observed this characteristic to a *considerable* degree.
- If you have observed this characteristic *almost all of the time.*

Space has been provided following each item for your comments.

Scoring. Separate scores for each of the three dimensions may be obtained as follows:

Add the total number of X's in each column to obtain the "Column Total."
Multiply the Column Total by the "Weight" for each column to obtain the "Weighted Column Total."
Sum the Weighted Column Totals across to obtain the "Score" for each dimension of the scale.
Enter the Scores below.

Learning Characteristics .... _____
Motivational Characteristics .... _____
Creativity Characteristics .... _____
Leadership Characteristics .... _____

PART I: LEARNING CHARACTERISTICS

	1*	2	3	4

1. Has unusually advanced vocabulary for age or grade level; uses terms in a meaningful way; has verbal behavior characterized by "richness" of expression, elaboration, and fluency. (National Education Association, 1960; Terman & Oden, 1947; Witty, 1955) □ □ □ □

2. Possesses a large storehouse of information about a variety of topics (beyond the usual interests of youngsters his age). (Ward, 1961; Terman, 1925; Witty, 1958) □ □ □ □

3. Has quick mastery and recall of factual information. (Goodhart & Schmidt, 1940; Terman & Oden, 1947; National Education Association, 1960) □ □ □ □

4. Has rapid insight into cause-effect relationships; tries to discover the how and why of things; asks many provocative questions (as distinct from informational or factual questions); wants to know what makes things (or people) "tick." (Carroll, 1940; Witty, 1958; Goodhart & Schmidt, 1940) □ □ □ □

5. Has a ready grasp of underlying principles and can quickly make valid generalizations about events, people, or things; looks for similarities and differences in events, people, and things. (Bristow, 1951; Carroll, 1940; Ward, 1961 □ □ □ □

6. Is a keen and alert observer; usually "sees more" or "gets more" out of a story, film, etc. than others. (Witty, 1958; Carroll, 1940; National Education Association, 1960) □ □ □ □

7. Reads a great deal on his own; usually prefers adult level books; does not avoid difficult material; may show a preference for biography, autobiography, encyclopedias, and atlases. (Hollingworth, 1942; Witty, 1958; Terman & Oden, 1947) □ □ □ □

8. Tries to understand complicated material by separating it into its respective parts; reasons things out for himself; sees logical and common sense answers. (Freehill, 1961; Ward, 1962; Strang, 1958) □ □ □ □

	1*	2	3	4
Column Total	□	□	□	□
Weight	1	2	3	4
Weighted Column Total				
TOTAL				⬚

*1—Seldom or never
2—Occasionally
3—Considerably
4—Almost always

From: Scale for Rating the Behavioral Characteristics of Superior Students by J.S. Renzulli & R.K. Hartman, 1981, in W.B. Barbe & J.S. Renzulli (Eds.), *Psychology and Education of the Gifted* (3rd ed.), p. 158. Copyright 1981 by Irvington Publishers, Inc. Reprinted by permission.

One can also ask children directly about themselves rather than about their peers. Again, some tact is required. Older children can be asked to write their autobiographies, which can tell a great deal about their activities, beliefs, aspirations, and dreams and which also provide writing samples. Younger children can be asked a series of yes-or-no questions that relate to the characteristics of children being sought for the program.

To summarize, educators involved with the screening of students for programs for the gifted are well advised to seek information from as many sources as possible, including teachers, parents, and students themselves. Some assert that the resulting information is "soft" data, and I can only agree. However, information is information, and one is unlikely to suffer from a surfeit of data in making identification decisions. The identification of gifted students is such a problematic undertaking that one should take advantage of any source of information available in order to make intelligent decisions.

Standards for Screening

The methods referred to above—examining existing records, administering group tests, and soliciting referrals—are ways of generating information. Once in hand, this information must be used to make a decision regarding who will and who will not enter the candidate pool. There is no hard-and-fast rule for how this should be done. The priorities and resources of the school or school district are major factors that influence the process, and I will discuss below two parameters that come into play in this respect.

Matrices. First, however, I would like to spend some time discussing a practice that is often employed at this point in the process of identification. This is the use of screening or identification matrices. While the use of matrices has much to recommend it, I fear that in most cases they are misused and may be doing more harm than good.

A matrix, in this context, is a way of reducing a collection of data to a single index by setting up an array of rows and columns. The rows represent the various sources of information—tests, referrals, records—and the columns represent the values assigned to the performance or rating of the student under consideration. I will use as my example here the Baldwin Identification Matrix (Baldwin, 1978), since it is the best known, the most carefully developed, and the most widely used of the screening and identification matrices (see Figure 5.3).

The appeal of matrices is not hard to fathom. A matrix simplifies matters considerably by translating a number of scores and ratings into a single index. This index can then be used to rank students from highest to lowest for purposes of screening or placement. A matrix such as Baldwin's also has the

Figure 5.3: The Baldwin Identification Matrix.

Student _Joseph Matrix_ School _Loman Elementary_
Age _9_ Grade _3_ Sex _M_ Date _5-6-78_ School District _Eastern_

Assessment Items	Scores					
	5	4	3	2	1	B-NA
1. Standardized Intelligence Test	140+ ( )	130-139 ( )	120-129 (✔)	110-119 ( )	100-109 ( )	
2. Achievement Test Composite Score	95%ile ( )	90-94%ile ( )	85-89%ile (✔)	80-84%ile ( )	75-79%ile ( )	
3. Achievement Test—Reading Score	Stan 9 (✔)	Stan 8 ( )	Stan 7 ( )	Stan 6 ( )	Stan 5 ( )	
4. Achievement Test—Math Score	95%ile ( )	90-94%ile ( )	85-89%ile (✔)	80-84%ile ( )	75-79%ile ( )	
5. Learning Scale Score	32 (✔)	28-31 ( )	24-27 ( )	20-23 ( )	16-19 ( )	
6. Motivational Scale Score	36 (✔)	32-35 ( )	28-31 ( )	24-27 ( )	16-23 ( )	
7. Creativity Scale Score	40 (✔)	36-35 ( )	32-35 ( )	28-31 ( )	20-27 ( )	
8. Leadership Scale Score	40 ( )	36-39 (✔)	32-35 ( )	28-31 ( )	20-27 ( )	
9. Various Teacher Recommendations	Superior ( )	Very Good (✔)	Good ( )	Average ( )	Below Average ( )	
10. Psychomotor Ability	( )	(✔)	( )	( )	( )	
11. Peer Nominations	( )	(✔)	( )	( )	( )	
12.	( )	( )	( )	( )	( )	
Column Tally of Checks	4	4	3	0	0	
Weight	x5	x4	x3	x2	x1	
Add Across	20	16	9	0	0	
Total Score	45					

From: The Baldwin Identification Matrix by A. Y. Baldwin, 1978, in A. Y. Baldwin, G. H. Gear, & L. J. Lucito (Eds.), *Educational Planning for the Gifted*, p. 34. Copyright 1978 by the Council for Exceptional Children. Reprinted by permission.

virtue of suggesting to educators that there are many sources of information on which identification decisions can be based. The various rows on the matrix are graphic reminders that tests are not the only tools available. This is a repetition of one of the shibboleths of the gifted-education movement, the need to employ a "multiple-criterion" (more accurately, a multiple-measure) approach to the problem of identification. Given these advantages, why do I believe that matrices are usually a bad idea?

The primary, and in my opinion fatal, flaw in matrices such as Baldwin's has to do with the final index. In the example provided by Baldwin shown in Figure 5.3, "Joseph Matrix" achieved a score of 45. My question is, "45 what?" What does this number represent? If Joseph's sister Mary Matrix had earned a score of 50, of what quantity would this be an increment of five? I believe that there are no good answers to these questions, because the final index is conceptually and psychometrically uninterpretable, a classic apples-and-oranges situation.

In the Baldwin Matrix, my example here, one is asked to add together IQ, achievement test scores (double weighted due to the inclusion of a composite score), four disparate subscales from an unvalidated teacher nomination form, other teacher recommendations, peer nominations, and some unspecified index of psychomotor ability. What is the result? One ends up with a mélange, a hodgepodge whose meaning is unclear. This is analogous to combining a family's income, home equity, number of children, average height, and number of food-processor attachments in order to derive a "quality-of-life index." These things cannot be added; the sum cannot be interpreted. By using the Baldwin Matrix or a similar device, one loses information that could be very useful and merely gains a questionable index of "giftedness."

This alone should be sufficient to discourage the use of such matrices, but there are other problems. Again using as my example the Baldwin Matrix, which has probably been given more careful thought than any other, one can question the manner in which scores are assigned. A matrix serves to reduce the range of scores on each variable, in this case to a scale of 0 to 5. If this is a good idea—and it may not be—it should at least be done consistently. But take the case of Marvin Matrix, a student who outscores 78 percent of his age peers nationally on the Wechsler Intelligence Scale for Children (WISC) and the mathematics and reading scales of the Iowa Test of Basic Skills. Being at the 78th percentile on each measure, Marvin should receive the same number of points for each on the matrix.

However, on the Baldwin Matrix, a WISC IQ of 112, which would correspond to the 78th percentile, would give Marvin two points. Since the row for reading achievement-test scores is marked off in stanines, Marvin's 78th percentile ranking would give him three points (seventh stanine). However, the same rank on the mathematics test (78th percentile) is worth only one point. This inconsistency is a problem of this particular matrix, and it is likely to be a greater problem in the case of less carefully designed matrices.

One should also be concerned about the probability that matrices obscure important differences between students. Take the case of two more members of the fecund Matrix family, Max and Mabel. Max is a brilliant student whose social skills are less than adequate and who has ill-disguised contempt for his teachers and peers. He scores 5 on the first five rows of the Baldwin Matrix and 0 on the rest. Mabel is an indifferent student, but she is athletic, popular with peers and teachers, and a budding actress with a flair for imitation and improvisation. She receives no points except on rows 7 through 11 on the matrix, where she receives 5s. Both Max and Mabel achieve an index of 25; according to the matrix they are equal. However, quite obviously they are very different, and these differences ought to bear upon their admission to a program for gifted students. This is a good example of how information can be lost through the use of matrices.

Another problem relates to one of the cardinal principles of programming, the need for consistency between the definition of the target population and the identification procedures. Those schools and school districts that buy the Baldwin Matrix or devise a similar one are, almost invariably, violating this principle. The reader is invited to glance over the rows of the Baldwin Matrix and to attempt to abstract a coherent definition of giftedness from the various measures found there. It is highly unlikely that any meaningful definition could encompass all of the qualities being assessed by those scores. By adopting this matrix, one also adopts the rather indiscriminate definition of giftedness it implies. A well-defined target population virtually precludes the use of this device.

Most important, the use of a matrix results in the loss of quite a bit of information that required considerable time and effort to collect. Each test score, recommendation, and other item of information, some of which could be of significant interest to those who must make identification decisions, disappears into the composite index. Were this index psychometrically valid or interpretable, the trade-off might arguably be worthwhile. In actuality, however, the loss of information in a situation in which information is a precious commodity is too great a price to pay for such a small return.

In summary, therefore, I would caution against the use of matrices in the manner in which they are commonly employed. Too often, good information is lost, obscured, or mangled when it is fed into such devices. They should be used with extreme caution and considerable forethought.

A better approach. Rather than combining scores into a single, possibly meaningless, index, educators should instead look at each score and rating individually and place into the candidate pool any student who reaches a cutoff on a single instrument. This is preferable, because screening involves the search for any likely candidate, whether that student reveals himself or herself on tests, grades, ratings, or products. Especially when the student body is diverse in terms of ethnicity, culture, social class, or language used in the home, it is necessary to look at profiles, not global indexes.

It is difficult to specify a general rule for setting cutoff scores for screening. A certain amount of trial-and-error is involved, and local conditions need to be considered. For example, in a fairly homogeneous district where a candidate pool of 20 percent of the student body is being sought, choosing the top 10 to 12 percent on each instrument may well result in the desired figure. Many students will qualify on more than one measure, and the overlap will keep the total down. If the population is more heterogeneous with respect to its performance on the various indicators employed for screening, lower cutoffs will be needed if the pool is to be kept to 20 percent. In any case, the decision is an educational one, not a mechanical or statistical one. Educators should make the decisions by interpreting, not merely adding, the scores.

Efficiency and effectiveness. There are some guidelines that can be helpful in establishing standards for screening. Two parameters, which unfortunately cannot be measured or estimated, should be kept in mind. These are *effectiveness* and *efficiency*. They were first discussed by Pegnato and Birch (1959), in an article that has had some influence in the years following its publication. Effectiveness and efficiency affect the size of the candidate pool, and they reflect the intentions and priorities of the school or school district with respect to the identification of gifted students.

Effectiveness is related to how many gifted students in a population actually make it into the candidate pool. Let us suppose that we are omniscient (thus rendering the entire identification process unnecessary, of course) and that we know that there are 100 gifted students in the student body of the Boss Tweed Junior High School. Let us further suppose that, as a result of the screening, 90 of these gifted students are placed in the candidate pool and 10 are overlooked. In this example, the screening procedures would be 90 percent effective. Effectiveness is the number of gifted students in the pool divided by the number of gifted students in the school or school district.

Efficiency is an index of the number of students in the pool who are actually gifted. Going back to Boss Tweed Junior High, let us now suppose that the pool contains 180 students altogether (we have already stipulated that 90 of these students are gifted). The efficiency of the screening at Boss Tweed would be 50 percent, computed by dividing the number of *gifted* students in the pool by the *total* number of students in the pool.

Keeping in mind that our lack of omniscience renders it impossible to compute actual values for these parameters, the formulas would look like this:

$$\text{Effectiveness} = \frac{\text{No. of gifted students in pool}}{\text{No. of gifted students in the school}}$$

$$\text{Efficiency} = \frac{\text{No. of gifted students in pool}}{\text{Total no. of all students in pool}}$$

One may well ask of what use these formulas are if they cannot be used empirically. The answer is that although one cannot actually compute indexes of effectiveness and efficiency, one can affect the effectiveness and efficiency of one's screening in certain ways. It is important, first of all, to realize that these are antagonistic principles. As effectiveness increases, efficiency decreases, and vice versa. One must thus strive for one or the other; one cannot have a high degree of both.

Priorities and policy are paramount here. If the chief objective is to identify as many gifted students as possible, effectiveness should be stressed. If, on the other hand, time, personnel, and money are limited, efficiency will be of greater concern. The decision has to be made as to whether it is more important not to miss any gifted students or whether it is more important not to overtax available resources. Once this has been decided, one can take steps that will increase either effectiveness or efficiency.

Very simply, setting lower cutoff scores on screening instruments and allowing entrance into the candidate pool on the basis of one indicator will increase the size of the pool and maximize effectiveness. Setting higher cutoff scores and more stringent entrance requirements will keep the pool smaller and efficiency higher. The larger the pool, the fewer gifted students one will miss but the more time one will have to spend on the identification process. It is important to keep the trade-off in mind during this phase of the process.

However one proceeds, one's actions should be guided by policy. Striving for greater effectiveness or greater efficiency should be a conscious decision based upon an awareness of the needs of the school or school district. A determination must be made as to whether false negatives (ineffectiveness) or false positives (inefficiency) are more harmful in the given situation, and one should proceed accordingly.

Whichever parameter is assigned the higher priority, the goal of the screening phase of identification is a pool of likely candidates for the program. This sets the stage for the second phase.

THE SECOND PHASE: PLACEMENT

The goal of placement is to locate those students in the candidate pool who are most in need of the services of the special program and to place them in the program. A first, but optional, step in the placement phase is the collection of additional information.

Additional Testing

Figure 5.1 contains a box labeled "Additional Testing." This indicates that once a candidate pool has been formed, it may be possible or desirable to administer one or more tests, a more feasible proposition now that the number of students under consideration has been reduced appreciably. Whether additional testing is worthwhile educationally is another matter. Unless one of two conditions can be met, the time and expense involved may make the process supererogatory.

The need for more reliable information. First, if more reliable measurement of traits set forth in the definition of the target population is needed, additional testing is justifiable. For example, as I mentioned earlier, group aptitude tests are not as reliable as individually administered tests. More reliable measures may be especially useful if the students in the candidate pool are very able academically and their scores cluster near the ceiling of the group test. In such situations, one can make a good argument for the use of a more precise instrument with a lower standard error of measurement. One should consult test manuals and especially the Mental Measurements Yearbooks (Buros, e.g., 1978) for information concerning test reliability.

The need for more specific information. In a second, related situation, further testing is useful if more specific, as opposed to general, information is needed. For example, the IQ is an index of general intellectual (or, more accurately, academic) ability. This construct can be subdivided into (or replaced by) more specific factors that some view as the building blocks or constituents of human intelligence. J. P. Guilford's structure-of-intellect model (e.g., Guilford, 1967), which has been accorded a warm, if sometimes uncomprehending, welcome by professionals in the field of the education of the gifted, is an example of a model of intelligence that goes well beyond the notion of a single monolithic intellectual ability. Many of the 120 separate factors that for Guilford and his disciples constitute intelligence can be assessed using paper-and-pencil tests published by an agency known as the SOI Institute. Thus, if one's definition of giftedness specifies, say, the ability to think divergently, it is possible to assess this aspect of general cognitive functioning through the use of tests of some of Guilford's factors.

This seems to be a characteristically American approach to the problem of understanding intelligence. It has not found favor among British psychologists, who still adhere to the concept of *g*, or general ability. Howard Gardner's theory of multiple intelligences (1983), which has received quite a bit of attention of late, is simply one in a long line of multifactorial theories of intelligence that extends at least as far back as Kelley's *Crossroads in the Mind of Man* (1928). The reader should be aware, however, that there is considerable controversy surrounding the question of whether or not intelligence is validly or profitably divisable in this way. Even in this country there is skepticism regarding the legitimacy and utility of some of the more extreme models, such as Guilford's. Hagen's (1980) admonition that the SOI tests be used for experimental but not selection purposes is probably still germane given the tentative nature of the data supporting their validity.

Issues Relating to Tests and Additional Testing

Since I have raised the issue of IQ tests, and since the very mention of these instruments raises a red flag for many educators and laypersons, I would like to discuss briefly their use in the identification of the gifted.

IQ tests. The "IQ controversy" has been with us for some time, at least since the debates in the early 1920s between Lewis M. Terman and Walter Lippmann in the pages of the *New Republic* (see Block & Dworkin, 1976, for a reprinting of these exchanges). Arguments about the utility, validity, and morality of the tests continue today, and the battle has been joined by many within the field of the education of the gifted. (A special issue of the *Roeper Review* edited by Linda Silverman, 1986b, was devoted exclusively to this topic.)

While nobody could honestly deny that the tests have been abused in the past, their wholesale rejection by the field would be, in my opinion, a major mistake, a case of throwing out the baby with the bathwater (see Borland, 1986b). It would make considerably better sense to strive to end the abuse of the tests than it would to deny ourselves access to a potentially valuable instrument. Used correctly, with an awareness of their limitations, IQ tests can tell us quite a bit about the intellectual and academic aptitudes of some children. The tests do not, of course, comprehensively measure intelligence as that term is generally understood today. However, as Howley, Howley, and Pendarvis (1986) assert in their well-reasoned and extensively researched text, "Quite simply, IQ tests and other norm-referenced measures are about the best pedagogical tools we have from which to construct definitions that can be applied with some attention to fairness" (p. 376).

Owing to the fact that IQ tests are best defined as predictors of aptitude for academic achievement, they bear a direct relationship to the conception of giftedness that informs this book. Until better measures come along, in fulfillment of promises made by Gardner (1983), Sternberg (1984), and others, they will remain among the most useful instruments available to us. In the context of the multiple-measure case-study approach to placement advocated below, I have no hesitation about recommending their use in an informed and humane manner.

Creativity tests. Another issue concerns the use of tests that purport to measure creativity, such as the Torrance Tests of Creative Thinking (Torrance, 1966). In theory, this would be the place in the identification process where such tests would be used. The problem with their use, as numerous writers have pointed out (e.g., Crockenberg, 1972; Tannenbaum, 1983; Thorndike, 1966; Wallach, 1970), is that there is no persuasive evidence that they assess anything that can reasonably be considered to be human creativity. The very notion that a paper-and-pencil test could measure something as complex as human creativity is rather fanciful; in practice, there can be little doubt that such tests have failed to fulfill their creators' hopes. Thus, the unfortunate fact of their use in some programs for the gifted is reflective more of wishful thinking than of sound psychometric practice. Such measures have no place in a well-designed identification plan.

Other tests. What, then, can one use with confidence if additional measures of more specific abilities are needed? The question can best be answered with reference to the definition of the target population. If specific ability in one or more academic areas is mentioned in the definition, achievement tests of various sorts are available, although out-of-level administration will probably be required. The staff of the Study of Mathematically Precocious Youth at the Johns Hopkins University (see, for example, Stanley, 1981) has had great success administering the mathematics section of the Scholastic Aptitude Test to seventh-grade students in a search for high-level talent in mathematics. Similar approaches would recommend themselves to those interested in ability in other disciplines.

In terms of measuring specific cognitive factors, things become a bit problematic. In addition to the SOI tests, programs for the gifted have employed the Ross Test of Higher Cognitive Functioning (Ross & Ross, 1976), the Educational Testing Service Kit of Factor-Referenced Cognitive Tests (Ekstrom, French, Harman, & Derman, 1976), and the subtests of the Wechsler Intelligence Scale for Children–Revised (Wechsler, 1974). The jury is still out on the Ross Test; Educational Testing Service's kit is recommended for research purposes only; and the reliability of the WISC subtest scores is probably not high enough to warrant their use (Hagen, 1980).

Use of any test of specific cognitive factors ultimately becomes a matter of judgment and belief. Educators enamored of Guilford's SOI model will probably not be swayed by those who call for caution in its use (just as those who want to believe in the validity of "creativity tests" will not be deterred by their lack of validity). I hope, though, that the judgment made would be tempered and conditioned by an awareness of the most recent research and by common sense. It is usually the case that tests of specific cognitive factors are of little value in the identification process. Unless there is a very good reason for their use, the need to distinguish among a sizable group of very bright students, for example, they are probably more trouble than they are worth given the equivocal nature of the research data. To repeat one of the basic rules; the factors measured by the test must be part of the definition of the population one is seeking to identify.

Alternatives to tests. In those cases where more specific indicators of the desired abilities are required, Tannenbaum's (1983) notion of the curriculum as the identifier makes sense. Tannenbaum suggests exposing students to enrichment activities as the best way of predicting whether or not certain students will benefit from them or be able to handle them successfully. One is therefore predicting from like situation to like situation, not from a test to a classroom situation. This approach has been employed with success at the Hollingworth Preschool at Teachers College where, due to the age of the applicants, among other reasons, there has been skepticism regarding the absolute validity of aptitude test scores.

Thus, if one has a pool of candidates who have scored well on an aptitude test, it might make sense to expose them to activities similar to those that will be part of the special-class curriculum and to observe their reactions. The danger here, as Tannenbaum points out, is that this approach can become Procrustean. The goal is not to see which students fit the curriculum, but which students most need a special curriculum designed to fit their needs. This should be kept in mind by those who wish to adopt this logical approach to gathering additional data for making placement decisions.

By the same token, if creativity in a specific context, as opposed to the "stuff" (Perkins, 1981) the so-called creativity tests attempt to assess, is crucial to one's definition, this empirical approach is also dictated. Look for evidence of creativity in the students' work, not in their test scores. Student paintings, compositions, research proposals, projects, and other products can be judged for evidence of creativity, since past creativity is the best predictor of future creativity yet devised. The problem here is that too few students have had the opportunity to develop whatever potential for creative production they might have. The school curriculum simply does not give students as many chances to create as it does to memorize. So the idea of first exposing students to educational activities that stress creative work before looking at the students' products is especially crucial.

It may be concluded from the preceding paragraphs that additional testing is usually neither necessary nor desirable. This is probably an accurate statement. However, one should decide on a case-by-case basis. If one can justify further testing, one should carry it out. However, testing is not a panacea, and as I will argue below, it is no substitute for professional judgment.

The Placement Decision

Ultimately, a decision must be made. Certain students among those in the candidate pool must be selected for placement in the program, and some must remain in the pool. In general, there are two ways to make this decision (see Figure 5.1). The first is to combine all of the available data into a single score through the use of a mathematical formula, a tactic suggested by the matrix approach. The second option is to have the decision made by a committee of educators who decide on placement on a case-by-case basis.

The formula approach. The use of a mathematical formula appears to have distinct advantages. For one thing, it has the appearance of objectivity. Students are selected on the basis of a single score, mathematically derived, and the human bias factor would seem to be kept to a minimum. If the son or daughter of a school board member is placed in the program, it is because he or she obtained a score that exceeded the cutoff for placement. Thus, many educators favor this approach because it is easy to explain to parents and reduces the number of lobbying campaigns on behalf of certain students.

This method also connotes precision. Scores are often weighted differentially, so that each has its own coefficient in the formula. The final index is the result of a linear combination of factors that gives the appearance of being psychologically and scientifically sound.

Unfortunately, the soundness and precision of the approach are usually illusory. I have already discussed the problems encountered when educators mix apples and oranges in creating a "gifted index." That problem is usually not obviated by substituting a formula for a matrix.

Combining scores into a single index is a tricky business that requires resources usually not available to school personnel. University admissions departments can do this with some success, although far from perfectly, because they have the means and the time to derive and to validate the often complex regression formulas used to predict the probability of college success. In public school programs for the gifted, however, the coefficients in the formulas are usually the result of somebody's belief that, for example, teacher ratings ought to be given twice the weighing of parent ratings because they seem to be twice as important. Thus, in most cases the appearance of precision and objectivity is merely that—appearance—masking the fact that the procedure rests on a subjective guess as to what ought to work.

One of the most troubling features of such formulas (and matrices, which are simply formulas in which each variable receives the same weight) is that they represent an abdication of responsibility on the part of educators. Rather than making the difficult decisions themselves, those who use formulas and matrices are content to hide behind a facade of false objectivity. In fact, they are deciding rather subjectively to allow important placement decisions to be made by a process that, having no proven validity, is not assured of deviating significantly from chance.

Placement as a committee decision. Tests and recommendations are indispensable tools in the identification of gifted students. Without them, the placement of students in programs for the gifted would be an extremely difficult proposition. Indeed, some (e.g., Pintner, 1931) have suggested that the very fact that there are intellectually and academically gifted children went unnoticed until the advent of the psychological test. Tests, however, are only tools, and their utility depends on the degree of skill with which they are used by educators. Combining test scores and letting the numbers fall where they may can be politically expedient, but this is hardly a responsible use of such educational tools.

Placement involves a decision as to the proper setting for a certain child at a given time. This decision is too important to be left to what is little more than a numbers game in too many cases. Instead, decisions that affect the education of individual students should be made on an individual basis by a committee of educators who can act in an intelligent and informed manner. Thus, I recommend that educators adopt a case-study approach to the placement problem. Not only does this avoid the pitfalls described above, but it also puts the decision in the hands of educators, where it belongs.

The case-study approach allows each placement decision to be weighed in light of a specific child's particular needs. Circumstances that are relevant to a child's placement that do not enter into ratings or test scores, or that may confound them, can be considered. The fact that children come from different racial, ethnic, and socioeconomic backgrounds can also be taken into account, as it should be.

For example, the extremely intelligent child who is bored and senses that the school is indifferent to his or her needs and thus becomes a chronic underachiever may represent the type of child most in need of a special program. A mathematical formula might not reflect this child's needs accurately, since his or her underachievement would very likely depress the final index. The complacent but hardly brilliant child who is achieving to the limits of his or her potential in the regular classroom, and who should not be taken out of that classroom, is more likely to end up in the program for the gifted, although it is the underachiever who has greater need of this placement.

Or consider the child whom I encountered in a suburban school district. His computer skills were extremely advanced, well beyond those of any other student in his elementary school. The program for the gifted in that school district focused almost exclusively on computer programming. This boy, who was obviously gifted in terms of the specific aptitude that made up the bulk of the curriculum of that program, was denied admission because his scores did not add up to a high enough total according to the selection formula used. Had human beings, not a formula, been in charge, he would have received the placement he needed. Unfortunately, when formulas are employed, the predictor often becomes the criterion (see Sternberg, 1982), as was the case here.

Other examples, real and hypothetical, spring to mind. The brilliant but obnoxious student who receives low teacher and peer ratings, the street-smart child from the inner city whose test scores are relatively low, the highly able child whose classroom performance is affected by problems at home—all of these would very likely be passed over in favor of polite, capable, but not truly gifted achievers.

Human giftedness is too variegated a phenomenon to be captured in a single matrix or score continuum. It is a complex combination of traits and states that requires the sensitivity of caring human observers for its recognition; that is why I recommend that a committee be given responsibility for making placement decisions.

The composition of the placement committee. The makeup of the placement committee will vary from setting to setting, but it is important that it be broadly representative of those educational professionals who are knowledgeable of and affected by the operation of the program for the gifted. Regular classroom teachers, teachers in the program for the gifted, building and central administrators, psychologists, and program coordinators are likely candidates for membership in the committee. In some districts, school board members, parents, and students are represented as well. The type of program will determine the composition of the committee to some extent; music and art teachers are obvious choices for a program that stresses artistic creativity, for example. However the committee is constituted, every effort should be made to include a broad range of concerned individuals who are professionally interested in the program and who are able to contribute to the placement discussions.

These "discussions," by the way, may sometimes become rather heated. Tempers can flare up as disagreements over the placement of various students arise. Human judgment is rarely unanimous, and a perfect consensus cannot be guaranteed. However, the image of committed, sometimes passionate, flesh-and-blood educators putting themselves on the line on behalf of a student's needs and those of a program in which they believe does not bother me in the least. These are decisions affecting real children, and they should be made by real people who care. Eschewing questionable but noncontroversial formulas requires considerable effort and commitment, but so do serving on a jury and voting, which are analogous processes for making important decisions.

Moreover, in practice, there are usually quite a few candidates in the pool whose placement or nonplacement in the program is obvious to all. The number of placement decisions requiring serious discussion will always be significantly fewer than the number of places in the program. For the rest, there is no good alternative to having the committee members "slug it out" (in good faith, of course). This is a messy and probably unscientific approach, but compared with the meretricious precision of formulas and matrices, it is also reassuringly human and educationally more defensible.

THE NEED FOR REGULAR REEVALUATION

When all is said and done, as far as the identification of the gifted is concerned, all is not really said and done. This is because a good identification plan is ongoing and makes provisions for periodic reassessment of students. This is inherent in the special-educational model of education of the gifted advocated in this book. Since we should be less concerned with labeling students than with making appropriate placements, we should review these placements periodically in order to determine whether or not they are currently suitable.

The needs of students change over time. This is true of both the students placed in the program and those left in the candidate pool. Thus, the work of the placement committee is not really finished when the placements are made. In fact, this committee is better referred to as a placement and review committee, since a major aspect of its functioning should be the review of placements in order to see if they are still appropriate for the students in question.

If it is not apparent by now, let me state explicitly that anyone who undertakes the task of identifying children for a program for the gifted is going to make some mistakes. Students will be placed in the program who would be better served in the regular classroom, and some students who could benefit greatly from the program may not even make it into the candidate pool. It is even conceivable that some harm may be done in the process. This is an unfortunate but inevitable consequence of operating a program that should prove to be beneficial to many in the long run. This is why a placement and review committee, one that truly reviews its placements with some frequency, is so important. Placements are speculative; reviews are evaluative. Placements are made on the basis of predictive data of less-than-perfect validity. However, once a child has been in the program for a while, his or her placement can be evaluated in light of actual behavior. The goal is to recognize and to correct during the review process those mistakes made during the identification process.

This is especially crucial when children are identified as gifted early in their school careers. The younger the child is at the point of selection, the greater the likelihood of significant change over the course of his or her development. This is the case even with cognitive measures, such as the IQ, which many apparently view as being quite stable. On the contrary, as studies such as the Berkeley Growth Study (Bayley, 1955) and the Guidance Study (Honzik, Macfarlane, & Allen, 1948) have shown, IQ can be quite variable over the school years. In the latter study, for example, 59 percent of a sample of 222 students showed IQ changes of 15 or more points over the age span of 6 to 18 years.

Even among older children, change is a constant. Intelligence, as Jean Piaget has argued (e.g., Inhelder & Piaget, 1958), undergoes a process of evolution, not a simple linear process of accretion. The affective, conative, and attitudinal traits and states that bear upon a child's educational placement are even more subject to variation. Thus, in one sense, the child who was placed or not placed into a program for the gifted may be a significantly different person, with needs that have changed considerably, even over the course of one year.

One might say that there is a need to view placements as hypotheses to be tested empirically in the classroom. If the placement proves to be wrong for the child, there should be no hesitation about admitting and correcting the mistake. To make a special-educational placement and never to review that placement is a dangerous and irresponsible practice.

It is important, however, to make certain that students, parents, teachers, and administrators know that this policy is in effect and are aware of the process whereby reevaluations are done. Especially important is the need to make certain that all parties understand that reevaluation is not a matter of determining whether or not a child is "really gifted" but a practical matter of assessing whether a certain class placement has been in the child's interest. This is another opportunity to assert that identification involves placement decisions, not the labeling of children.

CONCLUSION

It may appear that the identification of gifted students as I describe it is an undertaking fraught with controversy and the potential for error, a thankless task that is likely to lead to some undesirable outcomes. There is no denying that these dangers lurk for the careless, or even the prudent, program director. However, I believe that attention to the issues raised above will minimize these problems. I also am convinced that the entire process is worth the aggravation incurred and the expenditure of time and energy that is required.

In far more critical situations, surgeons must live with the knowledge that their errors, an inevitable legacy of their humanity, can have adverse if not fatal consequences for their patients. However, if they were not willing to risk making some serious mistakes and to take the responsibility of living with them, fewer lives would be enhanced, prolonged, and saved. Similarly, if less dramatically, educators must recognize that the good that can come from special programs for the gifted will only be realized if they are willing to make such difficult decisions as those required for screening and placement, even if a few decisions result in educationally questionable outcomes.

The temptation to avoid this issue is great. It often seems more politic or expedient to resort to selection formulas or matrices, single test scores, or schemes such as the "Revolving Door" approach (Renzulli, Reis, & Smith, 1981). Although each of these has its seductive appeal, I strongly urge educators to avoid falling prey to them, even when the cost of doing so is greater in time and effort. Effective and appropriate education for gifted children is a difficult goal to achieve, but the message of this book is that it is attainable. It becomes more attainable in proportion to the willingness of educators to put themselves on the line and make the difficult decisions.

CHAPTER 6

Program Format:
The Effective Delivery
of Services

Pluralism lets things really exist in the each-form.
James, *A Pluralistic Universe*

Form ever follows function.
  Sullivan, "The Tall Office Building Artistically Considered"

To this point, I have for the most part been discussing the components of a program for the gifted that relate to the specification and selection of the students who will receive special services (the exception being the needs assessment, discussed in Chapter 4, which is concerned with every program component). With respect to the flowchart of Figure 3.1, I have discussed the components represented by the upper row of boxes. I wish to turn now to the lower row of boxes in Figure 3.1, the row that represents the various aspects of the program itself, the administrative and instructional arrangements required to deliver services to the identified students.

I will not discuss here the box in Figure 3.1 labeled "Program Goals." It should not be thought that this is a trivial component of a program for the gifted. On the contrary, the establishment of program goals based on the needs of gifted students and the resources of the school or school district as revealed through needs assessment is a central and indispensable aspect of the program-planning process. The components that will be discussed from this point on should all be designed as means to further the ends expressed in the program goals. I am taking for granted the absolute necessity of establishing clear goals for the program, goals that represent the intentions of the school or school district with respect to the needs of gifted students.

There is no need, however, to devote a separate chapter to the development of program goals. I discussed their importance in Chapter 3, and I will return to this topic in Chapter 9 in my discussion of program evaluation, where I will describe some problems that might be encountered in dealing with goals that fail to provide a sound basis for program evaluation. Beyond that, I believe that there is little else to be said on this topic in a book that deals with the practical issue of program planning, and I do not think that a methods chapter, dealing with the writing of program goals, is necessary for educators deeply involved in the program-planning process. Therefore, I will assume that program goals have been established and that we are discussing program format in light of these goals.

By *program format* I mean the various administrative provisions that allow for the convening of students for special instruction. Included under this rubric are all of the practical considerations that relate to bringing gifted students together in time and space with their special-class teachers, especially those considerations dealing with grouping, scheduling, transportation, space allotment, and so forth.

The issue of program format extends beyond the nuts and bolts of "administrivia," however. One of the central themes of this book is that a true *program* for the gifted is made up of components that flow from the identified needs of gifted students, are causally related, and must be considered together as interdependent parts of a carefully designed system. Thus, decisions about such seemingly mundane issues as transporting, scheduling, and grouping students for instruction resonate throughout the program system. How students are scheduled and grouped, for example, should be determined by the specifics of their need for special instruction. Scheduling and grouping, in turn, obviously affect decisions about curriculum and instruction.

Numerous questions must be confronted in the fashioning of a program format; among them are the following:

- What did the needs assessment reveal concerning the nature and instructional needs of gifted students?
- What resources does the school or school district possess that will enable it to respond to these needs?
- What limitations with respect to resources are likely to be encountered?
- What are the attitudes of teachers and the other educational partners regarding such issues as taking students out of the regular classroom, homogeneous grouping, acceleration and enrichment, elitism, and so forth?

As one can see, these questions deal with a variety of issues and program components, and I have only suggested the range of questions that will arise.

The extensive range of possible issues that could be discussed in the context of program format dictates a concentration on the most crucial questions. Therefore, my discussion of program format will focus primarily on the issue of grouping. This narrowed focus stems from my belief that the grouping issue is the central one in any consideration of program format and that how students are grouped will determine in large part how, what, and how effectively they are taught. This is also the most controversial issue that can be subsumed under the heading of program format. Since it touches upon such topics as tracking and the possible segregation of gifted students, the question of grouping the gifted for instruction often gives rise to vigorous and impassioned debate. Moreover, other issues, such as those relating to scheduling and transporting gifted students, while important, are difficult to discuss in a general sense in the context of program planning. Once program goals are established and a program format is decided upon, scheduling and transportation can be left to those administrators whose tolerance for irritation is sufficiently high to permit them to deal with such things.

THE PROGRAM-FORMAT CONTINUUM

The bulk of this chapter will consist of an examination of the nature and of the advantages and disadvantages of various program formats. Two caveats are in order before we begin.

First, there is no authoritative catalog of program formats on which such a discussion can be based. One person's pull-out program is another's resource room. Where some see a single-program type, others discern distinct sub-species of programs, each of which merits discussion. One could argue per-suasively (and certainly in conformity with the major theme of this book) that each program in each school or school district constitutes its own unique program format; but that way lies anarchy. I have, in a manner that I hope is more logical than arbitrary, settled upon seven program formats. I will happily admit that there are many possibilities for consolidation or differen-tiation among my seven types (and I will discuss some other provisions that do not fit neatly into my typology later in this chapter). Furthermore, I am not proposing an ironclad taxonomy. Instead, I am trying to elucidate im-portant differences related to the various dimensions of program format in a way that makes sense in the context of program planning. Readers interested in seeing how other writers have classified program formats should consult some of the basic texts in the field. Among others, Gallagher (1985) and Howley, Howley, and Pendarvis (1986) present good discussions of this topic.

My second caveat hearkens back to my major theme: decisions relating to the planning of programs for the gifted should only be made in light of conditions obtaining in a particular school or school district. With respect to program format, this simply means that no given format is either good or bad in every circumstance. A format may be appropriate or inappropriate for a specific setting when the target population, program goals, and local resources are all considered, but this degree of appropriateness is very likely to change from one school district to another or even within one school district over time.

I will, however, explore below the potential pros and cons of various program formats. Each format has its particular characteristics, and these increase or decrease the probability that certain consequences, positive and negative, will ensue if the format is adopted under certain circumstances. I think there is heuristic value in looking at these possible advantages and disadvantages, although it might seem that I am ignoring the obvious fact that the terms *advantage* and *disadvantage* have meaning only in a given setting. I urge the reader to keep in mind that I am discussing these strengths and weaknesses in an abstract context, whereas program formats must be implemented in the real world.

I will discuss the seven program formats to which I referred by organizing them along a continuum defined by the degree of homogeneity of grouping required by each program type. This continuum is theoretically value-free; I am assuming that neither homogeneity nor heterogeneity should be taken a priori as a desideratum. While, like most educators, I have some definite opinions about the desirability of homogeneous and heterogeneous grouping, I am not attempting to array these program formats on a good–bad continuum from the best to the worst or vice versa.

I am emphasizing this point because in the field of special education there is a definite preference (and legal mandate) for programs that provide handicapped learners with the least restrictive environment. This is generally construed to mean the most heterogeneous grouping in which the handicapped child can successfully function cognitively and socially. For gifted students, establishing the "least restrictive environment" is more problematical. Howley et al. (1986, pp. 68–78) make a persuasive case for applying the term to the gifted by defining a "restrictive" environment as one that limits learning opportunities for gifted students by not providing sufficient "cognitive press." In their sense of the term, a heterogeneous classroom is a more restrictive environment for gifted students than is a self-contained class, exactly the opposite of what would be the case for a handicapped child who could be mainstreamed successfully. While I find this argument to be persuasive, I hesitate to assign a positive or negative value to either end of my homogeneous–heterogeneous continuum of program formats.

Having said that, let us begin exploring the seven program formats to which I referred above. I will begin with the most homogeneous format, the special school, and finish with the most heterogeneous format, provisions within the regular classroom.

SPECIAL SCHOOLS FOR THE GIFTED

The program format that results in the greatest degree of segregation and concentration of gifted students is the special school. As its name suggests, this is a separate, self-contained school designed exclusively for children identified as gifted. Students enrolled in a special school for the gifted take all of their classes with gifted students, including special or nonacademic classes. Admission standards are usually quite high, and competition for admission to some of the schools can be intense. Examples of this format are the Hunter College Campus Schools in New York City; the Roeper City and Country School in Bloomfield Hills, Michigan; the Calasanctius School in Buffalo, New York (Gerencser, 1979); and the Hollingworth Preschool at Teachers College, Columbia University, in New York City.

As is the case with every other program format, the choice of this approach shapes the curriculum in characteristic ways. In a special school, teachers of the gifted are responsible for instruction in the basic subject areas, not merely for enrichment, as is the case in most part-time programs. In some special schools, the curriculum is specialized, as in the special high schools in New York City (e.g., the Bronx High School of Science and the LaGuardia High School for the Arts). If the school does have a specific curricular emphasis, it will have an unusually rich array of courses in the area of concentration. Whether or not it is specialized with respect to subject matter, in nearly every case the curriculum will be a rigorous one, with instruction geared to a level appropriate for gifted learners. A certain degree of covert or overt acceleration is typical, and enrichment is usually built into the core curriculum.

Among the possible advantages of this program format are the following:

1. Students in a special school for the gifted spend their entire school day with other students who are their peers in both age and ability. This allows for a high level of peer support, and students are less likely to feel as if they are outcasts or oddities among their classmates.

2. The curriculum is designed to meet the educational needs of gifted students. Unlike the situation in most schools, there should be little need to try to adapt an all-purpose general curriculum to the demands of a few exceptional learners. The curriculum of a special school should, in theory, forestall both the boredom and the potential for the development of intellectual laziness that can result from a course of instruction that is not sufficiently challenging for the gifted. Moreover, the curriculum will have an articulated scope and sequence, something that is lacking in many enrichment curricula.

3. The faculty is more likely to be prepared, by virtue of education or experience or both, to deal with gifted students or advanced subject matter.

This can pay dividends both with respect to the level of instruction and with respect to the teachers' ability to serve as role models. Moreover, one could expect the physical facilities to be better adapted to the instruction of gifted learners, especially in special schools with specific curricular emphases.

4. Special schools, especially on the secondary level, are more likely than other program formats to offer advanced preparation for further studies within a given discipline. Students will generally graduate from such schools with advanced standing in college or at least a degree of knowledge and skill that is advanced in comparison with that of the age peers who attend other schools.

Among the possible disadvantages of this program format are the following:

1. Students in special schools have reduced exposure to age peers of different levels of ability, and this may lead to an unrealistic picture of the world and a skewed notion of human intelligence. In fact, some critics of this approach claim that students in special schools do not learn to interact with other children or adolescents or to adapt to the "real world." Others assert that the other students in special schools *are* "other children and adolescents" and that one's social development is facilitated when one can view oneself as similar to, not different from, one's associates. Moreover, there is a variety of "real worlds" to which one can adapt. Chances are that gifted students will choose to enter an adult real world, such as academia, that is somewhat rarefied intellectually (something that can happen immediately upon graduation from secondary school if they attend a selective college or university). For those children who do go on to highly selective colleges and universities and careers that require considerable exercise of the intellect, a special school may be the best preparation for their ultimate real world.

2. To the extent that the curriculum of a special school is concentrated in a particular discipline, students may be encouraged to specialize too early, leading to one-sided development and the lack of nourishment of latent interests and abilities. There is a delicate balance between avoiding what Stanley (1981) calls "irrelevant enrichment" for students with well-defined talents and prematurely depriving students of the curricular breadth that underlies a liberal education.

3. The competition for admission to some special schools, and the pressure for achievement once one is admitted, can be very intense, creating pressures to which children and adolescents should not be subjected. Although competition is a fact of life, it should not be the main feature of the education of gifted students. Maintaining the proper perspective on success and achievement is an important goal for gifted students and, indeed, for all students.

4. From the point of view of the educational planner, special schools are quite expensive and usually not a realistic option outside large school systems. One needs a school-age population base of sufficient size to support a separate facility that will serve that part of the gifted population (itself a small percentage of the school population) that will attend the special school.

Some of the soundest programs for gifted students are found in special schools for the gifted. However, it is unlikely that this program format will be seen as a viable option for most schools or school districts.

THE SCHOOL-WITHIN-A-SCHOOL

A somewhat more heterogeneous program format, although one that maintains the essential homogeneity of the instructional groupings, is the school-within-a-school, a format that combines many of the features of the special school and the self-contained class. A school-within-a-school is characterized by an autonomous educational program that is housed in a regular operating school. The coexistence of the special school and the regular school under the same roof is usually a matter of convenience or necessity. The school-within-a-school usually has its own administration, faculty, admission requirements, and curriculum, and its relationship with the host school is akin to that of a tenant with a landlord. Examples of this approach are not easy to come by, but there are three of which I am aware: the Academy Hill Center in Wilbraham, Massachusetts; the Academically Talented Program of the Orland Park, Illinois Schools; and the SEEK Program of the Watertown, New York, Public Schools.

There may be some integration of pupils enrolled in the school-within-a-school with pupils enrolled in the regular school for "special" subjects (physical education, music, and so forth), and there will certainly be integration of services (cafeteria and playground services, for example). However, there will be no heterogeneous grouping for instruction in academic subjects, and the features of a special-school curriculum discussed above will be found in the school-within-a-school. The main difference between the two program formats is one of housing. Like a home owner, the special school occupies its own building; like an apartment dweller, the school-within-a-school shares a roof with others.

In terms of curriculum, the school-within-a-school creates the same curricular responsibilities as does the special school. That is to say, teachers of the gifted are responsible for instruction in all subject areas, not only for providing enrichment. As was the case with the previous program format, students are likely to be accelerated, simply by virtue of their homogeneous grouping. Enrichment is usually worked into the content of the basic disciplines, although special enrichment courses may be offered (as is the case in some special schools). The only difference between the two formats with respect to curriculum is that in a school-within-a-school, there may be some heterogeneous grouping or, more likely, utilization of regular staff, for instruction in nonacademic areas.

Among the possible advantages of the school-within-a-school are the following:

1. As with a special school, there is the opportunity for continuous contact with age and ability peers and the exposure to an appropriate, articulated curriculum. In fact, all of the pluses associated with the special-school format are found in the school-within-a-school.

2. In addition, there is the opportunity for greater contact with students of a broader range of abilities in this program format. Even if the school-within-a-school is completely segregated within the host school, incidental contact is inevitable, and gifted students are likely to feel less isolated as a group.

3. As an option for a typical school or school district, a school-within-a-school is probably a more practicable format than a physically separate special school.

Among the possible disadvantages are the following:

1. The segregation of gifted students from the mainstream and the heightened level of competition for admission and grades that characterize the special school are possible liabilities of this program format as well.

2. With the increased opportunities for contact between gifted and non-gifted age peers comes the possibility of friction between the two groups. If the special school is an ivory tower, it at least affords some students a much-needed sanctuary. The school-within-a-school exposes gifted students not only to positive contacts with other children and adolescents but to the possibility of teasing, taunting, and even physical aggression.

3. As a relatively rare means of providing special education for the gifted, the school-within-a-school is often perceived as neither fish nor fowl. It may become something of a stepchild—in, but not of, a regular school. This can create confusion for building administrators, who may not know how much oversight they can or should exercise over the day-to-day operation of the special program. It can also be confusing for teachers within the program, who may feel isolated from regular faculty, unsupported by regular building administration, and generally unsure of their place in the scheme of things.

A novel and innovative approach to the problem of educating the gifted, the school-within-a-school holds promise for those who like the focus of the special school but who lack the wherewithal, economic and otherwise, to establish one. As is the case with other options, this program format has its pitfalls, but its promise is such that it warrants more consideration than it seems to have received thus far.

SELF-CONTAINED CLASSES

By the term *self-contained classes*, I am referring to a plan for the education of the gifted in which students are grouped into homogeneous class units in which they receive all or most of their instruction. In other words, there are designated "gifted classrooms," and identified students are assigned to these classes for the purpose of receiving instruction with other gifted learners. Usually, there are other, regular, classes, either grouped heterogeneously or according to some measure of aptitude or achievement, on each of the grade levels in a given building. In many respects, as the reader has probably already noted, this program format is indistinguishable from the school-within-a-school approach.

There is, however, one major difference: A school-within-a-school is a completely separate entity within the building in which it is housed. Not only do its students pursue a differentiated course of study under the tutelage of special teachers (as is the case with the self-contained–class format), but also they are usually drawn from a larger catchment area according to admission procedures that vary from those of the host school. Moreover, the school-within-a-school will very likely be under the supervision of a person outside the administrative staff of the host school.

A program for the gifted with self-contained classes, on the other hand, differs in that the students admitted to the program are drawn from the population of the host school, and the host school has the responsibility for the administration of the program. In fact, the term *host school* is inappropriate in this context, since it is more than a host; rather, it is the school that the gifted students actually attend. Whereas students in a school-within-a-school attend a program for the gifted that is merely *located in* a certain school building, students in a self-contained program for the gifted attend the program for the gifted *of* a given building.

Quite often, the impetus for the instituting of these two program formats differs as well. In the case of a school-within-a-school, the initiative nearly always lies with the central administration, which decides to place the program in a certain building. With self-contained classes, the impetus for the formation of the program may also derive from the central office, but might instead represent an initiative on the part of the building staff. Whatever its genesis, if it is a self-contained program, building administrators will be expected to exercise some degree of oversight.

Students in self-contained classes for the gifted are perhaps more likely than students in a school-within-a-school to be integrated with students not identified as gifted in such things as nonacademic classes, extracurricular activities, assemblies, and so forth. This reflects the fact that, unlike students in a school-within-a-school, gifted students in self-contained classes share membership in a school with other students.

The distinctions I am drawing between these two program formats are sometimes blurred in practice. A school-within-a-school can become effectively integrated into the daily functioning of a host school building, and self-contained classes have been treated as pariahs. However, I think there are sufficient differences between the two formats, especially with respect to administration and student selection, to warrant their differentiation here.

Perhaps paradoxically, a self-contained program for the gifted may be departmentalized, especially in grades above the primary level. As long as gifted students maintain homogeneous groupings, they are in what I am defining as a self-contained program, whether they stay with the teacher all day or move as a group from class to class (as in a strictly tracked system).

The curricular implications of the self-contained approach are basically the same as those of the school-within-a-school and the special school. As such, they require no elaboration here.

Similarly, the advantages and disadvantages of the self-contained format essentially mirror those of the school-within-a-school. The major difference is that the administrative confusion that can result from the host–guest relationship between a building staff and the staff and students of a school-within-a-school is rarely a problem with a self-contained program. This can be counted as a plus for this program format.

One possible disadvantage of this approach, as well as of the two previous ones, derives from the conception of giftedness that underlies these three approaches. In a self-contained program, for example, there is usually an assumption, perhaps tacit, that students in the program are gifted in all areas of the curriculum. They receive high-level instruction (and are subjected to high-level expectations) in every subject area, although certain students, even if they are quite high in measured general ability, may demonstrate peaks and valleys of achievement. This underscores the fact that there is really no such thing as a truly homogeneous group of students, even with respect to narrow academic-achievement variables. Teachers are sometimes surprised and disappointed to learn this, and they sometimes resent the fact that they have to group their students for instruction even though they are all gifted.

In some special schools with specialized curricula, there is less of an expectation of high aptitude and achievement outside the area of specialization. In a school for students with artistic gifts, students may not be expected to be highly capable in science and mathematics, for example. However, the assumption of general giftedness is usually characteristic of special schools, schools-within-schools, and self-contained classes. Although the contrary could be argued, it is probably fair to count this among the possible disadvantages of these program formats.

These first three program formats are somewhat controversial and are often rejected out of hand by educators as elitist or otherwise undesirable. Often, however, this is no more than a reflexive response that fails to consider the needs of gifted students. Howley et al. (1986), in their perceptive examination of this issue, state that although "total separation is viewed with suspicion by most educators, it may represent the best approach to education for some gifted students" (p. 90). If this cautious assessment is true, and, as stated with the qualifiers *may* and *some*, I think it would be difficult to refute, program planners have the obligation at least to explore the possible implications of adopting these formats for their programs for the gifted.

MULTITRACKED PROGRAMS

What I am referring to as a *multitracked program* is an adaptive form of homogeneous grouping that allows students to be grouped with gifted students only in those subject areas in which they demonstrate high achievement or aptitude. If a particular student requires a high level of instruction in science and mathematics, for example, but should be in the mainstream for instruction in other subjects, this program format would allow for that type of scheduling. Thus, students are placed in the program for the gifted on a part-time, subject-by-subject basis, eliminating the all-or-nothing quality that characterizes the special school, the school-within-a-school, and the self-contained class.

This program format results in the creation of a program for the gifted that is the least conspicuous of the options to be presented in this chapter except for the very last of the approaches. Since students shift from group to group depending upon their individual profiles of strengths and weaknesses, there is no unchanging, homogeneous group of gifted students that can be readily identified as the students in the program for the gifted. At any given time during the school day, there will be students receiving special instruction as gifted students in one or more subject areas, but the membership of this group will change over the course of the day.

Clearly, this program format is most appropriate at the secondary level where departmentalization and some flexibility with regard to scheduling are the norm. In terms of curricular implications, multitracked programs allow for acceleration and enrichment in each subject area, but not for enrichment outside the basic disciplines.

I suspect that this is a program format that is more often discussed than implemented, for reasons I will enumerate below when I discuss its advantages and disadvantages. If its potential disadvantages can be avoided, however, the multitracked program can be a flexible and effective way of delivering services to gifted students.

Among the advantages of this approach are the following:

1. As I have mentioned, this is a flexible approach. It permits schools to recognize that students are often talented in some areas but not others. This is an advantage with respect to both curriculum and identification, since students can be identified on the basis of demonstrated achievement in a given subject area and taught accordingly.

2. Whereas evaluating, and especially changing, student placements is problematic in the previous three program formats, it is more easily effected in a multitracked program. Student achievement is the primary index of appropriateness of placement, and if the placement must be changed, it is simply a matter of changing the scheduling of one class. In the special school, the school-within-a-school, and the self-contained class, changing a student's placement, should that placement be clearly inappropriate, is a difficult and disruptive process. In a multitracked program, a less massive change is required, and a student need not be completely uprooted and transplanted elsewhere.

3. As with the three previous program formats, the curriculum in a multitracked program will be articulated and will have an explicit scope and sequence.

4. The multitracked program tends to disguise placement in a program for the gifted, since the membership in the program changes with the regularly scheduled class changes.

Possible disadvantages of this approach are:

1. Scheduling is a major difficulty. Building the required flexibility into the schedule of every student who is talented in one or more subjects requires a genius for (or persistence applied to) scheduling that is not easily come by. Scheduling students in the typical school day, especially students who take advantage of numerous electives and activities such as band and chorus, as gifted students often do, is difficult enough without having to shift students from track to track. A multitracked program may severely strain the ingenuity and patience of administrators.

2. Since the cast of characters changes from class to class, there is often the need to make compromises that can alter the quality of instruction. Should there only be 10 students who demonstrate high-level talent in a given subject area, it will probably be necessary to group them with a sufficient number of other students to fill the roster in a certain classroom in a certain period of the day. This could result in a watering down of the curriculum for the very able students. On the other hand, should there be a large number of talented students in a subject area, some of them may have to receive instruction in a more heterogeneous setting. The phenomenon of "discovering" that there are exactly as many gifted students on a grade level as there are places in the program for the gifted is a common one; it is multiplied in the multitracked program format.

3. The multitracked program, as its name suggests, is clearly a *tracked* program. In many schools and school districts, tracking is a dirty word and a forbidden approach to grouping students for instruction. In light of the various abuses that have been committed in the name of tracking, this wariness regarding homogeneous grouping is understandable. It is a shame that in the history of this practice there are examples of using homogeneous grouping for racist and other immoral purposes, and neglecting students in lower tracks in schools where homogeneous grouping has been the norm. In theory, grouping students on the basis of ability should result in benefits to all students; in reality, this promise has often not been realized. This being the case, it will not be possible to use a multitracked program format in a school or school district in which tracking is contrary to the stated policy or philosophy.

4. There is the danger, when using this approach, of the promised differentiated curriculum never emerging. A multitracked program usually requires teachers to teach gifted students one period per day and students in the mainstream for the rest of the day. I even encountered one school district in which teachers who taught the gifted track were assigned a remedial class in addition to mainstream classes to "balance" their teaching assignments. This requires teachers to prepare for at least two levels of instruction per day if the program for the gifted is going to be truly differentiated. Although some teachers will strive mightily to do this, others will simply not bother unless additional preparation time is provided. Such provisions are rare, in my experience.

Thus, although the multitracked program allows for a flexible approach to delivering services to gifted students, it also requires the cooperation and dedication of a large number of teachers (and at least one creative administrator to do the scheduling). To the extent that every teacher does his or her part, the program will have a good chance for success. With less than total dedication on the part of the entire faculty, the program may disappear.

PULL-OUT PROGRAMS

By whatever name it is designated, what I am referring to as the pull-out program is the most commonly used program format for gifted students in the United States (Cox, Daniel, & Boston, 1985). In this approach, gifted students spend most of their time in a regular heterogeneous classroom, but they are removed or pulled out for a given period of time each week for special instruction with other gifted students. The amount of time allotted for the pull-out program varies from school to school. In my experience, the range has been from a low of 20 minutes per week to a high of five mornings per week, or roughly half of the gifted students' school time. Each of these was a unique situation, the former for its egregious tokenism, the latter for its wholehearted commitment to special programming for the gifted.

Pull-out programs vary in other ways as well. Some programs involve the transporting of students to a central location within the school district. Other pull-out programs have sites within each building. In the latter case, multigrade grouping is often employed to constitute classes of sufficient size.

Instruction in a pull-out program is usually carried out by a special teacher, who designs a differentiated curriculum specifically for the gifted students. In almost every case, the curricular focus is on enrichment since instruction in the basic subject areas is the province of the regular classroom teacher. In fact, many teachers in pull-out programs for the gifted are told explicitly not to trespass onto the subject matter of the core curriculum. Thus, teachers of gifted students in a pull-out program must develop, as well as teach, a differentiated curriculum.

There are numerous advantages and disadvantages of pull-out programs. Among the former are the following:

1. Pull-out programs allow for both homogeneous grouping of gifted students for special instruction and for heterogeneous grouping within the mainstream for instruction in the basic subject areas. To the extent that there is a desire for some special grouping for the gifted but no desire for tracking or full-time homogeneous classes, the pull-out program can be an acceptable compromise.

2. The pull-out model is a familiar one for teachers and students as a result of its being employed for a variety of special provisions (e.g., speech therapy, resource-room help for learning-disabled students, band and chorus, and so forth).

3. This program format allows for a truly differentiated curriculum for gifted students during part of their school time. Whereas the degree of differentiation can be minimal when regular classroom teachers are responsible for the instruction of both gifted and nongifted students, pull-out programs

are usually the responsibility of special teachers, whose job it is to develop a special curriculum for the gifted.

4. The pull-out program format is a flexible one that allows for quite a variety of groupings. Students can be grouped in single-grade or multigrade classes in single buildings or across buildings. Thus, this program format is applicable in schools or school districts that differ greatly with respect to geography, population, resources, physical facilities, and so forth.

5. Since the cooperation of regular classroom teachers is required for the smooth operation of a pull-out program, a broad sense of ownership of the special program can be fostered. The program for the gifted is perhaps less likely to be perceived as an isolated entity when students maintain membership in the mainstream and the special program simultaneously.

6. During the time in which gifted students are in the pull-out program, the size of the remaining classes is smaller, and they are more homogeneous. This should allow the regular classroom teacher to concentrate on students who need special help, and it should also allow some students who tend to be overshadowed by gifted students to come to the fore.

Possible disadvantages of pull-out programs are:

1. As the national study funded by the Sid W. Richardson Foundation revealed, pull-out programs are "a part-time solution to a full-time problem" (Cox, Daniel, & Boston, 1985, p. 43). While a part-time solution is clearly better than no solution at all, too many pull-out programs for gifted students do not provide for nearly enough contact time to have an appreciable effect on the students' education. It is unlikely that a program that meets for less than one-half day per week could make much difference. More time than that is highly desirable; less time represents a futile or a cynical gesture.

2. Logistically, pull-out programs can be nightmares. Although they are adaptable to a wide range of schools and school districts, making the necessary adaptations can involve a great deal of work and diplomacy. If students are transported to a central location, temperamental buses and bus drivers must be dealt with. Accommodating the schedule of the pull-out program to that of various schools can also be a problem, especially when special events are scheduled, as is the case around holiday times and the end of the school year. There are times during the academic year when teachers in some pull-out programs resign themselves to meeting with decimated classes. The potential problems related to the practical, day-to-day operation of pull-out programs sometimes seem endless (it must often seem to teachers in programs of this type that Murphy's Law was formulated especially to describe their situations).

3. The professional demands made on teachers in pull-out programs are

heavy. These teachers are not only required to teach gifted students, they are also required to design special curricula for their students, being careful at all times not to infringe upon the regular core curriculum. It is a tribute to our profession that so many teachers perform this dual function so well. However, developing a curriculum is not an easy task, especially when a curriculum is being designed for students who devour in short order what will occupy other students for a considerable time. Thus, there is a danger, and in my experience often the reality, that special curricula in pull-out programs will consist of little more than trivia.

The proliferation of games and kits designed to promote thinking skills, the denigration of knowledge in so much of the writing on the education of gifted students, and the relative ease with which one can order materials compared with the difficulty involved in creating curricula all contribute to the sorry state of affairs found in some pull-out programs. When these factors are combined with a lack of adequate preparation time and the failure of schools of education to prepare teachers to become curriculum developers, not merely curriculum consumers, the result is a recipe for fun and games instead of real learning. Students are generally placed in pull-out programs for gifted students because they have the ability and the need to deal with challenging and important ideas. It is not uncommon, however, to find them spending their time completing mind-deadening work sheets, idly musing about "future problems," learning five-step methods for enhancing "creativity," and engaging in activities based on the worst sort of pop psychology.

Thus, while pull-out programs create the need for differentiated curricula, there is no guarantee that these curricula will be defensible. I suspect that one can find both the best of curricula and the worst of curricula for gifted students in pull-out programs. When teachers are skilled curriculum developers, with a clear sense of what constitutes valuable special education for the gifted, students in pull-out programs can soar. When teachers follow the fads of the moment and settle for fun and games, their students suffer. Programs for the gifted that are tied to the core curriculum, such as the program formats discussed prior to this one, occupy a safe middle ground with respect to curriculum. Although they are sometimes so constricted that opportunities for true differentiation are limited, simply because they are tied to the regular core curriculum, their curricula rarely degenerate into the exercises in mindless nonsense that characterize some pull-out programs.

4. Cooperative regular classroom teachers can contribute a sense of collegiality to a pull-out program, but uncooperative teachers can wreak considerable havoc. If, for whatever reason, classroom teachers are not favorably disposed toward the program for the gifted, they can exert significant pressure on gifted students and make their participation in the pull-out program

an unpleasant, and sometimes short-lived, experience. Teachers have been known to schedule examinations for periods reserved for meetings of pull-out classes; to refuse to give gifted students assignments for work they will miss; and to make comments designed to discourage children from leaving the regular classroom to attend the class for the gifted.

Lest it seem that I am portraying regular classroom teachers as the villains in this situation, let us take a look at their side of the story. In addition to having to teach in a day fragmented by ringing bells, needless announcements, fire drills, myriad procedural requirements, and a plethora of other pull-out programs, teachers must accept the fact that the students they are likely to refer to as their "best" students will be taken out of their classes when a pull-out program is created. While this may represent an opportunity of sorts, as discussed above among the advantages, it can also be viewed as a problem. Not only does it involve preparing assignments in advance and either condensing the curriculum or allowing for the making up of work missed, but it might also suggest that the regular classroom teacher is not capable of challenging gifted students sufficiently.

In situations in which there is conflict between regular classroom teachers and the program for the gifted, it is the gifted students who suffer. And while there are a few teachers who are cowardly enough to express their distaste for programs for the gifted by bullying children, I suspect that most teachers will cooperate if their professional status and prerogatives are respected. Therefore, it is incumbent on program planners to consult with and to consider the needs of regular classroom teachers in planning a program for the gifted, especially a pull-out program.

5. Pull-out programs make gifted students very conspicuous. Students attending such a program must get up and leave their classrooms, often while class is in session, sometimes having to raise their hands to remind the teacher that it is time to go. Their empty desks are constant reminders that they are elsewhere, and they usually have a difficult time making a subtle entrance once their special class is over. This high profile can be a problem for gifted students, especially for preadolescents and adolescents, who are invariably concerned with conforming and fitting in with the crowd.

6. Pull-out programs frequently are viewed as being something extra, rather than as something "instead." Thus, they can add considerably to the burden of work required of gifted students, many of whom are also engaged in numerous extracurricular activities. If the pull-out program meets for one full day per week and regular classroom teachers require gifted students to make up all missed assignments, the effective result is a six-day school week. Unless provisions are made for students to be excused from some of the more meaningless classroom requirements, there are likely to be many dropouts from our pull-outs.

7. Pull-out programs are not only a part-time solution; they are an expensive one as well. While a self-contained class, for example, represents a classroom that would have to exist on a given grade level anyway, a pull-out program requires an additional classroom, an additional teacher, and some empty seats in the regular classroom. Thus, even though it may appear that a pull-out program, being only a part-time proposition, must be less expensive than a full-time program, the reverse is usually the case.

8. Finally, the logic of the pull-out format is questionable. The existence of a pull-out program, or any program for the gifted, rests on, among other things, two basic premises. The first of these is that the regular classroom is not the right placement for gifted students. The second is that the school has the power to create a better placement for its gifted students—the premise that leads to the creation of a special program. The choice of a pull-out program implies that, given the existence of an inappropriate placement for the gifted and an appropriate placement, a decision has been made that the gifted should spend the majority of their time in the inappropriate placement and a minority of their time in the appropriate placement.

Judged by the relative space allotted above to the advantages and the disadvantages of pull-out programs, it would appear that the latter far outweigh the former as far as this particular program format is concerned. While that may be the case, I would not like to have the judgment depend on the amount of space I have spent on the disadvantages of the pull-out approach. Because pull-out programs are so plentiful, I have had the opportunity of observing and working with quite a few of them, usually as a troubleshooter of one kind or another. Thus, I have seen firsthand what can go wrong and what should be avoided. If I have been less explicit about the pitfalls inherent in other program formats, it is because I have seen fewer of them in operation.

The pull-out program as a program format for gifted students is no different from any other. Its suitability in a given situation depends largely on the particulars of that situation. In some schools or school districts, it is the best way to go. In others, it is a mistake. As always, it is dangerous to make general pronouncements about *the* best approach to take in providing for the special education of gifted students, and all such general pronouncements (except this one, of course) should be greeted with skepticism. Nonetheless, I think it is fair to state that the popularity of the pull-out format far exceeds its educational appropriateness for gifted students.

RESOURCE-ROOM PROGRAMS

The distinction between a resource-room program and a pull-out program can be a fine one, and many educators use the two terms interchangeably. However, I would like to define a resource room in such a way as to draw attention to some differences between it and a pull-out program that I think are worth noting.

By the term *resource-room program*, I am referring to a provision for gifted students in which students who are normally grouped heterogeneously report to a special site on a part-time basis for special instruction. In this respect, the resource room is identical to the pull-out program. However, the resource-room format differs from the pull-out format in the following ways:

1. The roster of students may change with more regularity than is the case in a pull-out program. Students may be placed in the resource room only when it is believed they require special services. In this respect, the use of the resource room as a format for a program for the gifted is similar to the use of the resource room in other areas of special education, especially the field of learning disabilities.

2. Students do not necessarily report to the resource room at the same time or for the same amount of time each week. Scheduling is much more flexible than it is in a pull-out program.

3. More than in other formats, activities in a resource-room program are likely to be individualized and to involve independent study. In fact, the Renzulli Enrichment Triad framework (1977), which culminates in small-group or individual projects, is probably the most frequent model for the resource-room approach to programs for the gifted.

4. The role of the teacher may be expanded. In keeping with the name of this program format, the teacher of the gifted may function as a resource for other teachers by making suggestions for enriching the curriculum of the regular classroom, conducting demonstration lessons, or helping to articulate the special and the regular curricula of gifted students.

Thus, the resource room is a pull-out program with a number of significant differences that suffice to make it a separate program format. As might be expected, this format shares many advantages and disadvantages with the pull-out program. In addition, it has a number of unique strengths.

1. It is very flexible. Students can go to the resource room when the opportunity presents itself, allowing the regular classroom teacher some relief from the inflexible pull-out format.

2. As a result of the above, the resource room model can make gifted students less conspicuous, since they do not leave and return to the classroom en masse at the same time on the same day of the week.

3. If the special-class teacher does serve as a resource for other teachers, the much discussed "spillover" effect, often promised as a consequence of programs for the gifted but rarely delivered, can become a reality.

4. If going to the resource room is contingent upon student productivity, as it is in many resource-room programs, there is little chance of there being the "dead wood" of which teachers in programs for the gifted often complain. If a student does not wish to participate actively in the program for the gifted, he or she does not attend.

There are, however, disadvantages as well. Among these are:

1. The curriculum can be nebulous or even nonexistent. With scheduling being so irregular, it is difficult to develop and to implement a formal curriculum. Thus, students in a resource room are likely to be encouraged to work on independent projects. While independent study is a worthy and desirable component of a defensible differentiated curriculum for the gifted (see Chapter 8), it is difficult to justify as the entire curriculum. Too often, individual projects degenerate into trivial activities as students with limited research skills and often minimal guidance are asked to identify, structure, and attack problems of some importance. However, in many resource rooms, there is no alternative to independent study, because there is no real curriculum.

2. The flexibility in scheduling afforded by this program format can be a real advantage, but the lack of a regular schedule can be a disadvantage as well. Some gifted students may never make it to the resource room, or they may be allowed to attend so infrequently that they are only nominally in the program for the gifted.

3. The requirement that students be productive in order to participate in the program for the gifted may be unfair to many gifted students. While this requirement helps eliminate those students who are unwilling to make any effort, it also eliminates some students who have real special-educational needs and who could become motivated if someone were to take an interest in them. Especially in the lower grades, it may be more reasonable to require the *program* to instill such qualities as productivity and "task commitment" in children with high potential than to require children to demonstrate these qualities as an entrance requirement.

4. There is reason to question the effectiveness of this format as it is presently used. The national study of programs for the gifted underwritten by the Sid W. Richardson Foundation (Cox et al., 1985) evaluated numerous program formats (their list of formats is somewhat different from mine). Applying "minimal" (p. 33) criteria, they determined the percentage of existing programs within each type that could at least be called substantial. While 75 percent of the special schools, 73 percent of the self-contained classes, and even 65 percent of the oft-maligned pull-out programs (here called "part-time special classes") nationwide were deemed substantial, only 48 percent of resource-room programs and 44 percent of independent-study programs were so judged. Although independent-study and resource-room pro-

grams ranked third and fourth in popularity across the nation, no doubt because of the successful marketing of the Renzulli model, these formats were ranked only seventh and eighth in terms of substance. The only program format to perform worse was what Cox et al. called "enrichment," a program format that appears to be the same as what I am calling "provisions within the regular classroom." Thus, one should consider the warning of Howley et al. (1986) that "placement in the resource room program is often mistakenly considered an adequate way for schools to fulfill their obligation to exceptionally able students" (p. 86).

In practice, programs bearing the "resource-room" label are often simply pull-out programs with different names. In those cases in which there is a true difference, it appears that there is often less happening instructionally than meets the eye. Nevertheless, the resource room as a format for programs for the gifted has quite a bit to recommend it, and it should be considered in those schools and school districts that must consider program formats at this end of the homogeneous–heterogeneous continuum.

PROVISIONS WITHIN THE REGULAR CLASSROOM

The final format I will discuss in this part of the chapter is one that has considerable appeal for many educators and administrators. By "provisions within the regular classroom" I mean any plan for the education of gifted students that maintains heterogeneous grouping on a full-time basis and makes the regular classroom teacher responsible for providing special services. In one variation of this program format, gifted students are identified, either by regular classroom teachers or by other school personnel, and some form of curricular differentiation—enrichment, acceleration, or both—is provided within the regular classroom. Another variation on this theme makes regular classroom teachers responsible for general enrichment for all students in their charge in an effort to help gifted and nongifted students alike.

Instead of delineating the possible advantages and disadvantages of this approach, I would like to violate my own rule and state that, on the basis of principle and experience, I am skeptical of the efficacy of this program format. The Richardson Study (Cox et al., 1985) found that while 63 percent of school districts in the country that had programs for the gifted reported using this approach wholly or in part, only 25 percent of these met the minimal criteria required for the program to be judged "substantial." In my experience, I have very rarely encountered a scheme of this sort that resulted in truly differentiated special education for gifted students.

Howley et al. (1986), whose book is cited favorably above, are characteristically lucid in their discussion of this issue. They assert that this program format represents "a universal principle governing the education of the gifted" (p. 69), the principle that the gifted can safely be ignored as a special-educational population. Moreover, in those schools where a conscious decision has been made to attempt to meet the educational needs of a gifted student in the regular classroom, one of two assumptions, explicit or implicit, must be operating: "(1) no alternative placements are available, or (2) this particular child is in need of very little differentiation of instruction, *in contrast to the majority of gifted students*" (p. 71). Stated in this manner, with the logic or illogic of this approach exposed, provisions within the regular classroom are seen either as an admission that no program for the gifted exists or is planned, or that school personnel are willing to ignore what research has revealed about the educational needs of gifted students.

Unfortunately, some writers in the field of the education of the gifted (e.g., Colon & Treffinger, 1980; Treffinger, 1982) and my own state of New York (New York State Education Department, 1982) have contributed to the myth that gifted students can be well served in the regular classroom. Nevertheless, there is little evidence to contradict the conclusion of Howley et al. (1986) that "these efforts . . . cannot transform the regular classroom into the most appropriate environment for gifted children" (p. 70). These authors go on to assert that "because of the enduring and perhaps inevitable practices of the regular classroom, full-time placement in the regular classroom is usually the least appropriate alternative for gifted students" (p. 73).

Why is this the case? What is it about the regular classroom that makes it "the least appropriate alternative for gifted students?" Certainly, it is not true that all regular classroom teachers are indifferent or antagonistic to the special needs of gifted learners. Nor is it true that they lack, to a person, the skills needed to work successfully with highly able students. Instead, the problem is a structural one, and it relates to the prevalence of heterogeneous grouping in today's schools.

Not only is heterogeneous grouping of students the norm in most schools, but it is now more pronounced than before as a result of the mainstreaming of a greater number of handicapped students, a development that by and large is to be applauded. However, this does make things more difficult for regular classroom teachers, who are held accountable, legally and ethically, for the transmission of a body of basic skills and knowledge to these heterogeneous (and often unconscionably large) groups of students over the course of fewer than 200 school days, each of which is punctuated by class bells, countless announcements over the public address system, and an array of noncurricular activities.

Working under these conditions, even the most conscientious teachers realize that they cannot completely meet the needs of all their students. Most, however, try to do the greatest good for the greatest number by gearing their instruction to the middle of the ability continuum and attempting to include as many students in each direction as possible. This may suffice for most students, but there will invariably be some students who will find themselves struggling to catch up and others who will find the material too easy and the pace too slow. The former are likely to be frustrated; the latter, including the gifted, bored. Any time that the teacher is able to make available for students outside the broad middle will probably, and understandably, be devoted to those students who are struggling, not to those who need a greater challenge.

This is the reality that obtains in the majority of classrooms today, and it is the reality that is ignored by those who advocate "meeting the needs of the gifted in the regular classroom." To expect teachers not only to deal adequately with this situation but also to develop a defensible, differentiated curriculum for their gifted students as well is wishful thinking at best, cynicism at worst. When one considers that most regular classroom teachers have no training and no experience in the field of education of the gifted, demanding that they institute provisions for able students within their heterogeneous classrooms becomes even more of an absurdity. In my opinion, it is better to admit honestly that one's school or school district is doing nothing for the gifted than to pretend to have a "program" in the regular classroom. I have seen a number of these phantom "programs" on paper; I have seen just one that came close to meeting the educational needs of gifted students.

Nonetheless, provisions within the regular classroom may have considerable appeal for those worried about elitism, labeling, and other real issues, for this is the only format that completely eschews the necessity of even part-time homogeneous grouping. Legitimate concerns have been raised about the consequences of homogeneous grouping with respect to its effects on students at each end of the achievement contiuum. Some contend that able students suffer socially, and less able students, academically when homogeneous grouping is instituted. Even if it could be demonstrated that gifted students thrive in schools in which there is homogeneous grouping, it might be preferable to sacrifice their potential for high achievement if, as some assert, other students suffer cognitive deficits as a result of being denied the opportunity to associate daily with the gifted in the classroom. It would at least make for an interesting moral debate.

However, there is a body of research that indicates that highly able students not only thrive academically (e.g., Begle, 1979; Tremaine, 1979; Whitmore, 1980) but also suffer neither socially nor emotionally (e.g., Maddux, Scheiber, & Bass, 1982; Whitmore, 1980) when grouped by ability. Moreover, one of the most comprehensive investigations of the issue of homogeneous grouping, the meta-analysis conducted by Kulik and Kulik (1982), found that other students incur no ill effects from being grouped with their ability peers. By combing the results of over 50 studies on the effects of ability grouping on gifted and lower-ability students in the secondary grades, Kulik and Kulik found that along with the expected positive effect for high-ability students, there was a small but positive effect for all students.*

The controversy over homogeneous versus heterogeneous grouping is likely to continue for some time. While the issue is still unresolved, there is no warrant in the research literature for the belief that homogeneous grouping is harmful to vast numbers of students, whereas there is ample reason to believe that it is beneficial for gifted students. In any case, there is very little to recommend full-time heterogeneous grouping for gifted students. Attempts to meet the needs of the gifted in the regular classroom do little or nothing for them. In fact, since these pretenses allow schools to point to their "programs" for the gifted without really addressing the needs of gifted students, they may impede actual progress toward providing special education for students with special abilities.

As I stated above, this list of seven program formats is not exhaustive, nor is it necessarily authoritative. One could well argue for the existence of a greater or lesser number of models for the delivery of instruction to gifted learners, and I will discuss below some additional approaches that do not fit into my homogeneous–heterogeneous continuum. Nevertheless, this discussion of program formats should suggest the range of options available, and I hope that it elucidates some of the factors that affect, and are affected by, the choice of a format. Let me now turn to some other approaches that fall outside the mainstream but deserve comment in this chapter.

SOME OTHER PROGRAM FORMATS

In this section I wish to discuss some arrangements for the education of gifted students that are either of limited applicability in the majority of schools and school districts or not comprehensive enough in their scope to merit treatment in the discussion above.

Richardson Report's "Promising Practices"

I would like to begin this section with reference once again to the national survey and report conducted under the sponsorship of the Sid W. Richardson

---

*Meta-analysis, like most tools used in educational research, is the source of some controversy. Slavin (1984) criticizes this approach in general and various meta-analytic studies in particular, including that of Kulik and Kulik, in a provocative and contentious article in the *Educational Researcher*. Readers interested in this topic should refer to Slavin's article, to the response in the same issue of the journal by Carlberg et al. (1984), and to Slavin's rejoinder.

Foundation (Cox, Daniel, & Boston, 1985). In addition to offering a critique of existing program formats and finding many formats lacking in substance as they have been implemented in our nation's schools, the authors of this document point to five program formats that, in their opinion, have demonstrated their effectiveness.

One of these, the special school for the gifted, has been discussed above. The other four "programs that hold significant promise" (p. 45) are briefly described below.

Education with an International Perspective. The best known example of this approach is the International Baccalaureate (IB) program. Administered by the International Baccalaureate Office in Geneva, Switzerland, this rigorous program of study concentrates on the mastery of at least two languages and a solid core that, in effect, provides students with an in-depth liberal education. During the two-year duration of the program, students take six academic courses selected from the basic disciplines plus an interdisciplinary course called Theory of Knowledge, which is unique to the IB program. In addition, each student enrolled in the IB program is required to participate in a creative, esthetic, or social-service activity.

The IB program is clearly a demanding and, ultimately, rewarding one for those students capable of completing it. In particular, the epistemological perspective afforded by the Theory of Knowledge course is by its very nature especially appropriate for gifted students, as individuals who are likely to become producers, not merely consumers, of knowledge (Jacobs & Borland, 1986; Tannenbaum, 1983). For eleventh- and twelfth-grade students whose school districts are willing to participate in this program (and to pay a fee for the privilege), this is a most worthwhile program.

Internships and Mentor Programs. Mentorships for gifted students have received some attention in the literature on the education of the gifted (e.g., Torrance, 1984), but relatively little has been done in terms of translating this into action. Typically, internships or mentorships place students with well-developed interests and high motivation in "real-world" settings under the tutelage of established professionals working in the students' fields of interest. This allows schools both to provide high-level, experiential opportunities unavailable within the school walls for students with specialized aptitudes and proclivities and to enable students to get a taste of the day-to-day life of a working professional before making an educational commitment to a given field. In one sense, a mentorship is work-study for able students.

Cox et al. (1985) describe some mentorship programs that seem to be functioning effectively and that have been enthusiastically endorsed by the students participating in them. What emerges most forcefully from reading these descriptions is the central importance of the choice of placement sites in determining the educational validity of this approach as a program format for gifted students. The programs operated by the Dallas Independent School District are a case in point. In one facet of this effort, students talented in the arts are brought together with artists and "master teachers," an approach to educating talented students that would be difficult to fault. The key exhibit of another aspect of this program, however, is a student who worked with a "buyer of kitchen utensils" at Nieman-Marcus. This might be good job training, but it is difficult to justify as high-level education for gifted students.

By their very nature, internships and mentorships are both promising and tricky. At their best, they provide the sort of advanced, hands-on experiences that gifted students need but cannot readily find in the schools. At their worst, they are little more than executive-training programs for students who are capable of higher pursuits or unstructured extracurricular activities with an educational rationale that is difficult to fathom. Considerable planning, screening (of both mentors and students), and monitoring of such placements is required if they are to be defensible as special-educational programs for the gifted.

Partnerships Between Secondary Schools and Colleges. A number of provisions fall under this heading. Perhaps the best known is the Advanced Placement (AP) program administered by the College Entrance Examination Board. This program allows high-school students to sit for examinations in a variety of subject areas found in most college curricula. If a student scores high enough on a given examination, college credit in that subject may be awarded by the college in which the student matriculates.

Other examples of this approach discussed by Cox et al. (1985) include concurrent enrollment in high school and college, and early entrance to college (see also Benbow, 1986, for some additional variations on this theme). Not discussed by these authors but fitting nicely under this heading would be the growing number of courses for elementary- and secondary-school students offered by colleges and universities across the country. The Center for the Study and Education of the Gifted at Teachers College, for example, offers a range of weekend classes for able students from ages 2 to 15, and other institutions of higher learning do likewise, although generally with a focus on older students.

These are all provisions that can work to the benefit of gifted students and are worthwhile; however, with the exception of early admission and perhaps concurrent enrollment, they are best described as supplementary provisions rather than as comprehensive programs (which, to be fair, is true of most "programs" for the gifted). Nonetheless, the opportunities for partnership between public schools and colleges have not been adequately explored. This is truly unfortunate, for both partners could derive significant advantages from such a relationship.

Summer Programs. Included under this heading is an array of programs, including the Johns Hopkins Talent Searches, the North Carolina Governor's Schools, the National Music Camp at Interlochen, and a number of summer offerings, many at colleges and universities, not mentioned by Cox et al. (1985). These require little explanation. They are characterized by stringent selection procedures and rigorous instruction by highly qualified instructors, and they have gained—and in most cases deserve—high praise for the quality of their efforts.

Summary. The "promising practices" described by Cox et al. (1985) have considerable merit, but I suspect that most educators concerned with meeting the needs of gifted students in the public schools would find this list of options disheartening. Unfortunately, these program formats have two salient qualities that lead one to wonder about how much thought was given to the practical problems of educating the gifted in the schools.

First, they ignore almost completely gifted students on the elementary level, where the need for differentiated education is perhaps the greatest. This curious myopia, which seems to imply that education prior to the secondary level is unworthy of consideration, is shared by most of the major reports that have called national attention to the need for excellence in education (see Passow, 1984, for a perceptive critical discussion of these reports).

Second, these approaches to the education of the gifted are not practicable ones in most settings. Few schools or school districts can launch special schools for the gifted. Summer programs of the sort described by Cox et al. (1985) are almost exclusively the province of agencies outside the public schools. And many joint school–college programs are dependent upon the fortuitous existence of a nearby college interested in outreach programs. Other provisions cited as exemplary by these authors, such as the International Baccalaureate and the Advanced Placement programs, require considerable expense, specially trained teachers, and a sufficient number of students to make them workable. Early admission is simply a method for getting gifted students out of the public schools earlier (which may be highly desirable), and mentorships are more difficult to implement at a high level of quality than Cox et al. (1985) admit.

Thus, the discussion of promising practices in this useful report is valuable as a way of conferring recognition upon worthwhile programs outside the reach of most schools and as a potential source of inspiration for individuals interested in launching similar efforts; but as a compendium of viable program formats for the education of gifted students in the schools, it has limited utility.

In addition to the formats discussed by Cox et al. (1985) there are two others I would like to mention.

Before-School and After-School Programs

In many cases, before- and after-school programs for the gifted consist simply of one of the program formats mentioned above in which the classes meet before or after the normal school day. In other cases, the flavor of these programs is that of a club or other extracurricular activity. In each case, there is one basic drawback to this approach, and that has to do with the message sent by the school or school district to students and parents: the program for the gifted is not worthy of being accommodated within the regular school day and should thus be regarded as just another extracurricular activity. This violates one of the basic requirements of a program for the gifted, that the offerings for the gifted be seen as an integral part of the curriculum of the school or school district.

There is nothing wrong with offering enrichment classes before or after school hours, especially if they are open to all students with a desire to learn about the subjects being investigated. In fact, any school or school district that has the willingness and the dedicated faculty required to make such offerings should be applauded. However, these should be something in addition to the special-educational program for the gifted, not something offered as a substitute for it.

In some schools or school districts, it may seem that there is no alternative to scheduling the program for the gifted before or after school hours, and this may be true in some cases. In fact, I taught in a very fine program in which classes for gifted junior high-school students began the equivalent of one class period before the normal beginning of school and continued into the homeroom and first periods. (It has been my experience that before-school classes are vastly preferable to after-school classes.) However, if a program for the gifted must compete with extracurricular activities, school personnel should not be surprised if gifted students consider the program to be just another club and choose other ways to spend their free time. Nor should they be surprised if students and parents question whether a good-faith effort has been made to provide a differentiated curricular program for the gifted.

Teams and Competitions

Of late, there has been a proliferation of organized interscholastic competitions that stress cleverness, ingenuity, and other mental abilities instead of the athletic prowess demanded of participants in more typical competitive events. Operating under such names as Creative Competitions, the Future Problem Solving Bowl, Olympics of the Mind, and Odyssey of the Mind, these programs offer opportunities for students who might not shine in more traditional interscholastic events to win some acclaim and to experience the pleasures of organized competition. On their own, as extracurricular activities, these competitions are at worst silly and at best often a source of pride for students, parents, and schools.

There is a potential danger, however, lurking in these events (in addition to the dangers of overcompetitiveness, loss of perspective, and too much adult pressure inherent in all organized competitions), and this danger is twofold. First, it is not rare to find that a school forbids all but students identified as gifted from trying out for these teams. This is not just unfair, but limiting to the team's prospects, since the sort of cleverness required to do well in these competitions is not possessed exclusively by gifted students.

A second and greater danger from a special-educational point of view is that the team will be passed off as the program for the gifted or that time set aside for the education of gifted students will be devoted instead to practicing for the competition. The activities involved in these competitions may be fun, and there is certainly nothing wrong with that, but this sort of activity cannot in any way be equated with the high-level intellectual activity that is required in a defensible differentiated curriculum for the gifted. A school or school district that claims that it has an Odyssey of the Mind team that is its program for the gifted is only half-right: It does have an Odyssey of the Mind team; it does not have a program for the gifted.

CONCLUSION

Although I have chosen to focus my discussion of program format primarily on how gifted students are grouped for instruction, this topic is a very broad one. It encompasses, in addition to numerous ways of grouping students, many issues not even touched upon in this chapter. I have, therefore, not tried to deal with the topic in a comprehensive manner. My intention has been instead to suggest the range of options available to program planners and to reinforce the central tenet of my approach to planning programs for the gifted: that every program component must be chosen or designed to work smoothly with every other program component to meet the unique assessed needs of gifted students in a specific school or school district.

Whatever decision is finally made with respect to administrative arrangements for delivering instruction to gifted students, this tenet, I hope, would be kept in mind. It is a great mistake to adopt a pull-out program simply because the adjacent school district uses that format; or to opt for provisions within the regular classroom because that approach is politically expedient; or to establish a resource room for the gifted because that approach was given the hard sell at a conference.

Choosing the proper program format does not differ from choosing any other program component in the system approach I have been describing in this book. It requires that program planners determine who needs the form of special education we refer to as education for the gifted; that they learn what the specific educational needs of these students are; that they assess the resources available to the school or school district in meeting the needs of these students; and that they make the most logical decisions possible in bringing to bear the available resources on the problem of meeting those needs. This is conceptually easy but, obviously, difficult in practice. It is the soundest approach of which I am aware, though, and the one that offers the greatest chance that the program format will be chosen to fit the students, not the other way around.

CHAPTER 7

Teachers and
Other Program Staff

There is probably more nonsense and less evidence dispensed
about the needed characteristics of the teacher of the gifted
than almost any other single issue in this field of gifted
education.

Gallagher, Teaching the Gifted Child

If we believe the lists of characteristics [of teachers of the
gifted] offered by researchers and writers in this field, we
would need to find a person who is so outstanding and
exemplary that few gifted programs could exist.

Clark, Growing Up Gifted

A few years ago, a survey was conducted in which experts in the field of the
education of the gifted were asked to rank "key features" of programs for the
gifted in order of importance (Renzulli, 1981). Although these authorities
deemed numerous program components to be crucial, "the teacher: selection
and training" was accorded the highest priority. This is hardly surprising.
Few would dispute the assertion that the quality of instruction in a program
for the gifted is directly, nearly entirely, dependent upon the efforts and skill
of the program's teachers and that teachers can make or break a program.
This is an article of faith in our field, and rightly so. However, translating
this credo into principles for planning programs for the gifted is another
matter altogether.

The problem is not one of assessing the capabilities of individual teachers
in the classroom, especially at the extremes of the teaching-ability continuum.
That is the easy part. Anyone who is familiar with gifted children and their
educational requirements needs to spend very little time in a given classroom
before realizing that he or she is in the presence of a remarkably capable or
a lamentably inept teacher. However, this is something that is done after the
fact, once a teacher has been hired, and it offers little help in the matter of
planning.

It is in attempting to generalize to teachers of the gifted as a whole, so that one may develop guidelines useful for program planning and hiring decisions, that one often comes a cropper. The popular and frequently encountered profiles of the ideal teacher of the gifted are for the most part no more persuasive than are the simplistic descriptions of the typical gifted child that abound in the literature, as the passages quoted at the beginning of this chapter are meant to suggest.

Although it is unlikely, given the exiguous body of data relating to characteristics of effective teachers of the gifted, that I will be any more successful than previous writers in adducing reliable evidence to support my recommendations and conclusions with respect to this issue, my aim in this chapter is also more modest. My goal is to avoid contributing to the accretion of nonsense that Gallagher (1985) laments and the possible paralysis that Clark (1983) envisions while suggesting some guidelines for selecting personnel and establishing an administrative structure as part of the process of planning a program for the gifted.

TEACHERS OF THE GIFTED

As is the case with every other component of a program for the gifted, teacher selection should not be conducted in isolation. By this I mean that it is important to consider the role of the prospective teacher in the context of the total program that is being planned. Care must be taken to match the characteristics of the teacher or teachers being sought with the requirements of the program. For example, a self-contained program for intellectually gifted fifth graders could very well require a teacher with a configuration of skills and knowledge quite different from that required of a teacher working in a senior high-school program for students gifted in mathematics.

This suggests one of the difficulties of stating a priori the desirable qualities of the successful teacher of the gifted. Just as there are children who are gifted in many and different ways, and just as there is a myriad of program formats in which these children can be served, so there is a wide range of personalities, abilities, and backgrounds that could predispose individuals to successful or unsuccessful tenures in various programs for the gifted. Therefore, any discussion of requisite traits or behaviors of teachers of the gifted, including the one that follows, should be tempered with the understanding that characteristics that are appropriate in general may be inappropriate in a specific program.

Traits versus Behaviors

Gallagher (1985) raises an important point concerning the lists of traits of effective teachers of the gifted found in the literature. Citing Bruch and

Torrance (1972), who advise us that "teachers [of the gifted] should be honest" (p. 384), Gallagher wonders what this means with respect to teachers in other fields. Would it be acceptable if teachers of children of average ability were somewhat less honest? And might a history of outright mendacity be tolerable in teachers of the mentally retarded? Or, rather, is not honesty a trait to be sought in all teachers, if not in all individuals? And if so, as most people would undoubtedly agree, what does Bruch and Torrance's statement add to our knowledge?

While we would all like to have honest individuals working with our gifted students, there is a paucity of research evidence that relates traits of this sort to efficacious educational practice.

To go a step further, there is reason to believe that the entire issue of desirable teacher traits may be of very little practical significance. Gallagher (p. 385), who, it should be clear by now, writes quite cogently on this issue, cites Benjamin Bloom (1980) in this context. Bloom asserts that "the characteristics of teachers have little to do with the learning of their students" (cited in Gallagher, 1985, p. 385). Perhaps this is just as well, at least from the point of view of those concerned with teacher education. If successful teaching depends upon the possession of a list of favorable personality traits that are fixed early in life and fairly resistant to change in adulthood, preservice teacher education would appear to be largely ineffectual for that vast number of aspiring teachers who do not possess what Gallagher refers to as the "all-encompassing virtues" (p. 384) that constitute most of these lists.

Happily, however, it is possible to distinguish between desirable teacher *traits* and desirable teacher *behaviors*. Unlike the former, the latter are both modifiable and demonstrably related to student behaviors. I will try, therefore, whenever possible in the discussion that follows to refer to teacher behaviors rather than to teacher traits or characteristics. This will sometimes be difficult, for there are enduring questions that are as much concerned with what teachers of the gifted should *be* as with what they *do*. Some of these questions cannot be ignored, especially that old chestnut, "Must one be gifted in order to teach the gifted?" to which I now turn.

Gifted Teachers and Gifted Students

One danger inherent in the promulgation of lists of desirable traits of teachers of the gifted is the possible effect of these lists on prospective teachers. As Gallagher (1985) observes, they "can have a rather paralyzing effect . . . [and] can give the impression that no human being can live up to such a list of characteristics" (p. 383). This is certainly true for the traits in the aggregate, but it is also true for one particular trait that is mentioned on nearly every list: the teacher's own level of intellectual ability.

Many writers have addressed this issue. Some, for example, firmly believe that high intellectual ability is a requirement for teachers who wish to work with the gifted. According to Ward (1961), for example, teachers of the gifted "should be deviant with respect to those qualities common to the gifted group" (p. 115). Newland (1976) agrees, stating that "the intellectual capability of teachers of the gifted should be appropriate to the educational level of their pupils" (p. 148).

In one of the very few empirical studies related to this question, Bishop (1968) asked students enrolled in the Georgia Governor's Honors Program to identify teachers in their home schools who the students thought were "most successful" in the classroom. These teachers were then compared with a sample of teachers who had taught these gifted students but had not been identified by them as particularly successful. Bishop found that the mean Wechsler Adult Intelligence Scale IQ of the "most successful" teachers of the gifted was 128, which is nearly two standard deviations above the mean for the population as a whole and significantly higher than the mean for the teachers not identified as successful.

Other writers, while no less insistent that teachers of the gifted themselves be highly intelligent, qualify their position by stressing that other traits are equally or more important. Gallagher (1985), for example, writes that "certainly the teacher [of the gifted] should be of superior intellectual ability, but, even more important, should possess the enthusiasm to continue to seek new ideas and to be a model of inquiry in the search for new knowledge" (p. 386). The same message comes through in another "expert survey" cited by Gold (1979). In *The Advocate Survey: A Survey of Experts in the Education of the Gifted,* 200 noted authorities were asked to rank characteristics of teachers of the gifted in order of their importance. Although "high intelligence" was one of the requisite characteristics, it ranked seventh, behind such traits as "proven teaching ability" and "flexibility."

Still other writers are less convinced of the absolute necessity of high intelligence among teachers of the gifted. Clark (1983), for example, asserts that "a teacher does not need to be highly intelligent to work effectively with the gifted learner" (p. 371). She does say, however, that to be successful with gifted students a teacher "should definitely value intelligence, understand its implications, and know how to nurture it" (p. 371).

Where does this leave the program planner who is wrestling with the task of writing a job description for the teacher or teachers in his or her program? How important is an intellectually gifted teacher to a program for the gifted? One way to respond to these questions is to equivocate a bit by pointing out the elusive meaning of the term *gifted.* In Chapter 2, I discussed the various meanings of this slippery word, and in Chapter 3, I argued for a definition of giftedness that is relative to the setting of the program. The same line of reasoning could be used to respond to the question of whether teachers of the gifted must be gifted themselves.

The essence of my equivocal response, then, is "It depends." The thing on which it depends is the conception of giftedness applied to children in the program. If the program is designed to serve children gifted in dramatics, it is less important that the teacher have extremely high intellectual ability than that he or she have a gift for drama. Similarly, if the program for the gifted uses Renzulli's (1978) definition of giftedness, merely above-average ability, coupled with some indicators of creativity and task commitment, should suffice. Thus, Ward's (1961) dictum that the teacher be "deviant with respect to the qualities common to the gifted group" (p. 115) would serve in the general case. The students' exceptionality should be matched in degree and kind by that of their teacher.

However, this is somewhat disingenuous and, in effect, finesses the issue. The vast majority of programs for the gifted are designed for students who are exceptional by virtue of high academic intelligence, and the question still remains: What should we expect of their teachers? Should teachers in programs of this type meet the same admission criteria as the students? Without equivocating further, let me answer in the affirmative. I think it is quite important that teachers of the intellectually gifted themselves possess very high intellectual ability. Let me list some of the reasons for this belief.

1. Teaching gifted students involves constant interaction with children who are highly knowledgeable, quick-thinking, subtle in their reasoning, and capable of sustained productivity under the right conditions. It requires considerable mental ability simply to keep up with such individuals and to survive in a classroom inhabited by them. It is difficult to conceive of a successful program for the gifted in which the teacher, whatever other positive characteristics and abilities he or she might possess, is the least intelligent person in the room.

2. Perhaps more than any other role in education, that of teacher of the gifted requires a secure sense of self-esteem with respect to one's own intellectual capabilities. Teachers of the gifted spend considerable time with children a fraction of their age who nonetheless in many cases possess more knowledge of certain subjects than they do. This can be disquieting. No matter how outdated one thinks the role of the authoritarian teacher may be, it is difficult for most people to disabuse themselves completely of the notion that the teacher should be the expert and the students the novices. This may be unfortunate, but I suspect that, human nature and adult–child relationships being what they are, it is nonetheless true. The potential for insecurity inherent in this situation and the deleterious effects it can have on the teacher's attitude toward his or her pupils can be mitigated by the

teacher's knowledge that he or she, too, is quite able and knowledgeable in a number of areas. It seems logical that a teacher who clearly is less intelligent than his or her gifted students is more likely to feel threatened than one who, while admitting that some students know more about certain things, knows that he or she and the students are equal in intellectual ability.

3. One of the most important functions of teachers of the gifted is to serve as effective role models. In their respect for learning, their seeking after truth, their willingness to risk failure by wrestling with difficult problems and issues, their playful attitude toward ideas, their ability to produce instead of merely to reproduce knowledge—in short, in their pursuit of the life of the mind—teachers of the gifted show by their own example that such a life is one of the highest callings in our society. The blandishments, material and psychological, of other activities are constantly paraded before gifted students. The rewards of the *vita activa* are obvious; those of the *vita contemplativa* are less so. It is often only through the personal example of and regular contact with those of an intellectual bent that the real though subtle joys of the intellectual life are realized. For gifted children, this is most likely to come from teachers of the gifted. And in order that this may happen, a high level of intellectual attainment on the part of their teachers is clearly required.

4. As I will insist in the next chapter, an effective curriculum for gifted students needs to be developed by the teachers who will be responsible for its implementation. This means that effective teachers of the gifted must also be capable of developing appropriate curricula for this population. Curriculum development in general is a demanding task; writing curricula for intellectually gifted students is, in some ways, even more so. To structure content, skills, and activities for able students is an intellectually daunting activity, one that requires significant intellectual ability.

These are some of the reasons why I believe teachers of the gifted ought themselves to be of high intellectual caliber. There are arguments against this position or in favor of more moderate positions, as I cited above, and they are not made by individuals who are advocating mediocrity in programs for the gifted. Moreover, I suspect that there are some instances in which teachers who themselves would never qualify for the programs in which they teach do wonderful and appropriate things for their gifted students. However, I also suspect that these teachers are the exception rather than the rule.

I would like to make two qualifications concerning the position advanced above. The first of these relates back to the question of program planning and selecting staff. High intellectual ability in teachers of the intellectually or academically gifted is, in my view, a necessary but not a sufficient quality for success. Although I have difficulty envisioning how a teacher of less than high intelligence could be successful working with intellectually gifted students, I have no difficulty envisioning (and remembering from experience) how a very bright teacher could, despite his or her intelligence, lack other qualities requisite for effective teaching with these students. Some of these other qualities will be discussed below.

Second, my argument in favor of seeking gifted people to be teachers of the gifted must be modified when we are speaking of giftedness or talent in areas other than the intellectual and academic domains, as I suggested above. Things get a bit more complicated here, however, than I acknowledged before. For one thing, it is still true that we would like to have intelligent individuals to constitute our corps of educational professionals, whatever and whomever they teach. Moreover, I do not mean to imply that it does not require intelligence to be gifted in, say, the arts or to teach those who are. However, the importance of highly developed academic intelligence is probably less critical in successful teaching with these gifted students than it is with the more conventionally gifted. Thus, as I stated above one could still argue that the teachers must be gifted, but, in accordance with Ward's (1961) dictum, they would be gifted in the way their students are gifted.

However, there are many examples of people who are gifted teachers in certain talent areas who were not gifted performers themselves. Nadia Boulanger was a gifted teacher of composition but a composer of slight attainments. Lee Strasberg did no acting of note until near the end of his life, but his success as a teacher of actors is indisputable. As a baseball player, Charlie Lau inspired no comparisons to Ty Cobb, but when he died he was widely eulogized as the most effective and most influential batting instructor in recent memory.

Thus, there is reason to suspect that the need for giftedness is less critical among teachers whose students are gifted in nonacademic domains. What *is* required is less than clear. One can glibly assert that for such students we need gifted teachers more than teachers who are gifted; but this is little help. It may be that the only reliable predictor of future success in working with these gifted students is a record of past success in the same activity.

Behaviors Characteristic of Successful Teachers of the Gifted

In this section I would like to discuss what I consider to be some of the indicators of potential for success in the demanding profession of educator of the gifted. To begin, though, a few disclaimers are in order.

First, I will try not to make this a list of traits or characteristics of effective teachers of the gifted. As I stated above, there is little research to link personal characteristics of teachers to effective teaching, as Bloom (1980) asserts.

There is reason to believe, nonetheless, that certain teacher behaviors can be linked to desirable student behaviors, so I will try to focus on what teachers should do, not on what they should be like. I will not always be able to do this, however, because there are some traits, such as high intelligence, that I believe to be essential.

Second, this list is not exhaustive. I will include the behaviors I think are most important; others might place more importance on behaviors that do not appear below, and they may be correct in doing so. Moreover, in certain programs and situations behaviors not on this list may be of critical importance, and some on the list may have no importance whatever.

Third, although I will refer in passing to some research, this list is not derived from my own research or a review of that of others. Research in this area is low in quantity, lower in quality, and lower yet in unanimity. The following is drawn as much from my experience and from my beliefs with regard to what programs for the gifted should be like as from the available research, perhaps more so.

Fourth, let us assume for the moment that what follows is the wisest and most convincing list of behaviors of successful teachers of the gifted ever written. Even in that unlikely case, there would be some excellent teachers of the gifted who do not fit this profile and some very poor ones who do. That is the nature of the profession in which we work and the species of which we are members. This is important for administrators to keep in mind when they are seeking teachers of the gifted.

Among the behaviors (and some traits) that, in my opinion, are characteristic of effective teachers of the gifted are the following:

1. *A teacher of the gifted should possess a considerable amount of general intelligence* (an assertion I discussed at length above).

2. *A teacher of the gifted should have a strong educational background in at least one substantive discipline.* Howley, Howley, and Pendarvis (1986) assert that "the most important role of the gifted education teacher is that of the scholar–teacher" (p. 263). I interpret that to mean that the teacher should also be a serious and capable student in a significant area of inquiry. This goes to the heart of an issue that is quite current in educational reform, namely, the preparation of teachers.

In too many cases, preservice teachers receive a considerable amount of instruction in pedagogical technique but receive little education of substance. As a result, our schools of education may be turning out many teachers who are well versed in methods and materials but who are relatively ignorant with respect to the essentials of a liberal education. A commonly advocated reform, recommended by the Holmes Group of deans of schools of education among others, is the abolition of undergraduate degrees in education. Under the terms of this proposal, instead of majoring in education on the undergraduate level, prospective teachers would earn a degree in the arts, sciences, or humanities. Then, as is the practice in such fields as medicine and law, specialized professional training would take place on the graduate level.

I think this is a solid educational model for the field of education in general and for the field of the education of the gifted in particular. Teachers of the gifted, if they are to work successfully with young scholars, must themselves be scholars. They cannot be experts in every field in which their students are likely to be knowledgeable, but they should each be able to say, "This is my field; I care about it, I know about it, and I can teach you quite a bit about it."

3. *A teacher of the gifted should consistently demonstrate a hunger for learning.* I mentioned this above as a concomitant of possessing high intelligence, so I will not belabor the point here. However, it is worth asserting that if a teacher is trying to instill a love of learning in his or her students, he or she must honestly model that attitude daily. For me, this means a love of knowledge and learning for its own sake, not just for instrumental purposes or material gain. Although there are those within this field who are dismissive of learning just for the sake of learning, I know of no other activity more characteristic of the life of the mind.

For the teacher of the gifted, moreover, this is a necessary component of his or her makeup. I implied above that a teacher of gifted students should be a specialist in at least one discipline (although a broad liberal education should be part of his or her background) and should expect that certain students will be interested and expert in other areas. In order to work with students whose areas of interest are different from one's own, the teacher of the gifted must be willing to learn something about those areas, quite likely from the students themselves.

4. *A teacher of the gifted should frequently say, "I don't know."* I am not advocating widespread ignorance among teachers of the gifted, just honesty when inevitable areas of ignorance are revealed. Too many teachers, when asked a question they cannot answer, refuse to admit that this is the case. This suggests to students not only that their honest inquiries are somehow disruptive and bothersome but also that ignorance of anything is a weakness, something that should be hidden and regarded as a source of shame. (This also suggests that such teachers are not to be taken seriously, since their students are not so gullible as to believe that teachers are omniscient.)

The old proverb, that there is no shame in being ignorant, only in remaining ignorant, has considerable validity in this context. There is no greater motivation for learning than ignorance, and acting on this motivation has to be modeled, not just preached to students. Fortunately, when one works with gifted students, one has many opportunities to reveal one's ignorance.

5. *A teacher of the gifted needs a solid sense of personal security.* This is not a job for the insecure or for those with fragile egos. Teachers of the gifted not only find themselves in day-to-day contact with children whose knowledge outstrips theirs in many areas, they also receive many reminders that this is the case. It is not unknown for gifted students to challenge their teachers for a variety of reasons, ranging from a desire to make a point intellectually to a desire to make points with their peers by embarrassing the teacher. This is hardly the place for a martinet who needs to prop up a flimsy sense of self by lording it over a group of students.

A strong ego is also required to survive some of the dealings one will have with other adults. Parents of students in programs for the gifted often have very definite opinions about what such programs should or should not be doing, and, acting on the educational expertise that comes with maternity and paternity, they are rarely reticent or moderate in the expression of their opinions. Similarly vocal are those parents who are convinced that their children should be placed in the program for the gifted despite the school's judgment to the contrary.

One's teaching peers will quite frequently express opinions about the program for the gifted, and they will not always do so tactfully. Their opinions will sometimes be echoed by frustrated school administrators weary of dealing with children, parents, and school board members whose concerns about the program occupy what the administrators may consider to be an inordinate amount of their time.

In short, teachers of the gifted often find themselves on the firing line, probably more frequently than other teachers. One cannot survive in such a pressure-cooker situation without a sufficient reserve of personal psychological resources (and a thick skin as well).

6. *A teacher of the gifted should tolerate diversity, originality, and off-beat responses to questions and assignments.* More than other students, gifted students are likely to respond to teachers' questions and assignments in ways that teachers do not expect but that may be far from inappropriate. By their nature, these students tend to see things from a variety of angles, to see connections where others do not, to be divergent in their thinking. In fact, encouraging divergent thinking is an explicit goal in many programs for the gifted.

Even in drill-and-recitation situations, the program for the gifted is not the place for teachers to regard teaching as a game of 20 questions in which the goal is to have the students guess the answer that is in the teacher's head. Few practices are more inimical to the teaching of thinking. If gifted students are to be encouraged to think for themselves—as they should—teachers must be open to the variety of ideas that will result.

7. *A teacher of the gifted should be well organized and well structured in his*

or her teaching. Let me be clear about what I mean by this. By "well organized and well structured" I do not mean to imply a mania for petty regimentation and inflexibility. I simply mean that the teacher should be able to organize the classroom, the daily routine, a body of knowledge, and a lesson and to communicate this organization to the students. This should be done to minimize confusion on the part of students, to encourage the responsibility that comes from knowing what is expected of one at a given time, and to encourage effective teaching.

One of the traits that characterized the teachers designated as effective teachers of the gifted in Bishop's (1968) study (one of the few good studies in this area) was systematic and organized classroom behavior. This behavior can be expressed in a traditional classroom or in an open classroom or in any type of classroom in between. In fact, I have long believed that nothing requires explicit and detailed structure more than a successful open classroom. However the classroom is structured, the students must be aware that things are organized, that the teacher is prepared, and that there is a purpose for what is being done, a purpose that is clear to them.

Implicit in this requirement and the one that follows is that the teacher should have strong curriculum-development skills. This will be the topic of the next chapter of this book, so I will not address this issue explicitly here.

8. *A teacher of the gifted should have some formal education in the nature, needs, and education of the gifted.* The education of the gifted, as I have argued in previous chapters, is best regarded as a form of special education. As such, it has its own pedagogy designed to meet the needs of a specific group of exceptional children. To function most successfully as a teacher of the gifted, one needs to be aware of the nature and needs of this special population and to have some familiarity with issues and methods relating to curriculum and instruction appropriate for the gifted.

Even though, as a member of the faculty of a school of education, I cannot claim to be completely objective in this respect, I believe that formal college or university courses in the psychology and education of the gifted provide the best form of preservice and in-service education for those who teach the gifted. Following a carefully designed sequence of courses and practice under the tutelage of one or more professors knowledgeable and experienced in this field allows for breadth and depth of study, as well as opportunities for interaction with students engaged in a similar educational program, that cannot be found anywhere else.

Few states require formal certification in the education of the gifted (a total of 17 according to Mitchell, 1988), and most of those that do so do not require more than a short sequence of courses. Despite this, I have seen an informal, de facto "certification" process operate in the job marketplace. I recall applying for my first position as a teacher of the gifted in the early

1970s. I appeared for my interview and was hired on the spot because of my training in the field: one three-credit course and no classroom experience with the gifted. Things have changed considerably since then. To use my own state of New York as an example, although there is no certification requirement for teachers of the gifted in this state, and although there are enough positions statewide for those qualified teachers who wish to teach gifted students, the posting of a teaching position that is particularly appealing will attract a number of applicants. Some of these applicants will possess master's degrees in the education of the gifted and will, as a consequence, have an advantage over their less-credentialed colleagues. Thus, although an M.A. or any coursework in the education of the gifted is rarely an explicit requirement for such a position, the job market functions in such a manner as to make formal education in this field an advantage, if not a requirement.

It may be the case, however, that more teachers of the gifted acquire their training in in-service workshops than in formal college coursework. This is certainly better than no preparation at all, and as one who does quite a bit of this sort of thing, I believe that carefully planned in-service courses of sufficient duration can do a great deal to educate teachers of the gifted and regular classroom teachers in concepts and methods related to the education of gifted learners. However, I also know that too many in-service programs are one-day "dog and pony shows" whose content is superficial and whose benefits are evanescent at best.

However acquired, through formal college coursework, through in-service workshops, or through autodidacticism, knowledge of this aspect of special education is essential for the effective educator of the gifted. I hesitate to call for mandated certification for teachers of the gifted for fear of precluding the participation in the field of many capable individuals, but I also have difficulty believing that professional preparation in the concepts and methods of this field is not requisite for success for most teachers. Thus, while acknowledging that there are no doubt incompetent teachers of the gifted who hold degrees in this field and excellent teachers of the gifted who have had no formal training in it, I view such training as highly desirable and as something whose presence on a curriculum vitae should be useful to administrators faced with hiring decisions.

9. *A teacher of the gifted should possess effective counseling skills.* By "counseling skills," I am referring less to skills developed through professional training than to patience, willingness to listen, knowledge of the nature and needs of the gifted, and a genuine concern for students. Gifted children are subject to certain stresses and pressures that are the direct result of their particular exceptionality (see, for example, Galbraith, 1985; Krueger, 1978). Although talking about their concerns would do these children much good, they are often reluctant to do so since it would call attention to their giftedness

and to things that make them different from their age-mates. But in a program for the gifted, they find themselves among their peers, and they often feel less reticent. It is not uncommon in such classes for discussions to turn from topics related to the unit of study to the problems associated with being a gifted child or adolescent in today's society.

Moreover, although a gifted child may feel that regular classroom teachers do not understand his or her problems or concerns, the teacher of the gifted may be regarded as being more sympathetic and more attuned to the gifted child's world. The teacher may feel unqualified to serve as a counselor, and I am not suggesting that in cases in which there are signs of a serious personal or family problem the teacher do anything other than make a referral to a qualified professional. However, in those situations in which a gifted student just needs a sympathetic listener or some help making educational decisions, the teacher of the gifted may well be in a better position to be of assistance than a guidance counselor who, unfortunately, has probably had no training in dealing with problems common to gifted children.

10. *A teacher of the gifted should possess skills of diplomacy, public relations, and public speaking.* Sine most programs for the gifted represent something other than business as usual in the schools, they require considerable explanation. Teachers of the gifted must frequently explain to administrators, other teachers, parents, and students what the program is doing and why. Often they find themselves called upon to represent the program for the gifted before hostile or skeptical audiences and to sell the program successfully. The ability to speak effectively to individuals and to groups is an invaluable skill for such teachers.

11. *A teacher of the gifted should be tough-minded and resistant to manipulation.* I suggested above that a teacher of the gifted should be sympathetic to the concerns of his or her students and understanding of their special problems and needs. This is quite true, but there is another side of the issue that needs to be addressed as well.

One of the things that students learn in school is how to go to school. By this I mean not just that they learn how to learn but also that they learn how to play the school game effectively. In some cases, this means that they figure out how to get the most effect for the least effort. This is not necessarily a bad thing; it is akin to what Sternberg (1986) talks about in his contextual subtheory of intelligence and to some of the metacomponents in his componential subtheory. Learning the rules of the game is an important part of one's initiation into any group, whether as a student or a professional, and gifted students are often particularly adept at this form of metalearning. This can have advantages, and it can also have negative consequences.

One negative aspect is that gifted students sometimes quickly learn that they can get away with less than their best work and still perform quite well in comparison with other students. Moreover, some teachers, although certainly not all, seem almost to be intimidated by the "gifted" label. They reason that if this child has been deemed to be gifted by people who should know about such things, whatever work this child submits must be praiseworthy, since it is the work of a gifted child. Thus, a sloppy essay is praised for its "creativity," and glib, unconsidered opinions are treated as examples of critical thinking.

Teachers of the gifted can perform a most valuable service for gifted students by refusing to fall for such manipulation. It is tempting not to be critical of the students one is nurturing, but honest criticism is essential to effective teaching and learning. Furthermore, these students are perceptive enough to realize that teachers who allow them to get by with doing less than their best are doing them no favor, even as they strive to get teachers to do just that. Honesty, tempered with humanity, is indeed the best policy in such situations.

12. *A teacher of the gifted should not be afraid to teach.* This is a somewhat cryptic statement that requires some explanation. There is a considerable amount of writing and rhetoric concerning the proper role of the teacher of the gifted, much of which implies or even states outright that the less the teacher does, the better. Some writers resort to ungainly verbal contortions, such as "teacher/facilitator" to avoid referring to the adults charged with the responsibility for the education of gifted students as "teachers." One popular performer on the lecture circuit urges teachers of the gifted to be "guides on the side" rather than "sages on the stage." The message these people are delivering is that teachers of the gifted should not actually try to teach anything to gifted students; instead they should "facilitate" the students' learning or even get out of the students' way and let them learn what they want to learn.

Now, there is certainly much to say in favor of encouraging independence in gifted learners, allowing the gifted to pursue independent-study projects on topics of their own choosing as part of their special curriculum, and insisting that students be able to challenge the ideas, opinions, and omniscience of their teachers. Moreover, gifted students, like most students, do not need dogmatic, pedantic, egotistical teachers who insist on always being the center of attention and permit their students only a passive role in the learning process.

However, there is also probably some merit in the idea that qualified teachers of the gifted should teach some things to their gifted students. Adult educational professionals with experience and training in the education of the gifted are likely to possess some declarative and procedural knowledge that they believe is important for gifted students to know and to believe that teaching is an effective way to impart this knowledge. While they may be convinced of the value of self-directed learning, they may *also* be convinced that the teacher has the responsibility to make informed curricular decisions about the education of gifted children.

Thus, I would urge teachers of the gifted not to be intimidated by simplistic slogans and exhortations to abdicate their responsibilities to their students. This is not an either/or proposition. Teachers of the gifted should be willing both to teach their students and to help their students learn on their own.

These behaviors and traits hardly exhaust those desirable or requisite for effective teaching of the gifted. The reader will no doubt be able to supply others or will dispute the importance of some that I have included above, but it is not my intention to supply a definitive profile of the effective teacher of the gifted. There is simply not enough known about what makes teachers excellent in general, let alone what makes teachers excellent in this field. Moreover, I believe that there is no single profile of *the* effective teacher of the gifted. In my experience, excellent teachers come in every size, shape, philosophy, background, and so forth. I hesitate to try to categorize such a diverse group or to promulgate a profile that might be used to screen out promising candidates simply because they do not fit my, or anybody else's, a priori conceptions.

Rather, I simply wish to suggest some considerations for those who, in planning a program for the gifted, must deal with the difficult issue of staffing. I hope my list is useful; however, I would be much happier if administrators would pay attention to the previous paragraph than to my imperfect list of traits and behaviors.

SUPERVISION OF PROGRAMS FOR THE GIFTED

I am reluctant to make sententious pronouncements about the ideal administrative structure of programs for the gifted. To do so would go against my theme, that program planning and implementation should be based on local needs and conditions. Given the diversity that exists among school districts, global assertions about the "best" administrative structure would make little sense for many, if not most, districts.

Similarly, it is difficult to generalize from current practice. Since there is little legislation governing programs for the gifted, and what does exist applies only to certain states and localities, practice varies widely. Some programs have elaborate administrative structures, and some operate as anarchies (these two categories not necessarily being mutually exclusive). In the two months preceding the writing of this chapter, for example, I visited a program in a rural/exurban school district serving fewer than 200 gifted students that had a full-time program director and a full-time assistant director. I also visited a program in a medium-sized city that served considerably more students in a variety of sites that was overseen by a school psychologist, only half of whose time was supposed to be devoted to the program for the gifted.

Instead of trying to prescribe how the administration of such programs should be structured, I will address some concerns and make some suggestions for avoiding common pitfalls I have observed in programs I have visited. I will leave it to local school authorities to make the specific decisions about who administers what, and under what title.

A question that is often asked about programs for the gifted is, Who's in charge here? Confusion usually derives from two sources: questions about who is directly responsible for the day-to-day operation of the program and questions about how that person (and the program) fits into the overall administrative framework of the school or school district. Both of these deserve some discussion.

Teacher, Coordinator, or Director?

Many programs for the gifted are the direct responsibility of a "coordinator" or a "teacher/coordinator." This is a slippery title, one that often connotes more power than it actually confers. The title of coordinator often has no meaning with regard to the administrative structure of the school or school district. It is simply a token designation given to someone who has the status and power of a teacher but is expected to do the job of a program administrator. When this title is appended to the word *teacher*, as in "teacher/coordinator," it usually implies that the individual in question is expected to perform all of the administrative and instructional duties of the program.

In some cases, this is a way for the school or school district to economize. Since the coordinator or teacher/coordinator has the rank of a regular teacher, the salary attached to the position is usually what the person would be earning in a regular classroom placement. Thus, the school or school district is able to obtain an administrator and a teacher for the price of the latter.

Moreover, although the coordinator or teacher/coordinator is expected to perform administrative functions, he or she is rarely assigned the administrative status necessary to carry out some of these functions. This is especially problematic when such duties require working with other teachers. Whereas an administrator can compel the (perhaps grudging) compliance of teachers with program requirements, a coordinator or teacher/coordinator must rely on powers of persuasion that are sometimes inadequate to the task. This places one in an awkward position and severely hampers one's effectiveness.

The answer to this dilemma is to make certain that the roles of those in charge are clear and that their responsibilities match their positions within the administrative hierarchy. Ideally, there should be a program director with day-to-day oversight responsibilities and an administrative title. If this is not possible—and it will not be in every school or school district—a coordinator or teacher/coordinator should be appointed.

However, this position should be carefully considered and the temptation to exploit the individual appointed to fill it should be avoided. This means that if extra duties are involved, extra pay should be forthcoming. It also means that if the individual who holds this position is expected to perform administrative functions, he or she should not also be expected to teach on a full-time basis. Thereby, both burnout and threats to the instructional quality of the program may be avoided. Finally, this means that tasks requiring the wielding of administrative authority should be carried out by someone in a position to exercise that authority. If the coordinator or teacher/coordinator is not to be given administrative status, those who have such status should not expect that person to perform functions for which they, the administrators, are being paid.

Need for an Unambiguous Chain of Command

Programs for the gifted are sometimes regarded as the stepchildren of their schools or school districts, for a variety of reasons. In some cases the program was put into place not because the administration felt that such a program was needed but rather in response to intense parental pressure. In other cases the program is an attempt to "keep up with the Joneses," to match program-for-program the offerings of a rival school or school district. In a few cases, the program is only a response to a mandate of the state education law, and thus a response that may be confused or lukewarm. In still others, the program may represent an honest response to student needs that does not fit comfortably into the district's administrative organizational chart.

Paradoxically, after more than seven decades of history in this country, programs for the gifted are still a new phenomenon for many if not most administrators. For a number of school authorities such programs are neither fish nor fowl, neither special education as they understand it nor "regular education." The practical result of this confusion is that the programs are often shoehorned into the system's organizational chart wherever it is convenient, with little thought for what this means for the day-to-day operation of the program. Lines of authority become blurred, and program personnel can be uncertain about to whom they should be responsible and to whom they can turn when help is needed.

As we saw in Chapter 6, this is a particular problem when a centrally coordinated program is placed in a particular building. This is a feature of such program formats as the school-within-a-school and, sometimes, a self-contained class. In such instances the role of the building principal is often unclear, both to the special program staff and to the principal himself or herself, and what should be rather routine situations can become difficult ones. This can raise some troubling questions. For example, if a special-class teacher has a difficult discipline problem, can the building administration be counted upon to help? Do teachers in the program for the gifted have access to supplies and other resources earmarked for the building in which the program is housed? To what extent does the building principal have a say in evaluating the performance of teachers in the special program? These and other questions can and do arise if they are not answered in advance.

On a higher level of the hierarchy, program coordinators or directors sometimes are not certain where their program fits into the larger scheme of things. Unfortunately, programs for the gifted are not always the direct responsibility of the central administrator whose daily activities, educational interests, or training make him or her the best person for the job. When this happens, the program director or coordinator lacks the protection and guidance afforded his or her peers whose programs are carefully watched over by superiors who have a stake in the programs' futures.

It is important, therefore, that a program for the gifted be clearly and logically integrated into the administrative structure of the school or school district. Ideally, the administrator responsible for special-educational programs would be the one with oversight of programs for the gifted, although this is not necessarily always the best way. The crucial factor here is that the program should not be an orphan (or even a stepchild). Like any other legitimate educational program, its role in the overall scheme of things should be carefully considered. Program personnel at least deserve a sense that their program belongs in the system, that there is an unequivocal chain of command affording the possibility of direct communication and, if necessary, appeal.

To the extent that a program for the gifted is truly programmatic and not merely provisional it will be clear to all where the program fits into the administrative structure. Moreover, a true program will be logically placed, with the implication that the school authorities view the program as a permanent feature of the school or school district, not as a temporary expedient or an extracurricular frill.

CONCLUSION

If a topic's importance were directly related to the length of its treatment, this would be the longest chapter of the book by far, for it deals with teachers, the most important component of any program for the gifted. However, the amount of our collective wisdom regarding teachers of the gifted does not correspond to the significance of the issue. This is perhaps inevitable. While I am usually quick to lament our disinclination as a field to carry out needed research to fill in gaps in our knowledge, I suspect that this issue is one that may be resistant to complete comprehension and easy summary. This is so because we must draw our teachers and other program staff from that pool of organisms known as human beings, who are a notoriously heterogeneous and quirky bunch. Those who have demonstrated their special competence as teachers and inspirers of gifted children have thus far not cooperated with our efforts to construct a neat profile of the ideal teacher of the gifted. I doubt that they will prove to be any more cooperative in the future.

This being the case, one is left with few guidelines for making personnel decisions. One can consult lists of desirable traits or behaviors of teachers of the gifted, keeping in mind, I hope, the limitations of such lists (including the one found in this chapter). Even better, one can use common sense and the principle that underlies this book: that every aspect of planning a program for the gifted should be guided by knowledge of assessed needs of the school or school district in question. Thus, the central question becomes not "What are the characteristics of the ideal teacher of the gifted?" but "What kind of person do we need for *this* program?" If that question is kept in mind, and if the program is developed in a logical, thoughtful manner, I am confident that the best person or persons for the program will be found.

CHAPTER 8

Appropriate Curriculum for the Gifted

Every choice of curriculum constitutes a valuative act, is essentially a moral choice.

> Sawyer, rejoinder to a response to his article, "In Defense of Academic Rigor"

Of all the issues with which we must contend, those related to curriculum go most directly to the heart of our profession. In fact, I would not hesitate to argue that we derive our very raison d'être from our curricular efforts. Above all else, the field of the education of the gifted exists to provide gifted students with differentiated curricula, that is, modified courses of study designed to make the schools more responsive to the educational needs of these exceptional learners. This is our primary goal and our defining mission. This is why we are needed as a field of educational practice.

As one might expect, given its importance, the issue of curriculum for the gifted has attracted much attention, and there is no sign of waning interest. Entire books devoted to the hows and wherefores of curriculum development and differentiation for the gifted have been, and will continue to be, written; graduate and undergraduate courses focusing on broad and specific curricular issues in the education of the gifted have been and will continue to be taught; activities, units, and models for differentiating the curricula of gifted students have been and will continue to be developed; and the fine points of curriculum have been and will continue to be argued. The issue is important, multifaceted, and, like other aspects of the education of the gifted, a source of no little contention.

I do not pretend to be able to deal comprehensively with the topic of curriculum for the gifted in a single chapter. Instead, I will discuss the issue as it relates to the theme of this book: planning and implementing programs for the gifted. I will treat curriculum as one component of a program for the gifted and focus primarily on how it fits into the overall program system, conceptually and practically. Thus, I will touch upon specific issues related

171

to instructional strategies, the efficacy of certain curricular models, and so forth only insofar as they fit into this larger programmatic context. I will, however, consider some fundamental questions concerning the nature of appropriate curricula for gifted students, questions of the sort that Robert Sawyer addresses in his penetrating essay "In Defense of Academic Rigor" (1988a). These basic questions are central to program planning; they must be considered by administrators and other educators who are engaged in program development, and they are quite apposite here.

DIFFERENTIATED CURRICULUM

The phrase *differentiated curriculum for the gifted* is a shibboleth in our field, and rightly so. The need for the field of the education of the gifted derives from the fact that gifted students need differentiated curricula. The only conceivable reason school personnel should wrestle with the program components discussed previously in this book—definitions, identification procedures, program formats—is to enable them to locate a group of exceptional children with special-educational needs and modify their curricula. Unless we make some change in the educational programs of identified gifted students, there is no logical justification for bothering with any aspect of a program for the gifted.

Although arguments rage with respect to what constitutes a differentiated curriculum for the gifted, there is no mystery involved. In a strict denotative sense, the phrase, differentiated curriculum for the gifted, simply means a course of study that is in some manner different from the one to which students in the mainstream are exposed. Thus defined, the requirements of a differentiated curriculum are far from stringent; anything that makes the curriculum different is sufficient to create a differentiated curriculum. This is a descriptive phrase, not an evaluative one, and it simply describes a minimal requirement: some deviation from the instructional norm.

It should be clear, then, that there are various sorts of differentiated curricula. Some are excellent; some are not worth the paper they are (usually not) written on. In discussion of a curriculum for the gifted, therefore, the issue of differentiation is important, but it is just the starting point. Differentiation is not enough. To be appropriate, a curriculum for gifted students must be defensible as well.

DEFENSIBLE DIFFERENTIATED CURRICULUM

The addition of the modifier *defensible* to "differentiated curriculum" introduces an evaluative dimension that complicates matters greatly. Differentiating the curriculum is relatively easy and confirmable; demonstrating that a curriculum is both differentiated *and* defensible is another thing altogether. Defensibility in this context implies that the curriculum is not only different from the norm, but educationally right for gifted students. And therein is the difficulty. Criteria for establishing the defensibility of differentiated curricula are elusive, value-laden, and rooted in one's philosophy of special education for the gifted. One could, therefore, argue that these subjective elements render meaningless any discussion of what constitutes a defensible differentiated curriculum for the gifted. However, while there will continue to be valid differences of opinion with respect to the specific elements of a defensible differentiated curriculum for gifted students, the diagnostic-prescriptive, special-educational, or system model described in this book provides some useful general guidelines.

A curriculum for the gifted is developed for a specific group of students, those students specified in the definition of the program's target population. They possess certain characteristics that affect their ability to think, to learn, to produce information, and so forth, and they possess these characteristics to such a degree that the basic core curriculum is not adequate for them and must, therefore, be modified or differentiated. In other words, these are exceptional students with unmet educational needs that are the direct result of their exceptionality or exceptionalities.

The characteristics that render these students exceptional and thus create the need for the form of special education we call the education of the gifted also provide the basis for the differentiation of their curriculum. This is consistent with a basic principle of special education: curricular modification must be based upon the personal characteristics that make students exceptional (and thus candidates for special education) in the first place. Put more directly, we must differentiate according to the specifics of the exceptionality.

Applied to the education of the gifted, this means that a defensible curriculum for the gifted is one that is differentiated in response to the characteristics of the gifted children as specified in the program's definition of its target population. To the extent that educators can demonstrate that there is a clear correspondence between their students' exceptionalities and the features of the differentiated curriculum, that curriculum at least has a fighting chance of being defensible. The specific components of a defensible differentiated curriculum for the gifted will vary among schools and school districts as their definitions of giftedness vary. Nonetheless, despite these differences in content, the formal requirement that there must be consistency between the characteristics of the target population and the manner in which the curriculum is differentiated is the sine qua non of a defensible curriculum.

Although it may seem that I am belaboring the obvious, my experience with numerous programs for the gifted has convinced me that, differentiated though they may be, the curricula of too many programs are far from defensible. In the majority of these cases, it is the law of correspondence between student characteristics and the features of the curriculum that is violated. Typically, what happens is something similar to the following.

A school or school district decides it needs a program for the gifted, adopts or fashions a definition of giftedness, and spends considerable time and effort identifying students for the program. In most cases, the students thus identified are characterized by such things as the ability to learn at an accelerated rate; the ability to deal with challenging content at a high level of abstraction; the ability to think critically, creatively, and analytically; the ability to produce, not merely to reproduce, ideas; and the ability to demonstrate and continually to increase a vast store of declarative and procedural knowledge. In short, these are highly able students characterized by unusually high intellectual capacity and interest. So far, so good. However, when these able students are finally assembled for special instruction, what often greets them is an array of faddish, meaningless trivia—kits, games, mechanical step-by-step problem-solving methods, pseudoscience, and pop psychology—exactly the sort of thing decried by Sawyer (1988a, 1988b) and other advocates of rigor and substance in the curriculum for the gifted (see, for example, Sosniak, 1987, Stanley, 1980). In other words, students of high ability are confronted by a so-called curriculum of the lowest level. There is no logical consistency between the students and their intellectual needs, on the one hand, and the demands of the curriculum on the other.

This situation, which obtains in far too many programs for the gifted, is, to borrow Sawyer's (1988a) words, "robbery of the gifted" (p. 8). To expose these students who have the greatest potential for learning from and contributing to our intellectual and cultural heritage to ideas and activities that are intellectually unchallenging and insignificant is miseducation of the worst sort. Furthermore, if, as Sawyer (1988b) asserts, a choice of curriculum is "essentially a moral choice" (p. 32), the consequences of intellectually shortchanging our gifted students are serious indeed.

ESSENTIAL ELEMENTS OF A DEFENSIBLE DIFFERENTIATED CURRICULUM

I have thus far been discussing the requirements of a defensible differentiated curriculum in the general, formal sense, with respect to the need for consistency between the characteristics of gifted students and the demands of the curriculum. But what about the specifics, the content of a curriculum for the gifted? Is it possible to discuss what features are necessary for a curriculum to constitute a valid course of study for gifted students? In part, the answer must be no, because to be effective, a special curriculum must be fashioned to meet the specific needs of the gifted students in a particular school or school district, and those needs will not be the same in every setting. However, there are some basics, some essential components of a curriculum for the gifted, that can be discussed in the general sense. While the presence of these elements would not guarantee that a curriculum is defensible and differentiated, their absence, I believe, would make a case for defensibility a difficult one to prove.

A True Curriculum

To start, I want to stress the importance of actually having a curriculum in a program for the gifted. This may strike the reader as being akin to recommending that automobiles have engines or houses walls, but there is a reason for this recommendation: the fact that a significant number of programs do not have something that could legitimately be called a curriculum. This begs the question of what is meant by the term *curriculum*, so let me address that issue briefly.

Definitions of curriculum, like definitions of giftedness, are many and varied, and no single definition has won widespread acceptance. However, Tanner and Tanner (1980) suggest a Deweyan conception of curriculum that is very useful. According to them, a curriculum is "that reconstruction of knowledge and experience, systematically developed under the auspices of the school (or university), to enable the learner to increase his or her control of knowledge and experience" (p. 43). Further light is shed upon the issue by Johnson (1977), who stresses that "curriculum has reference to what it is intended that students *learn*, not what it is intended that they *do*" (p. 7). These are just two examples from the panoply of available definitions, but they are sufficient to suggest some basic guidelines.

Each of these definitions implies some requisites for a valid curriculum: (1) A curriculum must result from a systematic study of a body of knowledge; (2) this systematic study should lead to a determination of what basic knowledge, declarative and procedural, students need to learn; and (3) this knowledge should be logically structured in a scope and sequence that allow one to plan instruction designed to result in the mastery of the specified knowledge by a particular group of learners.

It is my contention that many, perhaps most, programs for the gifted lack true curricula according to these criteria. Instead, most seem to operate on what Tannenbaum (1983) would identify as provisional level, exposing children to an array of activities determined more by whim, external events (space explorations, elections, and the like), and teacher interest than by anything that could legitimately be labeled a curriculum.

This is particularly true of part-time enrichment programs, the most typical format for programs for the gifted (Cox, Daniel, & Boston, 1985).

Teachers who are employed in such programs generally find that there are few if any explicit guidelines regarding what their students should study beyond the admonition not to duplicate or anticipate the core curriculum. These teachers are expected to provide enrichment and usually to develop certain, often ill-defined, thinking processes, but additional guidance is rarely given. Thus, most of them develop units of study as they go along, trying to keep one step ahead of the students who are involved and to pique the interest of those who are not. Some do not even do this. Instead, they rely on the seemingly endless supply of merchandised products—kits, games, dittos, prepared units, organized competitions, and the like—that masquerade as curricular materials for the gifted.

There are many problems with this approach, but the one I want to highlight here is the lack of structure, of scope and sequence, of even a rhyme or reason for what goes on in the classroom. For any given student, the special curriculum is a completely fortuitous thing. The activities to which he or she is exposed are determined in part by when he or she happens to enter and leave the program, not by any recognized process of curriculum development. What is lacking is the delineation of a body of essential knowledge missing from the core curriculum but requisite for the educational well-being of gifted students, along with a sequencing of this knowledge over the years of a child's attendance in the program. In short, what is lacking is a curriculum.

I do not want to appear to place all of the blame on teachers of gifted students. In many, perhaps most, programs there are few practical alternatives to the situation described above. Most programs for the gifted lack adequate curricular guidelines, and most school districts are unwilling to give their teachers of the gifted the time, compensation, education, and resources required to develop them. And even in the absence of a real curriculum, it should be pointed out, many teachers do a creditable job of providing provisional instruction. However, despite the best efforts of many dedicated professionals, in too many programs for the gifted there is no curriculum, and what a gifted student learns in his or her special program is not guided by any curricular structure.

At the very least, the following are required for a curriculum to be present in a program for the gifted:

1. *There must be a consensus with respect to what gifted students should learn that they would not learn in the mainstream.* This feature of the curriculum is essential if there is to be any sensible rationale for the program. The program should exist for good educational reasons, the most important being, to impart knowledge to which gifted students otherwise would not be exposed. What this knowledge is needs to be determined and made explicit. There are various ways of doing this. One example can be found

in Tannenbaum's (1983) discussion of his enrichment matrix. His concept of "expanded basic skills," that is, the skills and knowledge, beyond what is contained in the common core curriculum, that are required for students to begin to become producers and not merely consumers of knowledge, is particularly useful in this context.

2. *There needs to be a scope and sequence, an epistemological structure, to provide a meaningful organization for the knowledge and to serve as a basis for designing instruction.* One good framework for this is found in Bloom's (1956) famous monograph that outlines his well-known taxonomy of the cognitive domain. Popular as Bloom's taxonomy is, few are aware that the familiar six categories of knowledge, comprehension, application, analysis, synthesis, and evaluation represent just one level of the taxonomy. The knowledge category alone is divided into three subcategories, and each of these has finer divisions. These are arranged hierarchically within the knowledge realm, and together they outline an epistemological structure, ranging from knowledge of terminology to knowledge of theories and structures, that can serve as a framework for sequencing a body of content within a discipline field. This is a plausible general structure. Others exist (see, for example, Hirst, 1974; Phenix, 1964), as do organizations of knowledge specific to certain disciplines. What is important is that there be some logical sequence of the requisite knowledge.

3. *There should be planned articulation with the core curriculum.* Too often, the curriculum of the program for the gifted exists in isolation from the rest of what students learn. This is both inefficient and unsound instructionally. I do not mean to suggest that the special curriculum should adhere slavishly to and merely serve to enrich the common core. But I do mean to suggest that the total course of study of gifted students should be conceived of in a comprehensive manner, not as a "real" curriculum with some gifted-program frills. To return to the example provided by Tannenbaum (1983), his insistence on programs, not mere provisions, for the gifted leads to the idea that whatever enrichment is provided for the gifted is part of their expanded common core, not an adjunct to it. For the gifted, the expanded basic skills requisite for producers of knowledge are of a piece with the basic curriculum prescribed for all students, and this larger domain constitutes the curriculum for the gifted. This obviously requires careful articulation of the core with the special curriculum, which I am urging here.

These are the formal requirements for something that could credibly be labeled a curriculum. Their presence alone does not guarantee a defensible differentiated curriculum for the gifted, but their absence makes one impossible.

A Focus on Thinking Processes

Once the formal requirements for a true curriculum are met, one can specify some features that such a curriculum should possess. One such feature, which is rarely lacking in special curricula for the gifted these days, is an emphasis on the development of thinking processes. By this I mean that within the course of study there should be provisions for students to develop or to enhance their facility with certain types of thinking. This adds a dimension to the curriculum that would otherwise be lacking but is essential for gifted students.

It is possible for students to internalize an important and sophisticated body of knowledge by rote and to be able to reproduce it upon command without having any real understanding of the principles involved. This clearly is insufficient. While rote memorization, "knowledge" in Bloom's (1956) scheme of things, has been unfairly and foolishly anathematized, it is not enough for gifted students or for any others. Among other things, we want students to comprehend fully that which they have internalized; to recognize instances in which their knowledge should be applied; to be able to analyze their knowledge; to synthesize new information from the elements that they have learned; and to think critically and evaluatively about what they know and learn. Moreover, we want students to be able to think creatively and to solve problems effectively, even elegantly.

These goals are probably not realized even among our most gifted students unless they become explicit elements of our special curricula. Little more than what Bloom defines as knowledge is required for a student to survive in the basic school curriculum. Quite a bit more is required for students to become producers of ideas and for their potential to be challenged.

As I suggested above, this feature of a special curriculum for the gifted is present in most programs. In fact, many programs exist solely to facilitate the development of thinking processes. There has been, in the current incarnation of the gifted-child movement, a rejection of "the old content-centered curriculum" and an enthusiastic embracing of process-oriented education. To the extent that this leads to one-dimensional programs that focus on process development only, this emphasis is misguided. As Renzulli (1977) argues, process is a means, not the end, of special education for the gifted. Unfortunately, some educators have lost sight of this fact.

Thinking requires an object of thought. Some of the favorite words of those who urge us to focus on developing "higher-level thought processes"—words such as *analyze, synthesize,* and *evaluate*—are transitive verbs. One cannot just analyze; one must analyze *something*. This something may be trivial, such as the material found in many of the thinking-skills kits and games, or it can be as profound as the plays of Shakespeare or the paintings of Cézanne. I suspect that this makes a difference. A higher-level thought process brought to bear upon trivial content results in a trivial product of thought. In fact, given a choice, I would rather have gifted students memorize a sonnet by Shakespeare with little comprehension than have them synthesize fast food of the future, to cite an example from a lesson I once observed in a program for the gifted. Neither of these is an appealing option, but at least in the first instance the students would be carrying inside their heads something of transcendent beauty and worth.

This brings to mind the frequently encountered argument that learning is less important than learning how to learn. This notion is appealing on its face, but hollow and specious at its core. Now, it is unarguably true that it is of crucial importance that gifted students, in fact, all students, learn how to learn. They should learn how to learn for the same reason they should learn how to do anything of importance: because the thing learned is worth the effort required to learn it. In this case, learning how to learn is of great value because it permits students to learn, the end that validates the means; without learning there is no reason to learn how to learn. I am unable to think of a single verb that can take the place of the blanks in the sentence, "It is more important to learn how to _____ than it is to _____," without producing an illogical statement. The reader is invited to try the verbs *walk*, *talk*, *love*, *live*, or any others. They work no better than *learn*. In every case, the end outweighs the means in importance.

Thus, learning how to learn, while important, is subordinate to actual learning. Moreover, there is another crucial, but often neglected, component of this process: learning *what* to learn. This issue, the "what," is less frequently addressed than the "how," but it is arguably more important. The process of learning how to learn, while essential as a means to actual learning, is relatively value-free. The process of learning what to learn is anything but value-free. It involves making judgments, thinking critically, realizing that all ideas are not created equal. This adds another dimension to the role of the teacher and the curriculum developer. Since value judgments are required, the task is made more difficult. Nevertheless, it is a task that must be confronted by any conscientious educator of the gifted. As Sawyer (1988a) asserts, "It is robbery of the gifted merely to teach them how to learn without teaching something worth learning" (p. 8).

Thus, while I want to stress the importance of a process dimension in a curriculum for the gifted, I also want to stress the danger of making this the sole, or even the primary, emphasis, what Eisner and Vallance (1974) refer to as the "fallacy of formalism" in curriculum (p. 14). Process is a means to an end—even that most venerated process (if it is a process), creativity. What is important about creativity is not that one be or become creative but that one use one's creativity to produce knowledge, beauty, and meaning. To the extent that we make the development of creativity or any other thinking process the overriding goal of our special curricula, we are trivializing the education of our gifted students.

Appropriate, Meaningful Content

To insist that a curriculum for the gifted have some content may seem once again to be insisting on the obvious, but experience has convinced me that this is not the case. I argued above that our obsession with the development of thinking processes has sometimes led to a confusion of the means with the ends of education and to "curricula" that are essentially content-free. Let me relate an incident that emphasized for me the need for content in our curricula for the gifted.

A number of years ago, I was asked to evaluate a program for gifted children in a school district in the Northeast. As part of my data gathering, I visited classrooms in order to observe firsthand what gifted students were being asked to do in their special program. On my first day in the district, I walked into an enrichment class and encountered a group of third graders spread out on a rug and on beanbag chairs, each holding a clipboard containing a thick sheaf of papers. I was struck, first of all, by the palpable lack of energy and enthusiasm in the classroom, the last thing I expected to encounter in a group of eight- and nine-year-olds. The students were listlessly and intermittently doing something to their papers with their pencils, but they were certainly far from excited by what they were doing.

Curious, I approached one child and noticed that the top sheet on her clipboard was a reproduction from a ditto master. The entire sheet was covered with rows of circles. The girl had drawn faces on some of these circles and was now staring idly into space.

I asked her what she was supposed to be doing, and she said, "Oh, we're supposed to turn these circles into something—whatever we want."

"What do you want to turn them into?" I asked.

"Nothing," she replied.

I asked her if I could see the other papers attached to her clipboard, and she showed me sheet after sheet of similarly mind-numbing material: rows of squares, parallel lines, and so forth, all marked in a desultory manner.

After the class was dismissed (an event that finally evoked some enthusiasm from the students), I asked the teacher what the students had been doing. She pulled out a book of ditto masters, one of a series of well-known commercial materials, and told me that the particular exercise I had observed was designed to help the students develop their synthesizing skills, all a part of the "creativity" series that was the backbone of her curriculum. In truth, what these students were developing, if anything, was their ability to deal with ennui; and if what I saw was the backbone of the curriculum, the curriculum was utterly invertebrate.

This sad incident has stuck with me ever since. It is, I will admit, an extreme case, a program for the gifted trying to function without a content base. But while this example hardly typifies programs for the gifted in degree, it is not necessarily atypical in kind. For, if my experience and that of many others is representative, there is a significant number of programs for the gifted whose curricula are lacking in meaningful content.

What constitutes meaningful content? I cannot answer this in a definitive, comprehensive sense. In a general sense, though, I would point to the existence of an established and growing body of art, scholarship, and experience, the valued products of the world's cultures, the essentials of a broad liberal education, that provide at least a starting point for a rational discussion of content in a curriculum for the gifted. I hesitate to assert the existence of a canon or to subscribe to the arguments advanced by Allan Bloom (1987) and E. D. Hirsch (1987), which I find to be ethnocentric, intellectually myopic, and insufferably smug. However, I do share the belief of these and other critics of education that we are often too ready to sacrifice what is valuable for what is modish, unchallenging, and ultimately trivial.

James DeLisle (1988), responding to the article by Sawyer (1988a) from which I previously quoted, makes an assertion that I find troubling but to which I suspect many educators in this field would subscribe. He writes that "an innovative teacher can create a heaven, educationally, with seemingly 'weak' materials" (p. 22). The ultimate implication of this statement is that *what* is taught does not matter; what matters is *how* it is taught. This is surely not the case, however, for what is taught—much of it at least—ends up in the minds of students. I defy anybody to argue persuasively that it does not matter what our students, gifted or not, know.

Of course it matters what we teach our gifted children. Some things are worth learning, and some things are not. This does not mean that there will not be valid differences of opinion with respect to what constitutes the former and what constitutes the latter. We may disagree, for example, over whether John Donne is more important than Sylvia Plath; whether Handel is more worthy of appreciation than Duke Ellington or the Beatles; whether Sophocles has more to tell our youth than Eugene O'Neill, Ingmar Bergman, or Woody Allen. Moreover, we must acknowledge that human perception is too rooted in time, space, and fallibility for us to construct a hermetic canon of great works from the study of which we should never deviate. This does not mean, though, that we cannot and should not attempt to distinguish the mindless from the mind-enhancing, the meaningful from the meaningless, the knowledge worth knowing from the trivial.

Gifted students are blessed with an enhanced capacity to wrestle with

challenging ideas of great significance. We are guilty of educational malprac-
tice if we do not attempt in good faith to include in our curricula that which
bristles with ideas and to exclude that which is intellectually barren. Agreement with this principle does not mean that we have to agree on what should
be included or excluded or that we must, as DeLisle (1988) suggests, "select
for the entire . . . field an approved list of curriculum materials" (p. 22). It
simply means that we must acknowledge that what gifted students know is
important, that it is our responsibility as educators to make choices that affect
what gifted students know, and, as Sawyer (1988b) argues, "that every choice
of curriculum . . . is essentially a moral choice" (p. 32).

If Sawyer is correct, as I believe he is, it becomes clear that our moral
choices carry moral consequences. Thinking of curriculum development as a
moral act with moral implications may be intimidating to some, perhaps to
most, educators. Perhaps this is how it should be, for the best educators are
those with a profound awareness of the far-reaching intellectual and moral
consequences of their professional activities. They realize that the choice of
curricular content is more than a decision as to how to fill a given period of
time. They regard it instead as a decision to commit their students' time and
minds to certain ideas. Those who are aware of the moral nature of this choice
are those who are likely to be our best teachers of the gifted.

Opportunities for Independent Study

Independent study has been oversold in the field of the education of the
gifted. It has been lauded as the only valid means and the only legitimate goal
of this form of special education, and it has been offered as the field's curricular panacea. Such hyperbolic excess notwithstanding, one can make a very
strong case for the inclusion of independent study as one valuable component
of a curriculum for the gifted.

For example, when such writers as Tannenbaum (1983) and Renzulli
(1986a) speak of the gifted as producers of knowledge, they strongly suggest
that there is a valid role in a special curriculum for activities that require
gifted students actually to generate knowledge, or at least to use the meth-
odologies of those who do. Much of what is required of students by any
curriculum entails the mastery of material that is directly presented to them
by a teacher in one form or another. Independent work—investigations that
are both planned and carried out by students—requires something else: that
students discover and structure problems and then fashion plans for gathering
knowledge that can be used to solve those problems.

Moreover, when we speak of differentiated curriculum, we are often
referring to differentiation with respect to the level of thinking required of
students exposed to the curriculum, and independent study is one educational
activity that in its more advanced forms requires students to do more than

memorize and regurgitate rote material. The problem finding and problem solving required in advanced independent study are of sufficient complexity to require the kind of higher-level thinking often held out as the hallmark of a differentiated curriculum for the gifted.

Another argument for including independent study in the curriculum of the gifted stresses the overlap between traits required to undertake independent study—for example, independence, initiative, and autonomy—and those often associated with gifted students. As I argued above, a curriculum for the gifted is defensible in part if it can be shown to be based upon the characteristics that make gifted students exceptional, and thus in need of a special curriculum in the first place.

Finally, to the extent that it is desirable, or in small districts necessary, to individualize instruction for the gifted, independent study is one possible vehicle. Although independent study can be conducted by small groups, it is usually an individual activity that requires monitoring and guidance by an adult, but not necessarily the existence of an entire class of students.

Numerous management plans for independent study exist; the one developed by Renzulli (1977) is probably the best known. I will not discuss how one can implement independent study in a program for the gifted, but I would like to offer some thoughts about what I see as its proper role in the special curriculum.

To start, I wish to suggest that not only is independent study not a panacea for our curricula, but it probably should not even be a requirement. By this I mean that not all students in a program for the gifted should be expected to engage in independent study, nor should we regard students who cannot or will not work independently as being not gifted, clear implications of models such as Renzulli's (e.g., 1977).

I base this belief on two facets of my own professional experience. In my previous work as a teacher of gifted children, I encountered many students who were not ready or willing to conduct their own research. Nevertheless, I was not willing to conclude, ipso facto, these students were not gifted. My experience with them indicated just the contrary, and it was clear to me that they needed the special program. I felt that as their teacher it was my responsibility to create a program that met their needs, not to insist that they fit into an independent-study program or leave.

The other element of my experience that has convinced me that independent study is not for all gifted students is my work as a dissertation advisor to doctoral students. I have encountered more than a few highly able adult students who have had serious difficulty initiating their doctoral research. If this is a problematic undertaking for capable adults, it is reasonable to conclude that it will be even more so for many gifted students, who by definition still require special programs.

Another point I would like to make is that, contrary to those who contrast the "doing" of independent study to "mere knowing," I believe that a great deal of knowledge is required for the successful initiation and completion of an independent-study project. It is obvious that considerable procedural, methodological knowledge is needed. Students need to know how to do what must be done in order to complete their independent study in an acceptable manner; but students also need considerable declarative knowledge. They need to "know about" as well as to "know how."

Some writers stress methodological over content knowledge and argue that independent study is a superior form of learning because it requires the former instead of the latter. This, I think, is highly questionable. For one thing, declarative knowledge, that is, knowledge about something, is the usual goal of independent study. We study something in order to learn more about it; we try to solve a problem so that we may have its answer. Moreover, it is difficult to imagine proceeding in any investigative field armed only with procedural, methodological knowledge, ignorant of the facts and ideas of the field. Take the commonplace example of cooking. One may know all there is to know about cutting, seasoning, sautéing, and so forth, but one would find it difficult to cook if one could not distinguish a pan from a knife, an ounce from a gallon, veal from peanut butter. To return to a common theme of this chapter, knowledge is essential. It is both a necessary means and the validating end of independent study.

In a sense, then, independent study is not really a curricular issue. The knowledge that is required for independent study and that results from independent study is curricular in nature. Independent study itself is really an instructional strategy, important still, but only a means to a higher end. Conducting independent study is useful, as are learning how to learn and being creative, but each of these is subservient to what really matters: the generation, acquisition, and appreciation of knowledge.

The final point I would like to make about independent study concerns its inability to stand alone as the curriculum for the gifted. This is one curricular component, and an optional one at that, not the sum total of the curriculum. What gives independent study part of its motivating force, the fact that it involves students in the exploration of their own interests, also constitutes one of its chief curricular limitations. Students' interests may be narrow, even trivial, and as such they may be a poor foundation for a curriculum. I love sports and rock and roll, but as a teacher I quickly tired of them as topics for students' independent projects.

One of our major obligations as educators of the gifted is to expose students to new ideas, new experiences, and new realms of meaning. We cannot do this if we rely exclusively on students to choose the objects of their study. I hope it does not sound repressive to suggest that teachers are, or should be, in a better position than are students to make the majority of curricular decisions. It is our moral duty to think long and hard about what our students should know and then to commit ourselves to helping them learn it. This may well require independent study on the part of our students; it certainly will require teacher-developed curricular activities.

Lest it seem that I find little merit in the inclusion of independent study in the education of the gifted, let me repeat that I see much value in this instructional strategy. I am concerned, however, that too many people have accepted uncritically the claims of those who have made independent study both the test of a child's "true giftedness" and the sole basis of their educational models. Independent study has its place, and this place is alongside other instructional approaches.

Provisions for Acceleration

By *acceleration* I refer to educational provisions whereby students meet curricular goals at an earlier age or at a faster pace than is typical. Well-known forms of acceleration include grade skipping; early entrance to kindergarten or college; ungraded schools; and special-progress classes, in which a class of students completes, for example, three years' worth of work in two years.

Acceleration is one of the most curious phenomena in the field of education. I can think of no other issue in which there is such a gulf between what research has revealed and what most practitioners believe. The research on acceleration is so uniformly positive, the benefits of appropriate acceleration so unequivocal, that it is difficult to see how an educator could oppose it. For example, Pollins (1983) conducted a review of the literature on acceleration and concluded that "No study, regardless of its orientation . . . , has demonstrated any significant negative effects of acceleration on social and emotional development" (p. 176). Julian Stanley (1981), the best-known advocate of acceleration for the gifted, writes that "We do not know of a single careful study of actual accelerants that has shown acceleration not to be beneficial" and that "anyone who can read . . . [the research literature on acceleration] and still oppose such acceleration certainly has the courage of his or her preconvictions" (p. 265). Nevertheless, many do have the courage of their preconvictions and oppose acceleration vigorously, warning parents and teachers against its dire consequences.

This concern is heightened by recent publications alerting educators and parents to the dangers of pushing children to achieve beyond a level or pace that is appropriate for them. The current fad, summed up in the phrase *a gift of time*, for holding children back a year, for example, by repeating kindergarten or entering kindergarten at age six, reflects a fear that children are being asked to grow up too fast (although I suspect that in some cases the motivation is to give children a competitive edge). This is in part a reaction to another fad, the so-called superbaby mentality. Spurred by the likes of Glenn Doman and his Better Baby Institute, a considerable number of anxious but naive parents (like the father described in Chapter 5) are so eager to start their children on the fast track to career success that they subject their babies to formal educational regimens shortly after birth, in some cases earlier. Given the seemingly obvious potential for danger in this approach, a vigorous reaction is to be expected.

Most prominent among those bruiting the dangers of premature formal education is David Elkind, whose books *The Hurried Child: Growing Up Too Fast Too Soon* (1981) and *Miseducation: Preschoolers at Risk* (1987) sensibly and persuasively alert us to the dangers of hastening the end of childhood and extending the formal academic curriculum into the preschool years. One might ask, therefore, whether the reasoned concerns of such eminent authorities as Elkind argue against acceleration in any form? I submit that they do not, and, further, I submit that a categorical refusal on the part of school authorities to consider acceleration for any students is a variant of the miseducation of which Elkind writes.

To simplify Elkind's major point somewhat, the problem with the form of miseducation to which he calls attention in the book bearing that title is that it ignores the developmental level and the needs of young children and, indeed, the very nature of childhood. Formal education is imposed on preschoolers, Elkind argues, without any consideration of what young children are like cognitively and emotionally. Thus, the problem is that adult desires, not children's developmental needs, drive the curriculum, the result being miseducation and the potential for real harm to children.

Elkind's argument is difficult to refute, and we ignore his warnings at our own and our children's peril. However, I believe those who cite Elkind's work in support of a blanket proscription of acceleration have missed the point. The point is not to make sure that all children move at a slow, uniform, deliberate pace dictated by birthdates and norms tables from developmental psychology texts. Rather, the point is to meet children's current needs, neither to push them to conform to adult expectations nor to hold back those who are eager and able to learn, solely for administrative convenience.

Thus, I would argue that in addition to pushing, there is a parallel danger of "pulling back" children whose cognitive and emotional development demands more flexibility in making educational arrangements than rigid, lockstep school sequences will allow. I agree that it is miseducation to try to teach a six-month-old to read, but it is also miseducation to insist that a precocious five-year-old who reads fluently and with great pleasure be subjected to a year of kindergarten and the empty charade of "reading-readiness" activities. In short, it is miseducation to ignore children's needs in deference to adults' needs that center on issues extraneous to children's welfare, whether these relate to status, one-upmanship, parental egos, maintaining orderly schedules, or choosing to ignore the research on acceleration.

My sympathy for those who, like Elkind, worry that our children are in danger of having their childhoods stolen from them derives in part from experiences in my professional life. As the director of a preschool for precocious children at Teachers College for four years, I was frequently in the position of having to resist the demands of a few well-intentioned but misguided parents who insisted that we introduce formal academic study into the curricula of our three- and four-year-olds. But professional experience has also given me cause to worry about the danger at the other extreme. Thus, I find encouraging Elkind's response to a parent of a gifted child who asks what should be done for his or her child in school in order to prevent boredom. Elkind (1987) suggests that the parents should "ask that your child be promoted one grade. . . . Research suggests that gifted children can adapt well to being the youngest and have no problem making friends, playing, and so on" (p. 195). Rather than being part of the problem of hurried and miseducated children, then, acceleration, instituted with concern for and awareness of a child's development and educational needs, is part of the solution.

In fact, the form of acceleration suggested by Elkind, grade skipping, is probably the least desirable form of acceleration available, since it involves a dislocation of the child from his or her accustomed classmates and results in the gifted student's becoming the youngest and probably smallest child in the class. Group forms of acceleration, such as special-progress classes, are less disruptive, and early admission alternatives, although they, too, result in the child's being the youngest and smallest, at least do not require the readjustment required when a child skips a grade. Nonetheless, even grade skipping should not be rejected out of hand as an option for gifted students. If a child is unhappy in a grade placement that is clearly educationally wrong for him or her, if the child's age peers are not his or her ability or interest peers, and especially if the child himself or herself wants to make the change, there is no sound reason to refuse to consider grade skipping, nor does the research reveal anything but positive consequences when all factors are considered.

Enrichment has been the curricular modification of choice for gifted students in recent years, and there is much that can be said in favor of some types of enrichment; but enrichment alone is not enough. It is usually pursued for only a fraction of the time a child is in school, despite the fact that gifted students are gifted full-time. There is no justification for school authorities to think they have met the educational needs of their gifted students if, after spending one morning in an enrichment class, these students are consigned to the tedious lockstep of the regular curriculum for the remaining 90 percent of their school week. Some form of acceleration is needed so the majority of the time these able students spend in school will be spent in an educationally appropriate manner.

Two millennia ago, Ovid, writing of Julius Caesar's precocious development, asserted that "Genius divine outpaces time, and brooks not the tedium of tardy growth" (cited in Hollingworth, 1942, p. 2). Twenty centuries later, too many school authorities have still not received the message. Considering the unanimity of the research evidence in favor of acceleration, this state of affairs is clearly untenable. Gifted students, if they have a right to an appropriate education, have the right to acceleration if it can be shown that it is in their best interest.

Curricula Developed by the Teachers Who Will Implement Them

The argument in this section can be reduced to a single recommendation: develop your own curriculum; do not try to buy one. Good curricula for the gifted come from teachers, not business managers. I base this advice on two observations.

First, my examination of the increasing number of catalogs selling materials for the gifted and of a number of the wares peddled therein has convinced me that the educational value of much of what is sold is slight or nil. The education of the gifted is a hot item among educational publishers today. (As editor of a series of books on the topic, I offer this statement as an observation, not a condemnation.) Nowhere is this field of education hotter than among those entrepreneurs who offer for sale materials to be used with children in the classroom. Books, units, kits, games, filmstrips, charts, simulations, software, hardware, and so forth abound, each guaranteed to develop higher-level thinking skills, to make children more creative, and to add a spark to the classroom.

I have often entertained the fantasy that enterprising publishers, realizing that "gifted" is what is selling these days, have had printed thousands of decals bearing the words "FOR THE GIFTED." Then, my fantasy continues, they go into their warehouses, dust off boxes of worthless materials that have languished there unsold for years, affix the decals to the boxes, and presto! Spelling FOR THE GIFTED! Driver Education FOR THE GIFTED! Study Hall FOR THE GIFTED! This, I admit, *is* a fantasy and certainly does not accurately portray the activities or motives of publishers of educational materials. It does, however, offer a clue with respect to the quality of a considerable amount of what is sold with the label "for the gifted."

I will not regale the reader with specific descriptions of the trivial and fanciful materials hawked by various firms. Robert Sawyer, whose *Journal for the Education of the Gifted* article (1988a) has been cited several times, includes some descriptions of materials on gnomes, future studies, and other fluff in his fine paper, and these serve as both comic relief and a source of sorrow and shame. The reader, who I hope has by now resolved to seek out Sawyer's article, can amuse and anger himself or herself by reading Sawyer's description of this educational pabulum.

I need not belabor or support this point further. I believe that the bulk of the products offered for sale as curricular materials for the gifted is worthless at best, harmful at worst since, in a curricular version of Gresham's Law, the bad material tends to drive out the good. That is to say, the utilization of this material takes time away from more serious and worthwhile pursuits. The reader is encouraged to peruse a number of the catalogs available and to decide whether the adoption in a program for the gifted of the materials advertised within would result in a defensible differentiated curriculum.

My second point brings us back to the system model that underlies the program-development approach described in this book. Throughout, I have urged program developers to base every component of their program on the needs of students in their own school or school district and on the resources, limitations, and specific conditions that are characteristic of the locality and its schools. I see no reason why this should not apply to curriculum development as well. A curriculum should be developed to meet the needs of the students who will be in the program as revealed in the needs assessment. These will vary from district to district. To attempt to respond to these needs directly and accurately by shopping around for commercial materials is a hit-or-miss proposition at best. Even were the available materials not of almost uniformly embarrassing quality, there is no guarantee that a collection could be put together that would be right for the students in a given program.

To ensure that students in a particular school or school district will be exposed to a curriculum that is uniquely appropriate for them, that curriculum must be developed by the people responsible for planning the program and for teaching the gifted students. No other approach can offer as much hope for effecting a match between student needs and curricular content and demands. Moreover, in light of the need to develop a true multiyear curriculum with a logical scope and sequence and some form of articulation with the core curriculum, it will be necessary to develop, not to buy, a curriculum.

This does not mean that commercial materials should be banished from programs for the gifted forever. They can sometimes prove to be useful components of curricular scope and sequence if they are of sufficient quality and are valid means to established curricular goals. However, the curriculum itself, the specification of learning outcomes for gifted students, must be the product of the thinking of individuals who know the school and its students, who have a stake in the outcome of the special program, and who will be responsible for the implementation of the curriculum.

The substitution of locally developed curricular materials for the commercial variety should not be undertaken as a cost-cutting measure. Rather, the money that would have been spent on kits and games should be spent to compensate teachers of the gifted for the additional time required to develop a true curriculum. If consultants or other resources are needed, they should be provided. The curriculum is no place to skimp: the outcome of the curriculum-development process is too important.

The foregoing are some of the elements of a defensible differentiated curriculum for the gifted. They hardly constitute an infallible recipe for curricular success, but I doubt that a curriculum for the gifted can have much chance of being defensible if these elements are lacking. Before closing this chapter, I would like to discuss an issue that poses some difficult and perplexing questions for educators of gifted students: the issue of whether everything that is done in a program for the gifted must be uniquely and exclusively appropriate for gifted students alone.

GOOD FOR SOME OR GOOD FOR ALL?

An indelible experience of my professional life occurred at a school-board meeting in Brooklyn. I was invited by a friend, the coordinator of the program for the gifted in one of the Brooklyn school districts, to talk about the whys and hows of special education for the gifted. This program was the focus of some controversy, my friend told me, and a speaker was needed to reassure the skeptics and to counter the program's critics at the next board meeting. The meeting was to be open, and I was assured that I could count upon a sizable audience, since there was some interest in this program among the public at large.

I arrived at the elementary school designated as the meeting site on a miserably hot June evening, and I noticed immediately that there actually was some public interest in this particular program for the gifted. The meeting was scheduled to be held in a large, airless cafeteria-cum-auditorium, the sort of thing referred to as a cafetorium in some schools (presumably those schools in which the faculty bewails the students' lack of respect for the English language). People were crammed into every square foot of the room, and most of them seemed quite animated. "Good," I thought, trying to view the situation positively, "at least this audience will be interested in what I have to say."

And interested they were. Every time the superintendent, an old-style politico quite enamored of the sound of his own booming voice, mentioned the program for the gifted, program adherents and detractors sent up competing volleys of cheers and boos, with the latter predominating handily. Finally, after what seemed to me to be an irrelevant, rambling peroration that included denunciations of a host of borough, city, and state politicians, the superintendent mispronounced my name and turned the floor over to me.

I was, to say the least, somewhat curious about the reception I would receive. Nevertheless, I plunged into my talk, editing as I went along, dropping such phrases as "I'm sure we would all agree that . . . ." I had been asked to speak for 20 minutes. About 12 minutes into my talk, which had been at least politely received, the superintendent cut in, thanked me, and asked if anybody in the audience had any questions for Professor Borgman.

A forest of arms sprouted. I pointed vaguely toward a dense concentration of waving hands, and a woman stood up. She identified herself as the mother of a boy who was not in the special program. Her son, she explained, had missed the cutoff on the selection matrix by one point.

"Now, I've been told that these kids in this gifted program are learning critical thinking and creative thinking," she stated.

"I believe that's true," I replied helpfully.

"Well," she continued, "my question is, if those kids are learning critical thinking and creative thinking, what is my son learning? Uncritical thinking? Uncreative thinking?"

I do not remember what my response was. I am certain, however, that it was a feeble and unsatisfying one. What makes me certain is the fact that I have thought about that woman's question very frequently over the past five years or so, and I still do not have an answer that begins to do justice to her excellent question.

I wish every educator concerned with the education of the gifted could have an experience similar to the one I just described. We speak glibly and confidently about defensible differentiated curricula in our classes, our books, our workshops, our teachers' meetings, but I suspect that we rarely have the question "How can you defend what you are doing?" put before us so forcefully and effectively. I suspect that if we were all to have this experience, it would be in most cases an unpleasant one, for I suspect that much of what we do, we cannot defend.

I am speaking of defensibility in a manner somewhat different from the way in which I discussed it earlier in this chapter, although the same basic principle is involved. What I am most concerned with here is not the question of whether what happens in classrooms for the gifted is appropriate for the gifted, but whether it might not be appropriate for all students. I have seen quite a few special programs. I would venture to conclude that in the majority of cases, after ruling out the things that were so trivial or mindless as to be educationally useless for anybody, most of what was happening in the special classes consisted of activities that would have been comprehensible to, enjoyed by, and beneficial for most students, gifted or not. In these schools, and in others like them in which the curriculum of the program for the gifted consists of activities from which any child could benefit, another test of defensibility is failed—the test of ethical defensibility.

Educators concerned with the needs of gifted students are often accused of fostering elitism in the schools. Many times such criticism is reflexive anti-intellectualism; sometimes it is a natural response to practices in the field and at least partially justified. To the extent that we set aside certain enjoyable, beneficial learning experiences for a select few with no educational reason for withholding these experiences from the majority, we are engaging in an elitist activity. Whenever a school's microcomputers are reserved for the exclusive use of the gifted, whenever only the gifted are allowed to go on field trips, whenever tryouts for the Odyssey of the Mind team are limited to students in the "gifted program," elitism is being practiced. These are obvious cases. But I suspect that more subtle abuses are closer to being the norm.

Returning to the plaint of the mother in Brooklyn, how many of our programs for the gifted stress the development of certain thinking skills—critical thinking, creative problem solving, or whatever—in schools in which no similar instruction takes place in the regular classroom? I suspect that this is anything but a rare situation; probably just the opposite. I also suspect that it is instruction of this sort that is pointed to as the keystone of the program's differentiated curriculum. If so, what is the logical implication of all of this? It is simply that children not labeled gifted have no need to learn to think critically or creatively. That statement may strike the reader as ludicrous or offensive, as it does me, but it is the logical implication to be drawn from a situation in which a special curriculum is differentiated along such lines.

If, as I suspect, much of what passes for differentiated curriculum consists of knowledge and skills learnable by and useful to most students, a basic and troubling question arises: what kind of curricular differentiation will result in a curriculum that is appropriate only for the gifted? Is there any body of knowledge to which we can point with certainty as being the exclusive province of gifted students? Is a defensible differentiated curriculum really possible?

I must confess to being less than completely certain myself as to how these questions should be answered. I find my lack of certainty difficult to shrug off, because, as I suggested at the beginning of this chapter, if we cannot find a way to differentiate the curriculum of gifted students in a manner that is defensible, then our very reason for existing as a field is called into question. Earlier, I suggested that the defensibility of a differentiated curriculum depended upon its congruence with and responsiveness to the characteristics that differentiate the target population and thus create the need for special education in the first place. This notion may be of some help here.

Each of the elements listed earlier in this chapter as requisite for a defensible differentiated curriculum for the gifted—a true curriculum, focus on thinking skills, appropriate content, opportunities for independent study, provisions for acceleration, and teacher-developed curricula—would contribute positively to a sound general core curriculum. What would make these the elements of a curriculum that is appropriate only for the gifted? Without getting into the issue of whether this is what makes the gifted gifted, perhaps it would be a matter of differentiating in degree rather than in kind.

Thus, although all students should have an opportunity to develop their thinking skills, gifted students will be able to spend more time at the higher levels, since such thinking will come easier to them and they will need to spend less time memorizing basic content. Although all students certainly should be exposed to a curriculum rich in meaningful, challenging content, the gifted will be able to deal with more abstract, more complex, more ambiguous issues and will be able to acquire a greater amount of knowledge. Although independent study is perhaps likely to be appealing to and appropriate for a number of students who are not gifted, gifted students are more likely to have the foundation of knowledge and skills, as well as the extra time, to explore independent research. And although most students would benefit from a break in the curricular lockstep, gifted students, if set free from such constraints, will travel the farthest in less time and with greater comprehension. In other words, it makes sense if the attractive elements of a curriculum for the gifted are not treated as an all-or-nothing proposition but are rather included in the curriculum according to students' capacities to profit from them, and the extent to which their inclusion answers distinct educational needs.

This, I think, provides a way of differentiating that is both educationally and ethically defensible. We do not find ourselves, if we proceed in this manner, stating implicitly that only the gifted need to think or to develop their creativity, and we can point to the way in which our curricula are differentiated with some hope of defending what we are doing.

CONCLUSION

Differentiated curricula are the reasons for the existence of programs for the gifted. They are what make this form of special education special. They are also, in too many cases, difficult to defend.

If I have appeared to focus in this chapter on what is wrong with our differentiated curricula, it is not with the intention of defaming the field but of underscoring just how difficult a task creating an appropriate curriculum really is. Since it is a difficult task, we are going to make a lot of mistakes.

This is inevitable. But given the central importance of curriculum in our practice, it is also harmful, for our mistakes carry serious consequences. Most critically, they result in the waste of time, valuable time carved from an already too-busy school day, time that could be spent educating, not miseducating, our gifted students.

There is no simple answer, no magical ingredient, no easy path to a defensible differentiated curriculum for the gifted. It is a complex mix that varies from school to school just as students' needs vary from school to school. If there is one indispensable element, though, one quality that would be found in all curricula for the gifted, I would return to Sawyer's (1988a) concept of rigor. Rigor, for Sawyer, has nothing to do with dour, repressive schoolmasters or schoolmarms. Instead, it has everything to do with a curriculum worthy of the abilities of the special students for whom it is developed, a challenging, consequential curriculum that, in Sawyer's refreshingly jargon-free phrase, "helps young people learn to love their books and learn to love learning" (p. 14).

At the risk of having this chapter read as a gloss on Sawyer's article, I would like to close with two quotations from "In Defense of Academic Rigor."

> Academic rigor means posing big questions. Academic rigor means seeking answers to questions that truly matter. The teacher of such a course needs to be willing to show how the questions matter and needs to free himself or herself from the bondage of answer keys and teachers' manuals. The teacher of an academically rigorous course needs to *live* the content of the course, rather than merely administer it. Success in academic rigor is achieved by those who know *what* they teach and not simply *how* they are supposed to teach. (p. 17)

> Finally, the cause of academic rigor is the flowering of gifted education. We can make a difference in the lives of our students and even in the life of our society as a whole, once we resolve to return to the things that matter in academics. We can make ourselves indispensable in education only when we take on a task that itself is indispensable. And that is when we all begin to teach subjects and ideas indispensable to a democratic society—indispensable to people whose lives have meaning both to themselves and to their society. (p. 19)

CHAPTER 9

Evaluating Programs for the Gifted

The institution of education for gifted persons . . . is new in human annals. It therefore brings with it a large number of new problems which call for solution by experiment.

Hollingworth, *Gifted Children:*
Their Nature and Nurture (1929)

The problem of evaluating special programs for gifted children . . . in the public school system is fraught with many unusual difficulties. . . . The many programs for gifted children now being initiated in the country will eventually be called to account and asked to justify their expense by demonstrated results. How many will be able to provide these results?

Gallagher, *Analysis of Research on the*
Education of Gifted Children (1960)

Evaluation is one of the most critical facets of program development, but it is also one of the least employed.

Alexander & Muia, *Gifted Education:*
A Comprehensive Roadmap (1982)

The reader may have noted that in discussing the components of programs for the gifted in previous chapters, I have at times resorted to superlatives. I described the definition of the target population, for example, as the most important practical policy decision that a school or school district must make in planning a special program. I labeled identification as the most controversial program component, teacher selection as the most critical to the program's success or failure, and curriculum differentiation and development as the most central to our raison d'être as a field. Let me continue in this vein by asserting that the evaluation of programs for the gifted is the program component with which we, as a field, have had the least success and the one most likely to land us in trouble should this state of affairs not change. What do I mean by this?

What I mean is that we currently do not have many good ideas about how to evaluate programs for the gifted and that those who operate too many programs do not even bother to try. The consequences of this are many and serious. On the local level, information that could be used for program improvement is not being made readily available to program staff and to administrators. On a higher level, those who make decisions that affect the funding of programs for the gifted—for example, school board members, legislators, private foundations—lack effective ways of obtaining reliable information concerning the efficacy and accountability of such programs, and this lack of information could have serious consequences for those seeking continued funding of existing programs or seed money for new programs. On the most general level, this means that, despite our hopes, hunches, and convictions, our assertions that programs for the gifted make a positive difference in the lives of gifted students are based on an exiguous data base. The whole situation places the field of the education of the gifted in a tenuous position, where it will remain until we make some changes in our practice.

Although the primitive state of the art with respect to the evaluation of programs for the gifted has serious implications for our field on various levels, my concern in this chapter is with evaluation on the school or school-district level, where the problems and consequences, while not as broadly significant, are still considerable. Pursuant to that concern, I will use this chapter to discuss the meaning, functions, and importance of program evaluation; some of the problems endemic to the evaluation of programs for the gifted; and a framework for developing an evaluation design. First, however, I want to put the component of program evaluation into the context of the system model described in this book.

PROGRAM EVALUATION AS PART OF THE SYSTEM APPROACH

It is a serious but common mistake to regard program evaluation as something that happens *to* a program for the gifted. Those who make this mistake conceive of the chronology of programming in discrete steps: planning and implementing a program and then evaluating it. Evaluation, in this way of viewing things, occurs after the program is in place; it becomes an external process applied to the program. It is this kind of thinking that results in the telephone calls I and many others receive in April and May of each year from program coordinators seeking to have their programs evaluated, more or less after the fact. This approach, which could be called the "ethnographic" or "visiting expert" evaluation model, depending upon one's level of cynicism, involves having a putative authority in the education of the gifted visit the program in question in order to ascertain the degree to which it conforms to his or her ideas of what such programs should be like.

Now, there is nothing wrong with occasionally enlisting the services of an outside person with experience and expert knowledge in the field to assist in the evaluation of a program for the gifted. In fact, such a person can bring to the task a disinterested point of view, a wealth of experience with other programs for the gifted, and an immunity to in-district political consequences of his or her evaluation that can prove to be very valuable. However, this is not the sort of thing most schools or school districts can do every year, and it is rarely something that is given much forethought.

The problem with this evaluation-after-the-fact approach is that it is not programmatic, in Tannenbaum's (1983) sense of the term. It also deviates from the system approach recommended in this book in that it makes evaluation an add-on or afterthought to the actual program. In Chapter 3, I referred to the syntax of the system model as consisting of three phases: a diagnostic phase (needs assessment), a prescriptive phase (the development and implementation of the various program components), and an evaluative phase. Each of these phases, including the last, is integral to the program-proper and is essential to making the model systematic. To return to the medical analogy used in Chapter 3, these program phases correspond to a therapeutic approach consisting of medical diagnosis, medical treatment, and a follow-up visit to determine the effectiveness of the treatment. In medicine, none of these steps would be considered superfluous or external to the therapeutic regimen. The same should hold for educational programming.

What this means for programs for the gifted is that the development of an evaluation design is a basic aspect of program planning. The time to think about how the program will be evaluated is when the program is being planned, not after it has run its course for a year. Building an evaluation design into the plan of a program for the gifted increases the chances that the evaluation will function within the system, that it will focus on the important aspects of the system, and that it will be able to pinpoint strengths and weaknesses and thereby make the program more effective and accountable. In other words, instead of being something that happens *to* a program, evaluation should be *part of* a program.

SOME BASIC CONCEPTS IN PROGRAM EVALUATION

In this section, I will discuss some of the basic issues related to evaluation in general, with some comments about the evaluation of programs for the gifted in particular. Like so many of the objects of my focus in this book, evaluation means different things to different people, and thus it is necessary to reach an understanding of what educational evaluation is and what functions it can serve.

What is Program Evaluation?

One of the sources of difficulty in evaluating programs for the gifted is the multiplicity of meanings borne by the term *program evaluation*. The various conception of evaluation range widely in their connotations for program personnel; some are benign, some threatening. While evaluation probably suggests to most people a process whereby one makes judgments related to the value of an object of scrutiny, the judgmental nature of this process is not stressed in all conceptions of program evaluation. This is all to the good, for if one conceives of evaluation only as a matter of judging, one is likely to regard the prospect of undergoing an evaluation as an ordeal to be weathered, even as a threat to be countered.

Let us look at a few definitions of evaluation to get a sense of the range of ideas incorporated under this rubric, which will serve as a basis for fashioning a workable conception of the evaluation of programs for the gifted. Nevo (1983), writing in the *Review of Educational Research,* provides a concise survey of definitions of evaluation, which I have classified as follows.

Evaluation as judgment. There are, indeed, as suggested above, numerous definitions of educational evaluation that emphasize the judgmental nature of the process. Such writers as Eisner (1979), Glass (1969), House (1980), Scriven (1967), and Stufflebeam (1974) define program evaluation as the assessment of a program's merit or value. This is far from a minority opinion. The Joint Committee on Standards for Educational Evaluation (1981), representing 12 organizations involved with educational evaluation, promulgated a definition that describes evaluation as a "systematic investigation of the worth or merit of some object" (p. 12). While this may be the conventional view, other conceptions of evaluation have been proposed.

Evaluation related to objectives. In a similar but more specific vein is Tyler's (1950) widely cited definition of evaluation as "the process of determining to what extent . . . educational objectives are actually being realized" (p. 69). Although this conception also connotes judgment, it eschews such global terms as *merit* and *worth* and restricts the scope of the judgment to whether or not stated objectives are met. Since it can be assumed that these objectives exist prior to the actual data-gathering phase of the evaluation and that they reflect the intentions of the developers of the program, there is less sense of an imposition of outside values in this conception than is implied by the previous definitions. Under the terms of Tyler's definition, those who plan the program also establish the bases for its evaluation.

Evaluation as information gathering. Evaluation has also been defined as a completely nonjudgmental activity. Alkin (1969), Cronbach (1963), and Stufflebeam et al. (1971) are among those who conceive of program evaluation as the process of gathering information that is conveyed to an audience, usually high-level administrators, who then make decisions about educational programs. In such conceptions, those who carry out the evaluation are simply neutral data collectors; value judgments and critical decisions about the fate of the program are left to others. Even if my description of this type of definition ignores the limits of human objectivity and reflects a more naive conception of epistemology than Alkin, Cronbach, and Stufflebeam and his associates intended, it does reflect the definitions' shift in emphasis away from judgment and toward factual reporting.

Evaluation as a means of program improvement. Finally (although not exhaustively), evaluation has been defined as a force for program improvement and educational reform. The Stanford Evaluation Consortium (Cronbach et al., 1980) conceives of program evaluation as follows: "[a] systematic examination of events occurring in and consequent of a contemporary program—an examination conducted to assist in improving this program and other programs having the same general purpose" (p. 14). This is an appealing view of program evaluation. On the one hand, it avoids the adversarial aspects of judgmental definitions by stressing the goal of program improvement. The intended outcome is not a mere verdict but a plan for making the program stronger. Moreover, this definition presupposes the continuation of the program, something that is in doubt and is a source of uneasiness in some program evaluations. On the other hand, unlike definitions that mention only information gathering, the probably inescapable judgmental aspect of evaluation is not unrealistically ignored. Program improvement implies program imperfection, and the identification of program inadequacies requires critical judgment.

I would be loath to rely on any single conception among those mentioned above to the exclusion of the others. Each of these definitions has something to offer, since each stresses a legitimate aspect of the process of program evaluation. While not presuming to offer a definition of program evaluation that will be appropriate in all situations, I will base what follows in this chapter on the following combination of elements from the definitions surveyed above. Under the terms of the system model described in this book, *program evaluation consists of the collection of information related to the effect of an educational program on its students and the application of critical judgment to determine the extent to which the information suggests that important program goals have been met, all of this being done for the primary purpose of improving the program under evaluation.*

I will not engage in a tedious explication of this definition. Its major points have either been discussed above or, in the case of the emphasis on student outcomes and the notion that evaluation data are more suggestive than definitive, are self-explanatory. I would like instead to cite the definition of a *program evaluator* proposed by the Stanford Consortium (Cronbach et al., 1980), which is, I believe, compatible with my patchwork conception and illuminates further the process of program evaluation. According to Cronbach and his colleagues, an evaluator is best regarded not as a judge or a referee but as "an educator [whose] success is to be judged by what others learn" (p. 11).

This pleasing and revelatory conception of the role of an educational evaluator brings evaluation into the mainstream of the educational process by viewing the evaluator as an educator whose role is to teach, not as a judge whose role is to determine guilt and, perhaps, to impose punishment. It also stresses the need for evaluation to be seen as part of the program-planning process, as an ongoing part of the developmental sequence, not as a retrospective accounting of hits and misses.

What Are the Functions of Evaluation?

Michael Scriven's (1967) well-known and important distinction between formative and summative evaluation exhausts the list of the functions of educational evaluation as far as most educators are concerned. I will discuss these functions of evaluation along with two others cited by Nevo (1983) that, while more obscure, are no less interesting and important.

The formative function. Formative evaluation is the collection of evaluative data on one or more occasions during the school year. The function of formative evaluation is diagnostic. It serves to alert program staff to deficiencies and strengths in a functioning program, and it provides continuous in-process feedback that allows changes to be made in the program while it is in operation.

Although I suspect that the term *evaluation* connotes summative, after-the-fact assessment for most people, one can make a strong argument that formative evaluation is more important than summative evaluation. The most important advantage that accrues to one from formative evaluation is the ability actually to do something with the evaluation data at or near the time they are gathered. Armed with formative-evaluation data, program personnel can take action to make their program more effective for the students who are currently enrolled in it. Whereas summative data enable one to say "We should have . . ." or "We must in the future . . . ," formative data enable one to say, "Let's do . . . now."

Formative evaluation relates to the here and now, is action-oriented, and is less retrospective than summative evaluation. However, formative evaluation can also be used to affect the outcome of summative evaluation. To the extent that there are provisions for collecting formative data, there can be instituted changes that are likely to result in a favorable summative outcome.

The audience for formative evaluation is the program staff, not necessarily higher-level administrators. Formative evaluation data provide this audience with information they can use, as opposed to summative evaluation data, which provide one's superiors with information that may be used to make decisions about one's past performance and future prospects. Thus, formative evaluation will probably be seen by program personnel as considerably less threatening than summative evaluation.

The summative function. Summative evaluation differs from formative evaluation chiefly in that it is concerned with overall program effectiveness rather than with uncovering remediable deficiencies in an ongoing program. This is the sort of after-the-fact judgment of efficacy that most people think of when they hear the word *evaluation*.

Summative evaluation is almost (in a few cases, literally) experimental in nature. The basic strategy is to allow the program in question to function and then to assess its outcomes. The audience for the data revealed in a summative evaluation usually consists of higher-level administrators and others who are charged with the responsibility for making decisions about program continuation, expansion, termination, or substantive modification.

As Nevo (1983) points out, formative evaluation is carried out for the purposes of program development and improvement, whereas summative evaluation is used for purposes of accountability. Stufflebeam (1972) makes a similar distinction between proactive evaluation for decision making and retroactive evaluation for accountability. The distinctions between formative evaluation and summative evaluation are not particularly subtle or elusive. However, I am belaboring them here because my experience suggests that formative evaluation, which in many respects is more useful, is usually slighted in favor of summative evaluation.

In addition to the formative and the summative, there are two additional functions of evaluation that are less well known but hardly trivial (see Nevo, 1983, p. 117): the psychological, or sociopolitical, and the administrative.

The psychological or sociopolitical function. There are instances in which it is difficult to discern either a formative or a summative purpose of a particular evaluation. Rather, it appears that the evaluation is being conducted in order to publicize a program, to motivate or otherwise to shape the behavior of those being evaluated, to comply with a requirement that a program be evaluated, or to achieve a goal unrelated to diagnosis or accountability. This catchall category has been labeled psychological or sociopolitical. While one might piously insist that these are improper functions of evaluation, one cannot credibly argue that evaluations are never carried out for these and other "irrelevant" reasons.

With respect to programs for gifted students, it is not difficult to imagine that evaluation will be used for these purposes. For example, the coordinator of an excellent program for the gifted who feels that his or her program is not being treated as a high-priority offering by the powers that be within the school district may seek to have the program evaluated by the state education department for possible inclusion on a list of exemplary programs. This would serve neither a formative nor a summative function, but its sociopolitical implications would be considerable. Or a state director of programs for the gifted who believes that the majority of programs within his or her purview are lacking in substance may push for a statewide requirement that all programs receiving state funds be evaluated annually. The goal here would be to affect the behavior of local program personnel by making them aware of the need to submit the results of their program evaluations on a yearly basis. In this case, the function would clearly be psychological.

Neither of these uses of evaluation is particularly offensive. Anyone who has tried to win recognition for a neglected program would sympathize with the coordinator in the first example, and most would applaud the efforts of the state director in the second example to effect widespread program improvement. Thus, evaluations that serve these functions are not necessarily bad; they are merely outside the boundaries of more typical formative and summative functions. However, the last functional form of evaluation, the administrative, is less benign.

The administrative function. Administrative evaluation, as defined here, is nothing more than a demonstration of organizational authority. X evaluates y simply to remind y that x occupies a superordinate position in the hierarchy as shown by x's ability to exercise a nonreciprocal evaluative function. This is clearly an abuse of evaluation, since the desired result is not formative, summative, sociopolitical, or even psychological except in the one-upmanship sense. It is evaluation for the purpose of browbeating or bullying.

Gifted students are sometimes the objects of administrative evaluation. A child who is gifted may possess more knowledge about a given subject than a teacher and may even best the teacher in the unfortunate verbal power games that once in a while pass for class discussion. Nevertheless, both teacher and child know who holds the trump card—the ability to assign grades. Unfortunately, it is not unknown for an insecure or vindictive teacher to give a child a grade lower than is deserved just to take the child down a peg. This is a clear example of administrative evaluation.

It should be clear by now that evaluation is compounded of many activities, functions, and agendas. This process, which many regard as a bloodless, cut-and-dried exercise in psychometrics, is in fact often the occasion of intense human drama, intrigue, and manipulation. In practice, evaluations range from the disinterested to the disingenuous, from the experimental to the predetermined, from the cooperative to the confrontational. Nevertheless, an honest, competent evaluation is an essential aspect of sound educational practice.

Educational evaluation is problematic in any situation. The evaluation of programs for the gifted is an undertaking that adds new dimensions of difficulty to the enterprise. I will turn now to some problems peculiar to the evaluation of such programs.

SOURCES OF PROBLEMS MET WITH IN EVALUATING PROGRAMS FOR THE GIFTED

The evaluation of programs for the gifted presents certain difficulties not encountered in the evaluation of other types of programs. Some of these are the result of dealing with a population drawn from the extremes of ability continua. Others result from the differentiated goals of instruction in programs for the gifted. Combined, these factors render this form of educational evaluation one of the most problematic one is likely to encounter.

Program Goals and Instructional Objectives

As stated in the definition of evaluation proposed above, and as I will argue below, evaluation is in large part a determination of the degree to which the goals of the program have been met. The most important goals and objectives are those related to the outcomes of instruction. In Chapter 8, I discussed some of the features of a differentiated curriculum for the gifted, and it should be clear from that discussion that the goals of instruction in the classroom for the gifted will differ in many respects from those of the regular classroom.

Although one could argue that these should be the goals of instruction for all students, it is likely that it is in the classroom for the gifted that there will be an emphasis on higher-level thinking, creativity, critical thinking, affective outcomes, and so forth. There is a problem here for the program evaluator; these and other outcomes of special instruction are difficult to anticipate and to assess as observable behavior. In fact, in trying to couch these outcomes in terms of strict behavioral objectives, an exercise that is often valuable in other contexts, one runs the risk of trivializing the whole process.

Although I do not mean to suggest that program developers should be content with nebulous objectives or with sloppy specifications of desired student behaviors, it is necessary to acknowledge that developmental advancement in the cognitive domain involves a progression from the overt and the behavioral to the internal and the abstract. To the extent that we desire to further this progression, we will become less concerned with behaviors that can be observed objectively and unambiguously. This complicates the process of evaluation considerably.

Lack of Valid Tests

Related to the difficulty described above is the virtual absence of valid psychometric instruments for assessing some of the traits and behaviors we wish to affect in special programs for the gifted. Despite the possibility, even the necessity, of conducting a program evaluation without relying upon tests, there is no denying the utility of valid objective measures in this context. Although there exist published materials advertised as tests of creativity, critical thinking, "higher-level" thinking, and the like, the validity of these instruments is yet to be established in some cases and negligible in others.

Tests of creativity are perhaps the most popular of such tests, although their popularity appears to be waning. This is an encouraging sign, because there is no credible evidence that such tests actually measure something that could be plausibly identified as human creativity. Other measures exist that have not been unequivocally shown to be invalid, such as various tests of higher-level thinking, critical-thinking measures, and the test battery based upon J. P. Guilford's (1967) structure of intellect model developed by Meeker and Meeker (1977). In the main, however, these are usually poorly normed, of questionable validity, and certainly inappropriate for purposes other than research (see, for example, Clarizio & Mehrens, 1985).

Affective Goals of the Program

Quite appropriately, some of the goals of special programs for the gifted relate to affective outcomes. It is not uncommon to read program goal statements that stress instilling a love of learning in gifted students, increasing students' comfort with their exceptionality, helping students avoid intellectual boredom, and so forth. These are valid goals, but difficult ones to measure objectively. To my knowledge, no one since Francis Galton in the late nineteenth century has attempted to devise an objective test of such things as tedium (he ventured to develop a way of quantifying the degree of boredom caused by lectures, an enterprise that failed, to the relief of college professors everywhere). So, once again, one must depend upon less objective means of assessment.

Inadequate Evaluation Designs

Sometimes the design of the evaluation is the problem. By this I mean that the plan for collecting and interpreting evaluation data is beset by crippling limitations or logical fallacies that render the process of program evaluation meaningless. Among the problems frequently encountered in this respect are the following.

Limitations on the use of experimental designs. Program evaluation is different from psychological experimentation or quasi-experimentation in aim and function. Nevertheless, the control exercised by the researcher engaged in a true experiment is appealing to the educational evaluator, and the latter must think longingly of the possibility of evaluating a program in an experimental manner.

How much easier it would be if gifted students could be assigned randomly to treatment (the program for the gifted) and control (the regular classroom) conditions so that direct comparisons between outcome measures could be made. The problem of isolating the effects attributable to the program itself, uncontaminated by extraneous factors such as those described by Campbell and Stanley (1963), would be diminished considerably. Unfortunately, this is a condition more to be wished for than attained.

One stumbling block, a prohibitive one, is ethical: how does one justify denying a special-educational program to a child who is gifted? Another, equally if not more intractable, involves persuading the parents of half of a school's gifted population that their able offspring should be kept out of the program for a year for purposes of determining the program's effectiveness. True experimental designs are unlikely to play a significant or even appreciable role in the evaluation of programs for the gifted, no matter how dearly we may wish to employ them. And even if we could use such designs, they might not prove to be the panacea we seek.

Inadequacies of experimental and quasi-experimental designs. Let us assume that in some never-never land of educational practice we were given the opportunity to conduct a program evaluation using a true experimental design. Even then, we might fall prey to what Abraham Tannenbaum (personal communication) facetiously refers to as the "Sanskrit effect." This involves the following scenario.

In order to evaluate the effectiveness of a program for the gifted, gifted students in a school district are randomly assigned to the program or to a comparison group. The students in the program are exposed to the special curriculum, a year of instruction in Sanskrit, while the students in the comparison group receive no Sanskrit instruction. At the end of the academic year, a test of knowledge of Sanskrit is given to both groups, and it is found that the experimental group, the students in the program, significantly outperform the comparison group, the students not in the program, leading to the conclusion that the program is an effective form of special education for the gifted. In other words, students who were taught Sanskrit learned more Sanskrit than did students who were taught no Sanskrit.

That this would tell us nothing that we did not know before we started is obvious, but this exaggerated scenario makes an important point for program evaluators: evaluation of programs for the gifted requires one to do more than simply demonstrate the obvious (for example, that gifted students, when taught something, are likely to learn it). That this in itself should be obvious is true, but such situations do arise. Let us take an example from the literature.

The Creative Problem Solving (CPS) method (e.g., Parnes, Noller, & Biondi, 1977) is a popular follow-the-steps approach to solving problems that has found a niche in the field of the education of the gifted. It is widely hailed as an effective method. Torrance (1972), for example, reviewed 22 evaluations of CPS and reported that 20 of these showed the method to be effective. This looks impressive at first glance, but a more careful examination reveals what looks suspiciously like a variation of Tannenbaum's Sanskrit effect.

An example of this type of evaluation is the following. A group of gifted students is given a pretest using a "creativity" measure, invariably the Torrance Tests of Creative Thinking (TTCT) (Torrance, 1966). Then the students are taught CPS for an extended period of time, followed by posttesting on the TTCT. A comparison of pretest and posttest scores reveals a significant mean gain, leading to the conclusion that CPS is an effective way of enhancing students' creative thinking.

Leaving aside numerous objections deriving from the fact that what I just described is what Campbell and Stanley (1963) call a "pre-experimental" design that lacks adequate safeguards against internal and external sources of invalidity, we once again are left with an empty tautology. First of all, the measure being used, the TTCT, although not a valid measure of creativity is a fairly good measure of what Guilford (1967) calls divergent production. The bulk of variance on divergent-production tests (Borland, 1986a; Runco, 1985) is accounted for by ideational fluency, that is, the ability or tendency to produce a quantity of responses to a stimulus. This is essentially what is being tested here—the number of responses students give to a series of stimuli.

Now, if CPS preaches one thing over and over, it is the danger (probably overstated; see Perkins, 1981) of premature closure. This is the tendency to stop producing ideas when one thinks one has a good one. To forestall this, trainees in CPS are instructed to engage in brainstorming, to undertake a "long search," to produce ideas in quantity. This is one of the basic elements of CPS, and it is not difficult to grasp. After a few lessons, even the most obdurate student will generate as many ideas as possible. Thus, when it is time for the posttest on the TTCT, the students have been told so many times to generate a quantity of responses that that is what they will do on the test, and it cannot help raising their posttest scores.

In other words, the students have been given a test on which the scores rise when they produce a large number of responses; they have been told repeatedly to produce a large number of responses in such situations; and then they are given the test again, by which time they have learned what has been preached: in such situations, produce a large number of responses. This is just a variation of Tannenbaum's Sanskrit effect, the popular "Test; teach the test; then retest" variation.

I do not mean to single out CPS unfairly; it is just a prominent exemplar of this effect. One could point to Meeker's SOI method and others as similarly problematic in this respect. The important thing to keep in mind is that an evaluation should tell one something that one does not already know. These examples may fulfill the sociopolitical function of evaluation, but that is about all. They do nothing to help us judge the true effectiveness of a program or to show us how to improve it.

Psychometric and Statistical Factors

Certain tests that are valid in most situations and yield scores that ordinarily behave quite appropriately tend to go haywire when they are used with gifted students. Among the problems that can result are the following.

Ceiling effects. I discussed ceiling effects in Chapter 5 in the context of identification, and they are no less of a problem in evaluation. The reader will recall that the term *ceiling effect* refers to the lack of an adequate range of possible scores at the high end of the distribution. Some tests are simply not difficult enough for gifted students. When these tests are administered to a group of children varied in ability, a number of these children, gifted and nongifted alike, will attain the highest score possible. There may be real differences in ability between those who score at the highest level, but because the test-score ceiling is not high enough, these differences are not revealed. It is as if jumping ability were to be assessed by asking a number of persons—an assemblage including the infirm, normal adults, and world-class high jumpers—to clear a bar that could only be raised to a height of four feet. Although some in this group would not perform at the highest level, quite a few would, obscuring the fact that there are significant differences in jumping ability between average healthy adults and highly conditioned athletes with a special aptitude for flinging themselves into the air.

The problem this causes for program evaluators is often most apparent in pretest–posttest designs. The intention of evaluators using such designs is to assess gifted students' entering levels of competence, to intervene in some manner, and then to assess any changes in competence, which are then attributed to the intervention. This is a flawed design, but it is nonetheless frequently used, and it illustrates some of the havoc that can be wreaked by ceiling effects. For what sometimes happens is that a number of the students will hit the ceiling on the pretest, making the group pretest mean so high that there is no way for the group to show growth on that particular test, even if the treatment is effective.

Using gain scores and single-group pretest–posttest designs is bad enough; using tests with insufficient ceiling compounds the problem. Ceiling effects are related to two other difficulties, to which I will now turn.

Inappropriate norms. One reason that some tests lack a sufficient range of scores at the higher ranges is that the samples used to norm the tests did not adequately represent students of high ability. Test publishers generally envision their instruments as being used with students in the mainstream, and since finding a norming sample of sufficient size and heterogeneity is a difficult task, they see no reason to be very scrupulous about including large numbers of children at the highest extremes of ability. Thus, there is usually no appreciable representative sample of able children to establish norms that extend several standard deviations upward from the mean. In some cases, a considerable range of raw scores at the upper level will translate into the same scaled score, resulting in a low ceiling. In other cases, raw-score conversions are based upon unreliable extrapolations from the norming data, resulting in unreliable scores at the upper extreme of the distribution.

It is important, therefore, for purposes of both evaluation and identification, to look at the test manual carefully and to determine whether the test has been normed for the population for which its use is being contemplated—in this case, the gifted.

Regression effects. The phenomenon of regression toward the mean is a well-known but often misunderstood property of some aggregate test scores. It is simply the tendency for mean posttest scores for a group of individuals chosen because of extreme scores on a pretest to move away from the extreme and closer toward the mean, irrespective of any actual changes in the trait being measured. Take the following example. An IQ test is administered to all students in a large school in September, and the students who score in the top 3 percent are, on that basis alone, labeled gifted. (This is obviously a bad practice, but it makes for a good example of how regression works.) No program is instituted; the students are simply labeled gifted by an administrator, who does not even inform teachers of the labels. Then at some later time, this group of identified students is given the same IQ test. Invariably, unless the test is perfectly reliable (a virtual impossibility), the mean score for the group will show a decline from the pretest to the posttest, even though there is no reason to believe that the students' aptitudes have decreased.

The reasons for this are not important here (interested readers can consult Campbell & Stanley, 1963, for a lucid explanation). What is important is to realize that if students are originally chosen for a program for the gifted on the basis of high test scores, it will be difficult to show gains on those tests as a result of the program, in part because of regression effects. One basic rule, therefore, is that one should never use the same instrument for identification and for evaluation of student gains.

Even if the same instrument is not used, regression effects may still occur. A program may select students for a program for the gifted on the basis of high amounts of x, and they might use test y, a measure of x, for identification. Since a goal of the program is to increase the students' amount of x even more, program personnel may try to assess their effectiveness by pretesting and posttesting the students on test z, another measure of x. As different tests of x are being used for identification and evaluation of student growth, they reason, there should be no regression effects. This, however, is not the case. If there is real growth in x between the pretest and the posttest, then the pretest score on z will correlate with the identification score on y more strongly than will the posttest score on z. Thus, the students will regress downward more on the posttest of z than on the pretest of z, creating a drag on the pretest–posttest gain, which may obscure true growth.

This is perhaps more than enough discussion of regression toward the mean, but I suspect that it is more of a problem in evaluating programs for the gifted than is realized. It is likely that in most cases in which evaluators attempt to measure gains in aptitude resulting from program activities, the test used for this purpose will correlate with the test score or composite of scores originally used to identify the students for the program. In such cases, there is likely to be some regression, creating a difficult situation, which is compounded by the following problem.

Unreliability of gain scores. The most common method of assessing educational growth is to assess students' levels of aptitude or ability both before and after a treatment, or a program, is instituted and to compute a gain score for each student by subtracting the pretest score from the posttest score. As common as this practice is, it is also difficult to defend because gain scores are notoriously unreliable (Cronbach & Furby, 1970). Both the pretest and the posttest have error components, and the gain score, being a combination of the two, has a compounded error component.

There is usually no reason to use gain scores. If some method of comparing gains in a treatment group with gains in a control group is needed, one is better off doing no pretesting and simply comparing posttests *if* students have been randomly assigned to the groups. If there has been no random assignment, direct comparison of posttest means is still indicated if there are no significant differences in group pretest means; if pretest means differ significantly, analysis of covariance with pretest scores as the covariate should serve.

Inequality of percentile units. One last property of tests that is potentially problematic for program evaluators is the fact that percentile scores, which seem to be evenly spaced, may result from raw scores that are quite skewed. Let us assume that a student has a raw score, x, that places him or her at the 50th percentile of the test distribution. This student is tightly bunched with many other students at the modal point of the distribution, like a racer in the pack in the middle of the field. Now, if this student were to retake the test and achieve a raw score of $x + 2$, he or she would pass quite a few other students in the original distribution. And just as a racer bunched in the pack can increase his or her standing by passing a number of close competitors with a sudden burst of speed, this student will increase his or her percentile rank significantly by adding 2 points to the raw score.

Let us also take the case of a student who achieves a very high raw score—not at the ceiling, but very high—on the same test. This student is like a racer far out in front of the pack who trails just a few other runners, who are well spread out. This student could add to his raw score significantly but pass no one, just as the racer could begin a vigorous sprint and pass no one, simply because there are few individuals to pass. In the case of this second student, considerable gain in the raw score translates into a small gain, or none, in percentile ranking; yet the raw score gain might represent an increment in skill or aptitude.

It should be clear from the preceding that the evaluation of programs for the gifted poses numerous technical problems, some of which are unique to this population. This explains, in part, why program evaluation is infrequently and badly done in most programs. However, these difficulties are not sufficient to justify the woeful state of program evaluation in the field of the education of the gifted. Programs can and should be evaluated effectively, and I will turn to that issue in the remainder of this chapter.

A FRAMEWORK FOR PROGRAM EVALUATION

What follows is an approach to designing a program evaluation that, in my experience with various school districts, has been accepted and used effectively by program personnel, many of whom were initially wary of or confused about the prospect of carrying out an evaluation. It certainly is not the only way to structure an evaluation, or necessarily even the best, and it is not presented as such here. Rather, it is offered as one way to organize one's thinking about program evaluation.

I will not discuss the fine points of evaluation design, data analysis, and so forth. Those seeking more technical information about the mechanics of program evaluation should turn to one of the many texts and other resources that deal with this far-from-neglected topic in education. More specifically, readers interested in evaluation as it relates to programs for the gifted should consult the work of Callahan (e.g., 1983; Callahan & Caldwell, 1986).

In thinking about evaluation, the logical place to begin is with program goals.

Program Goals as the Basis for Evaluation

One undertakes a program evaluation in order to assess the degree to which a program is working as planned so that the program can be improved, and accountability assured. For this process to be defensible, it must refer to and be predicated upon the goals of the program. As I stated in Chapter 3, program goals are a delineation of what the school or school district wants the program for the gifted to accomplish. These program goals thus become the benchmarks against which program effectiveness can be evaluated.

This, then, must be the clear and singular focus of evaluation. Too often, however, program personnel become enamored of a particular test or other instrument, or of a particular design that appears to be "tight" and well controlled. This, unfortunately, can result in the fallacy of misplaced precision, in other words, a situation in which something is carefully and reliably measured, the measurement of which tells one nothing about the program in question. In this context, relevance is much to be preferred to precision if a choice must be made. As Tannenbaum (1983) asserts, "Evaluation makes sense if the methods and instruments relate directly to the educational objectives, even if it means sacrificing some precision for the sake of relevance" (p. 443).

Thus, the main objective of evaluating programs for the gifted is not to use the best tests, or to employ the design with the tightest controls, or to engage in the most abstruse statistical analysis. These can all provide some interesting answers; unfortunately, too often they are answers to the wrong questions. It is more important in evaluating programs for the gifted to ask the right questions, even if the answers are hard to come by or promise to be ambiguous or equivocal. The central question is "How effectively is the program doing what we want it to do?" And that can only be answered by comparing program goals with program outcomes.

The foregoing assumes the existence of appropriate program goals, something that unfortunately cannot be safely assumed in every situation. Although program evaluation must be built upon a foundation of program goals, this foundation is in some cases nonexistent or inadequate. A brief look at program goals and the problems that attend them in some programs for the gifted is in order.

Nonexistent program goals. It is not unheard of that a program for the gifted lacks any written program goals. While it is logical and, I would argue, essential to delineate clearly what the goals of a program for the gifted are, more than a few programs have omitted this step of the process altogether. In some cases this simply means that the program staff, while united and in agreement with respect to what the program is and ought to be doing, have not bothered to commit their implicit goals to paper. In most cases, however, I suspect that the lack of written program goals reflects the absence of a sense of purpose beyond the desire to provide a program and to keep it going.

It is difficult, if not impossible, to defend this inaction. Given the minimal effort required and the importance of the task, it is just as difficult to excuse. Programs for the gifted that do not have a set of clearly stated and validated goals are like rudderless ships whose course is set as much by situational factors as human guidance. There is really little more to say on this topic. All programs for the gifted should have written, workable, consensually validated program goals that reflect the desired outcomes of the program in response to demonstrated student needs.

Program goals that are too lofty. Not all program goals are suitable for evaluation purposes. Some, for example, are so general, abstract, or grandiose that evaluating whether or not they have been met is practically impossible. In fact, some are perhaps unattainable in the context of an educational program.

I am thinking here of the sort of goal statements found in so many written program descriptions (usually on the inside of the front cover, perhaps embellished with a scroll border), suggesting that what the reader is perusing is more akin to the Declaration of Independence than the goals of a program for the gifted. For example, a goal statement that reads "to make the world a better place for humanity," as desirable as that end is, is probably quite out of the reach of a typical school or school district. Even more common program goals, such as "to educate the leaders of tomorrow," can be a bit much and should raise some questions for the reader. Is the program an educational failure if the gifted students served by it do not all become leaders of some sort? Is this the only group in the school from which tomorrow's leaders will emerge? And how will one evaluate progress made toward such a goal over the course of this academic year?

It might be argued that these pie-in-the-sky program goals are harmless, that they express unexceptionable sentiments, and that they provide a sugar coating for the program that forces its detractors, in effect, to argue against the educational equivalent of motherhood, apple pie, and baseball. However, it can also be argued that program goals of this type do no real good, provide no sound guidance for program personnel, and certainly do not assist in the process of program evaluation. If it is necessary to assert the school's or school district's belief in truth, justice, and the American way at every turn, then the inclusion of such banalities among the goals of the program will be inevitable. It then becomes the responsibility of those more concerned with the needs of children to make certain that some educational goals are interspersed among the platitudes.

Confusing means with ends. To shift our focus precipitously from the airily vapid to the mundane and earthbound, let us look at another kind of program goal that is no help in terms of program evaluation. I am referring here to goals such as the following: "To identify 3 percent of the students as gifted;" "To conduct in-service training for all regular classroom teachers;" "To extend the program for the gifted into the junior high school." These goals are certainly not too general or abstract, and their attainment can be easily and unambiguously determined. So, one might ask, what is the problem?

The problem is that program goals of this sort reflect a confusion of means with ends. They state what the school or school district will do, not what is desired for its students. These things could easily be accomplished without any appreciable benefit accruing to gifted students. Thus, they are sometimes referred to as instrumental or enabling goals or objectives, stressing their identity as means rather than as ends.

There are various means to valid ends, and they should be discussed, debated, and implemented, but they should not be confused with valid program goals. The goals of a program for the gifted must reflect the desired outcomes of the program expressed in terms of its effect on students' behaviors, states of knowledge, attitudes, and so forth. The most pertinent question to bear in mind in evaluating goal statements is, So what? So what if teachers sit through an in-service workshop? So what if the program is extended? So what if students are identified? None of these is an end in and of itself. Affecting the ways that students learn, think, create, and feel is a valid end for programs for the gifted.

The foregoing underscores the need to think clearly and carefully about program goals during the program-planning process, and it further underscores the prominent placement of the box labeled "Program Goals" in Figure 3.1, the flowchart that schematically illustrates the program-planning process. Once valid goals have been established, the basis for a sound evaluation design exists.

Designing a Program Evaluation

Figure 9.1 shows one page of a form that can be used to design the evaluation of a program for the gifted. If adopted, this form should be carefully considered and partially completed by the staff of the program for the gifted before the school year begins so that provisions for both formative evaluation and summative evaluation can be incorporated into the design. In order to complete this form, the staff must address the following questions.

Which goals will be the focus? Some programs for the gifted have numerous—perhaps too numerous—goals. To try to evaluate the program's progress toward each of these goals every year would be an onerous task and a disincentive to conducting a real evaluation. Thus, it makes sense at the beginning of each year to establish priorities for the year to come, at least insofar as evaluation is concerned. For example, three, four, five, or six goals might be chosen as those on which the program staff would like to focus in a given year. Some of these might be chosen because they are the most important and will be included in the program evaluation every year. Others will be selected on a rotating schedule, serving as a basis for evaluation every few years.

However they are chosen, the limiting of the goals for evaluation is a practical necessity unless the program has only a few. Once they are chosen, a form as shown in Figure 9.1 can be completed for each program goal. The goal is written across the top of the form, and one then proceeds to the next step. The example has been completed for the goal of the development of independent-study skills.

What program activities will serve to further the attainment of the goal? It makes little sense to have a program goal unless instruction is geared toward

Figure 9.1 The program-evaluation form.

PROGRAM GOAL: To encourage the development of research skills

ACTIVITY	OUTCOME	OBSERVATION POINTS	CRITERION	PERFORMANCE	ANALYSIS
Complete programmed unit on research	Unit examination	End of unit	All students meet test criterion	All at criterion	Satisfactory
Presentation on library resources by librarian	Library activity and written log	Class following presentation	All students complete activity and log to teacher's satisfaction	All completed satisfactorily	Satisfactory
Evaluate research of previous students after presentation on research methods	Written evaluations of the reviewed research	One week after presentation	90% of evaluations judged acceptable by teacher	40% judged acceptable	Unsatisfactory, but see below
Develop research proposal	Research proposal	End of second grading period	90% judged acceptable by teacher	92.5% acceptable	Satisfactory
Initiate and carry out research	Research report	When completed	80% of projects will be completed	40% completed	Criterion not realistic
Initiate and carry out research	Project evaluation form	When completed	80% favorably evaluated by expert judges	50% favorably evaluated	Unsatisfactory, but see below

Synthesis: Good progress was made toward the goal, but not to the extent hoped or expected. Students did learn about research methods, but they had trouble evaluating other students' research when asked to do so. This was probably due to the poor presentation made by the guest instructor, who did not make his material comprehensible to the students. Poor performance prompted follow-up instruction by the program staff, and the students later demonstrated that they could evaluate research reports competently. Fewer students than expected completed projects; fewer yet completed good projects. Clearly, our criterion was not realistic for elementary students. We will retain this goal next year, and we will include the same activities, but we will establish more realistic criteria for student performance based upon our experience this year. See narrative for elaboration.

it. If program goals truly guide program design, as they should, their influence will probably be most evident in the development of the curriculum and the choice of instructional strategies. Thus, it should not be too difficult to think about the academic year ahead and to identify instructional activities that are related to the particular program goal in question. For example, for the goal listed in Figure 9.1, the development of independent-study skills, the following classroom activities might be among those planned to help students develop such skills:

1. Students will complete a programmed unit designed to acquaint them with the elements of research.
2. Students will attend a presentation given by the school librarian dealing with the full range of library resources that can be used by students pursuing their own research.
3. Students will examine examples of research proposals and evaluate their suitability, practicality, importance, and so forth.
4. Students will evaluate the products of the research of students from previous years.
5. Students who so desire will develop proposals for carrying out their own research.
6. Students will carry out approved research projects under the guidance of the teachers in the program for the gifted.

These and other major activities designed to further the attainment of the program goal are then listed in an abbreviated form, as shown, in the column of Figure 9.1 labeled "Activity." These activities will provide opportunities to observe student behavior that can shed some light upon progress toward the goal in question. One should not worry about whether the activity will yield behavior that can be observed objectively or measured precisely. To repeat a previously stated admonition, relevance, not precision, is of paramount importance here. What one is striving for is an accumulation of data that will enable one to draw logical inferences with respect to whether or not the goal has been attained. Thus, final determinations will hinge upon the accretion of evidence, not absolute, incontrovertible proof. This is an inescapable reality in any program evaluation; I am simply stating it explicitly as a feature of this framework for program evaluation.

What will be the outcomes of the listed activities? Each of the activities listed in the first column of Figure 9.1 will have one or more outcomes that can be observed and recorded. These should be listed in the second column. The reader will notice that in only one case is a test score a specified outcome. This is a feature of this particular program goal, which is rather product-oriented, but it also illustrates that it is permissible, and in fact necessary, to go beyond objective psychometric measures as means of collecting data for evaluating programs for the gifted.

When will outcomes be observed? The outcomes of the activities are the opportunities for data collection, and these opportunities may present themselves on one or more occasions. Anticipating these occasions on the evaluation-design form is good planning. In addition, it also suggests that there are times other than the end of the academic year at which program evaluation data can be collected. This reinforces the tendency to plan for formative evaluation as well as for summative evaluation (the importance of which was discussed earlier in this chapter). The observation points for each activity outcome should therefore be listed in the third column of the form in Figure 9.1 as shown.

What level of performance will be expected? In the column headed by the portentous word "Criterion" in Figure 9.1, one should specify the level of performance, with respect to the outcome of the activity, that one would accept as reflecting appreciable progress toward the program goal. Here things get a bit tricky; there may be no basis for establishing a criterion other than the best judgment of the educators designing the evaluation. This, however, is a resource upon which the program will be drawing many times over the course of the academic year, and it might as well be called into service here. In some cases, previous experience will serve as a guide for establishing an appropriate level for a given criterion. From time to time, absolute criteria, which specify that all students will perform to a verifiable level of acceptable performance, will be appropriate.

One of the outcomes of a program evaluation is a more realistic idea of what performance criteria are appropriate for a given outcome of an activity related to a program goal. This is an experimental process, and one should not become overly concerned with establishing, a priori, the right criterion. There is no need to set criteria so low that they will inevitably be met, since the results of the program evaluation do not hinge upon one source of information related to a single program goal. The program staff should simply make their best effort to determine the level of performance they would like to see students attain and, if it is not attained, decide afterward whether there was a problem with the instruction or the criterion was unrealistic.

When the evaluation form in Figure 9.1 has been completed through the first four columns for each targeted goal, one has an evaluation design. At this stage of the process one has established certain program goals as priorities, scheduled observations of student behavior in response to instructional activities related to these goals, and set performance levels for the student behaviors. Once this has been accomplished, the actual conducting of the program evaluation is a rather straightforward matter.

Conducting the Program Evaluation

Conducting the evaluation itself, once the design has been established, is a process that can be guided by the forms discussed above. At this point, the data to be collected have been specified as outcomes of instruction, and criteria with which the outcomes can be compared have been established. The succeeding step is indicated by the next column of the evaluation form in Figure 9.1.

What is the actual level of performance? At the specified times, student behavior can be observed and the level of performance can be recorded on the form in the column labeled "Performance." This is a simple matter of reporting what was observed in most cases, although there may be some complications or mitigating circumstances. These, however, can be described later. All that is required here is the recording of the level of performance that was observed, as shown in Figure 9.1.

How does the performance compare with the criterion? The last column carries the heading "Analysis." Here, one succinctly indicates the degree to which the performance satisfied the criterion. The reasons for this determination and the various subtleties involved do not need to be spelled out here. There will be room for that later in the narrative that accompanies the form in the final report. As shown in the example, this column simply provides a summary of the hits and misses related to each behavior guided by instruction designed to further progress toward the program goal in question.

Often, "Satisfactory" and "Unsatisfactory" will suffice in this column. At other times, brief statements, such as "Criterion too stringent" or "Activity not completed," will be needed. In any case, the point is to provide a concise summary of the various outcomes relative to expectations that can serve as a basis for drawing inferences with respect to goal attainment.

What does it all mean? At the bottom of the form is a space headed by the word "Synthesis." It is here that one begins to pull everything together and to draw some evaluative conclusions. The synthesis is a brief integration of the outcomes detailed above in which some conclusions are drawn and some background factors discussed, as illustrated in Figure 9.1. One may conclude that there was considerable progress toward the attainment of the goal; that very little progress was made; or something in between. In some cases, conclusions such as these may not even be appropriate.

The goal is to provide a brief summary of the evaluation as it relates to the program goal under discussion. One should not strive to tell the entire story here—that should be saved for the narrative that accompanies and expands upon these forms.

Reporting the Evaluation

In and of themselves, these forms do not constitute an evaluation. They must be incorporated into a narrative that gives the evaluator the space to say what needs to be said. More detail can be supplied about the specifics of the evaluation of each goal, and the summary presented in digest form under "Synthesis" on each form can be expanded upon. Moreover, the entire set of goals can be discussed in a larger synthesis that reflects upon the program as a whole. General conclusions can be drawn, and summative judgments made. (It is assumed that the observation of student behavior at the various observation points will be incorporated into formative evaluation.)

One should keep in mind and communicate to one's audience that an evaluation done in this manner is more closely akin to the unfolding of a logical argument than to a sudden revelation of the truth. The goal is to collect data from a number of sources that the evaluator can interpret in a way that will lead to program improvement. Inevitably, many or most of the data will be "soft" data from the point of view of an orthodox psychometrician, but this is a typical consequence of assigning a higher priority to relevance than to precision of measurement in program evaluation. Valid, reliable measures of the traits and abilities of concern to educators of the gifted are in short supply, and the factors I described above often preclude the use of experimental evaluation designs. However, opportunities to observe gifted students engaging in activities designed to further the goals of the program abound, and these can yield data that in the aggregate can be put to good use in evaluating programs for the gifted.

Most important, the narrative is the place to discuss what steps will be taken to improve the program in the future. Improvement is, after all, the ultimate purpose of program evaluation. Whatever of an evaluative nature is learned about the program is only a starting point for planning steps to make the program better. Thus, recommendations for improvement should be the centerpiece of the evaluation report. They provide the entire process with a rationale and a goal.

CONCLUSION

Repeatedly throughout this chapter, I have asserted two points that may at first appear to be antagonistic to each other. The first of these is that the evaluation of programs for the gifted is a difficult process that we have not really mastered as a field. The second is that the evaluation of programs for the gifted is essential to the viability of our field. I hope that I have convinced the reader of the truth of the latter and of the modifiability of the former. While evaluating programs for the gifted will never be an easy task or one that is free of controversy, it can be carried out successfully if one relies upon common sense, good faith, a smattering of measurement know-how, and some knowledge of gifted children.

I have no doubt that the current state of affairs, in which program evaluation is the exception rather than the rule, will change. The only question that remains concerns the identity of the agents of this change. If educators of the gifted come to view evaluation as an indispensable aspect of program planning and part of the obligation owed to gifted students, guidelines for evaluating programs for the gifted will emerge from the field and will be consistent with what we collectively are trying to accomplish. If, however, we continue to temporize on this issue, those who underwrite our programs will inevitably lose patience and impose upon us ways of demonstrating accountability that could prove to be quite inappropriate.

There have been many examples in the history of education in which the tail of evaluation has wagged the programmatic dog. One only has to look to the closest public-school classroom to see how achievement tests drive curriculum and instruction to one degree or another. Those who believe that such a thing cannot happen in programs for the gifted can continue to ignore the issue of evaluation, at least for the time being. The rest have some work to do.

CHAPTER 10

Final Thoughts and Conclusions

When thou hast done, thou hast not done
> Donne, "A Hymn to God the Father"

Now this is not the end. It is not even the beginning of the
end. But it is, perhaps, the end of the beginning.
> Churchill, *Speech at the Lord Mayor's Day Luncheon*

Having reached the end of my discussion of the components of a program for the gifted, I wish, in this final chapter, to try to put the program-planning process into perspective and to deal with some issues that, while they do not fit neatly into the schematic outline of this book, nonetheless deserve consideration. Thus, after stressing the importance of regarding program planning as an ongoing process, I will discuss some concerns relating to gifted students who are too often overlooked or underrepresented in programs for the gifted. Then, before concluding, I will briefly touch upon the necessity of attending to the affective needs of gifted students.

PROGRAM PLANNING AS AN ONGOING PROCESS

With the discussion of program evaluation, the component-by-component description of program planning outlined in Chapter 3 is completed. I do not wish to give the impression, however, that planning and implementing a program for the gifted is simply a matter of following a linear process, checking off one box at a time until the entire program is in place, and then sitting back and resting.

In Chapter 3, I described the "syntax" of program planning and implementation as diagnosis (needs assessment), followed by prescription (actual program planning and implementation), followed by evaluation. That is an accurate outline as far as it goes, and it goes far enough to cover the processes of planning and implementation, which are the major topics of this book. But for the administrator of a program for the gifted, there is more work to be done, work that relates to program modification and fine-tuning.

As I stressed in the previous chapter, program evaluation is valuable not so much because it enables one to render after-the-fact verdicts but rather because it can serve a formative, diagnostic function, providing information that enables program staff and administrators to effect changes in the program to make it more effective and more efficient. Program evaluation, therefore, instead of being the end of the line is really just another stop along the way.

Figure 3.1 shows an arrow pointing backward from the box representing the evaluation component. This is meant to represent the chief function of program evaluation, program improvement. An effective evaluation should supply data that pertain to the operation of each of the functional aspects of the program for the gifted: identification procedures, choice of program format, teacher selection, curriculum development, instruction, even the evaluation procedures themselves. Armed with such data, those in charge can take steps to improve the operation of these components and to design a future evaluation that will shed light on the effects of these program-improvement efforts.

Moreover, evaluation data may reveal the need to change aspects of the program that relate to policy or educational philosophy. For example, the definition of the target population may need to be modified if evaluation data suggest that the students with the greatest educational need are not being served. Program goals or curricular objects that seemed to be sound in prospect may appear to be less so in retrospect and may have to be rewritten.

Even if the program in its first incarnation is an appropriate response to the needs of the school or school district and its students, these needs can change rapidly as a result of demographic and population changes in the community, new curricular emphases in the mainstream program, and the like. A successful program for the gifted may itself change the state of affairs within the school or school district to such an extent that the overall picture with respect to student needs changes. If this occurs, the initial step of the process, needs assessment, may have to be repeated, although it will probably not have to be done in as detailed a fashion as it was originally.

Thus, looking at Figure 3.1 more sequentially than one ordinarily should, one sees that once the evaluation component is reached, there is a need to recycle the process and at least to think about going back to or near the beginning. Program planning is, in this way of viewing things, not a process of fashioning a masterpiece to be placed on display, unalterable for all time. Instead, it is an iterative process resulting in successive approximations of the idealized program. In fact, it is almost a process of advancing, testing, and refining hypotheses. The hypotheses being tested relate to theories about what makes the best educational sense for gifted students in a school or school district, and they take the form of different approaches to the program components discussed in the previous chapters. Each successive approach represents, it would be hoped, an advance on previous ones, guided by what has been learned through the process of program evaluation.

Another way of looking at this is to conceive of a program for the gifted as a dynamic rather than static entity. Too often, my experience has convinced me, programs are implemented and, especially if they are successful, never change appreciably. Perhaps nothing succeeds as well as success, but in a dynamic system like a public school district, success is not constant for long. A program for the gifted is not a closed but an open system, receiving significant input from the larger systems of the school and the community. If it does not adapt to changes in its environment, it becomes progressively less effective. Often, change only comes in response to a crisis—perhaps a widespread lack of confidence in the program by educators, parents, and students—and in some cases the change either is too little or takes place too late.

A program for the gifted that is envisioned as an adaptive, self-evaluating system is less likely to suffer such a fate. This does not imply that such a program should not have a foundation of enduring principles that are immune to fads and passing fashions, a firm commitment to academic rigor for gifted students, for example. It is simply that the means employed to further these principled ends should be sufficiently flexible to prevent them from becoming ends in themselves and thereby displacing the goals that were the original inspiration for bringing the program into being.

I hope that by now the point is clear that when it comes to planning and implementing programs for the gifted, one's work is literally never done. Success with such programs, once achieved, is not guaranteed to be permanent. In his wonderful film *Annie Hall*, Woody Allen's character, Alvy Singer, compares a relationship between two people in love to a shark, an animal that, should it stop moving, will die. This is probably true of programs for the gifted as well. Unless those responsible for such programs envision them as dynamic, open systems responsive to changes in the larger dynamic systems on which they depend, they, like Alvy and Annie, could end up with a dead shark on their hands.

THE INCLUSION OF "SPECIAL POPULATIONS" OF GIFTED CHILDREN

Let me turn now to a topic that I mentioned briefly in Chapter 5 but to which I did not devote an amount of space commensurate with its importance. This is the issue of fair representation of what are often referred to as "special populations" of gifted students—black, Hispanic, and other gifted children outside the white mainstream; gifted girls; gifted handicapped children—each representing minorities within our population who, in the aggregate, are anything but the minority among the gifted except in some programs for the gifted.

A charge frequently leveled at programs for the gifted and those who advocate their implementation is that they foster elitism in the schools. I believe that the charge is baseless in the manner in which it usually is intended; that is, as an assertion that special education for this population of exceptional children is contrary to egalitarian principles because these children are exceptionally able. Stripped of its rhetorical trappings, what is really being argued is that adjusting the curriculum to meet the needs of *this* group of children and thereby making their education an appropriate one, a goal we profess to hold for all children, is not fair. Presumably, what would be fair, would be that these children, because they happen to have an unusual capacity for learning, be denied an education designed to nurture that capacity. It is not too far off the mark to interpret this as an argument for punishing gifted children in the name of equality. This is not only nonsense, but pernicious nonsense.

There is, however, another form of the elitism indictment that I am not convinced we can dismiss as easily. This is the charge that, with many creditable exceptions, programs for the gifted do not fairly represent or serve our country's pluralistic society. Specifically, one can fairly criticize this branch of educational practice for underrepresenting children of color, gifted children with handicapping conditions, and, in some subject areas and at some grade levels, girls.

I doubt seriously that, except in a very few instances, this is the result of a conscious policy of discrimination. However, I suspect that were even the most liberal and egalitarian of us to engage in serious and honest introspection, we would discover that we are sometimes blind to our own follies, subtle assumptions, stereotypes, and ethnocentric perceptions that limit our ability to regard each person and each group as equal. We are human, after all, with all the limitations on perfection that condition confers. And even were we all blameless of any trace of prejudice, stereotypical thinking, or condescension, we would still have to face up to the failures of our good intentions. For it has not been an uncommon experience for me, or for many others with whom I have discussed this issue, to enter a school building, to walk down a hallway and see white, black, and brown faces, and then to enter the classroom in which the program for the gifted is housed and see almost nothing but white faces. This is elitism, and it is a problem in some programs for the gifted.

It is also a danger to our field and to the society that, however ambivalently, supports us. I hardly need to establish through detailed argument the validity of my assertion that prejudice and discrimination—whether it be racism, sexism, or hostility toward the handicapped—are clear and present dangers to society. These forms of ugliness have poisoned our country from its very beginnings and have, to a degree, tempered the pride we can derive from the more noble qualities that, to a greater extent, have defined our national character. It is an admittedly lesser danger to our field that may go unremarked by some of us, even some who acknowledge that a problem exists.

Those, like the writer and most of the readers of this book, who believe that programs for gifted students are essential to fair and effective education and those who, on the contrary, believe that such programs are unmitigated evil are, I strongly suspect, very much a minority of the nation's population. It is only through the sufferance of that majority of society that neither enthusiastically supports nor actively opposes programs for the gifted that our efforts have at times been allowed to succeed. Now, the history of our field suggests that as long as we are not seen as perpetuating gross inequities, we, and not our detractors, will be mildly encouraged or at least tolerated by society at large, especially if society perceives gifted students as a national resource. This seems to be the situation that obtains at the present time.

It is a troubling historical fact, however, that the most progressive decades of our recent history, the 1930s and the 1960s, have been the decades that witnessed the greatest neglect of, even hostility to, programs for the gifted, while such programs have thrived in the mean-spirited 1980s. However it may trouble us morally, the present attitude of relative indifference to human suffering and the slackening of our efforts on behalf of society's have-nots coexist (and I would like to think merely coincide) with a moderate enthusiasm for the encouragement of excellence. In such a climate, whatever problems we as a field have experienced with respect to fair representation of all groups in programs for the gifted have not caused us too many practical difficulties, although what this has done to our collective moral well-being is another matter.

This situation is not likely to last indefinitely. Just as over the last decade our country's moral pendulum has swung, I would argue, in the direction of meanness and selfishness, it is likely to swing back. Should that occur, those who automatically regard all of our efforts as antidemocratic will find a more receptive audience for their arguments, and our field, like Caesar's wife, will have to be above suspicion. It will not be enough to point to the fact that neither general education nor society at large is doing a better job than we are of eradicating every trace of inequality. Should we fail to redress the inequities that are found in some of our programs for the gifted, society is likely to intervene, perhaps by concluding that the whole barrel is rotten, not just a few apples. In such a case, the very children we are trying to serve would suffer the most as a result of our inability to correct this unfortunate situation.

It is ironic that a field that can accurately be included among the helping professions, one that is composed of educators who are, in my experience, almost invariably compassionate and humane individuals, has had what has perhaps been its greatest national acceptance in such a morally impoverished time, but I think that is demonstrably the case. I have no doubt that the vast majority of educators in this field would welcome a return to the true American values of compassion and decency—a kinder, gentler nation as a reality, not a cynical political slogan. But we have to be prepared for the possibility that an efflorescence of the nobler aspects of our national character could bring with it a greater scrutiny of our activities, especially with respect to our success in achieving equal representation of all groups in our programs. And we also must be prepared to be held to a higher standard than other fields as a result of the tension between excellence and equality that has permeated our country's history.

I think it is also apposite to ask what this situation is doing to us as a field, to our collective conscience, our soul if you will. How much have we been willing to overlook as long as an appreciable number of gifted students finally get their due? Which of our principles have we subordinated to our increasingly successful efforts to reclaim the educational birthright of our country's gifted children? I think we must ask ourselves these questions, and I am sure that most of us would agree that we cannot comfortably excuse the injustices inflicted on some by pointing to the benefits accruing to others. We do not have to trade one inequity for another.

Lest I be misunderstood, let me repeat that the overwhelming majority of individuals I have met in this field are decent, caring, moral people, and that I have never discussed this problem with anyone in this field who did not share my concern over it. Moreover, it is important to acknowledge that it is extremely difficult, to say the least, to insure that the many programs for gifted students that exist within our far from perfect society will be free from the sins of the larger culture. We exist, in part, to respond to excellence, and while the potential for excellence exists in all segments of our society, opportunities to develop that potential do not. A child who is not white, who is poor, who is handicapped, or who is a girl will not always be as easy to identify as gifted as will the children who now predominate in some of our programs.

Moreover, despite these conditions that make discrimination easy, many within our field have worked hard to avoid the easy route. Mine is hardly the first expression of concern over this problem, and many practitioners are doing more than merely lamenting the fact that the problem exists. Nevertheless, we are not doing enough or well enough. Although our intentions are laudable, the results have not always been acceptable. We need to do much more than we are now if children from minority cultures, poor children, handicapped children, and girls are to get their fair share of the services we wish to extend to all gifted children.

How can we redress the situation? At the risk of seeming simplistic, we just do it. The problem, our part of it at least, is a problem of identification. In Chapter 5, I strongly urged that placement decisions be made by people working in committees, not by matrices or formulas. People alone, not tests or convoluted ways of combining and interpreting them, can make things better. No amount of fussing with test-score weightings, no seeking after "culture-fair" or "culture-free" tests—those chimeras of years past—will aid us in this respect. Tests, which are essentially predictors of success in schools that subserve an imperfect society, will, and should, continue to reflect the bitter truth of society's failure to provide quality of opportunity. To do otherwise would gloss over the harsh reality and make it harder to change.

The way to begin is for educators who are responsible for placing children in programs for the gifted to operate according to an assumption that I believe is unassailable: that race, ethnicity, socioeconomic status, gender, and handicapping conditions are not factors that have to militate against a child's requiring services in a program for the gifted. In other words, there must be an initial assumption that gifted children exist in every segment in our society, and there must be a result that supports that assumption. Placement committees must make it their goal to find those children in each group, not necessarily on the basis of strict numerical quotas, but in such a way that reasonable people, looking at the composition of our programs for the gifted, will not draw the conclusion that a pattern of systematic discrimination exists.

It is not enough to complain that nonbiased tests do not exist or to assert that patterns of achievement in our society are such that, unfortunately, certain groups must be favored. Nor is it acceptable to point to definitions of giftedness that feature traits that are more likely to be found among the affluent, the comfortable, the nonhandicapped, and males. The present condition exists as a direct result of decisions made by people—ironically, by good people, for the most part. These same people can change this situation, not easily, but effectively. And while there may well be arguments among people of goodwill over how we should change things, I do not see how there could be arguments over *whether* we should change things. We must, and we can. We must do it soon.

ATTENDING TO THE AFFECTIVE NEEDS OF GIFTED STUDENTS

We now turn briefly to the need to address the affective issues related to and raised by the institution of programs for gifted students in the schools.

There is no support within the research literature for the popular, although hardly universal, belief that gifted individuals have a tendency to be eccentric, emotionally unstable, even slightly mad. Although this view was for a while accorded a surprising amount of respect as a result of the work of the criminologist Cesare Lombroso (1895), his claim that genius and insanity are closely linked is now regarded as a quaint pseudoscientific relic of a more credulous age. Nonetheless, there is no warrant for the assumption that gifted children, by virtue of their intellectual ability, are somehow immune to or unusually capable of surmounting the difficulties inherent in being different in the society of the schools. The stereotype within the field of the gifted child as an invariably healthy and well-adjusted person, part of the legacy of Terman's work (e.g., Terman, 1925; Burks, Jensen, & Terman, 1930), has perhaps caused us to ignore or to minimize the pressures brought to bear upon gifted children by society, school personnel, parents, peers, and the children themselves.

I suspect that it is also the case that we tend to give short shrift in general to children's complaints that their lives can at times be difficult. As adults, we can fall prey to the temptation to romanticize our childhoods. Selectively recalling only the pleasures of our youth, we sometimes remember our younger years as halcyon days of freedom from responsibility and from what at times seem to be the nearly overwhelming burdens of adulthood. Compared with such responsibilities as supporting a family, maintaining a marriage, sustaining and advancing a career, and confronting the inevitable passing of one's time, the concerns of childhood—dating, peer acceptance, and so forth—seem to shrink in importance. It is easy to forget that for children and adolescents, these are the major concerns of their lives, and they can exert pressures on the individual equivalent to those exerted on adults by adult concerns. Moreover, many children and adolescents must deal on a daily basis with such problems as drugs, crime, violence, teen pregnancy, and family tensions, problems that only in the most trivial sense can be labeled children's issues.

Definitions of giftedness tend to stress intellectual, academic, artistic, and motivational characteristics of gifted students. As a result, and understandably so, our educational programs for these children are predicated upon these cognitive and volitional traits and give little attention to affective considerations. Yet, one of the bases for advocating the creation of programs for the gifted is that the mainstream is not a very congenial place for gifted students to spend their time. Not only is the regular school program intellectually unsuited to the needs of the gifted; prolonged exposure to it can have negative affective outcomes with respect to the children's attitudes toward learning, school, society, and themselves. We frequently argue, therefore, that special programs are required in order to minimize the potential that these outcomes will be the lot of our gifted children.

However, this also means that programs for the gifted will at least initially be serving students whose school experiences have not been consistently pleasant and who are, in many cases, likely to bear the scars of and hold negative attitudes toward a heretofore unresponsive school system. Furthermore, the solution, a program for the gifted, can sometimes be part of the problem. Such programs effect changes in the school lives of the children they serve, disrupting schedules, interfering with friendships, and calling greater attention to the children's exceptionality.

It is important, therefore, that this situation be acknowledged and that some provision be made within the system for attending to the unique emotional needs of the gifted. I have no special prescription for accomplishing this, nor have I space in this book for a detailed discussion of issues related to counseling gifted students. However, no conscientious discussion of programs for the gifted can ignore the fact that school personnel will be called upon at times to deal with students' social and emotional problems deriving at least in part from the students' giftedness.

In Chapter 7, in my delineation of some desirable behaviors and characteristics of teachers of the gifted, I mentioned that such teachers need to possess effective counseling skills, because their classes are likely at times to become forums for the airing of gifted students' concerns and complaints. While it is true that teachers can, will, and should listen to their students' concerns, it is hardly enough. Most teachers do not possess the professional skills required to counsel children and adolescents in their most trying circumstances. Unfortunately, it is also the case that most guidance counselors and other helping professionals lack knowledge of the characteristics and needs of the gifted.

In planning a program for the gifted, it might be wise to assign a guidance counselor or school psychologist, if possible, to the program for the gifted. It would not have to be this person's only responsibility; few schools or school districts are so rich in human resources that they can allocate someone exclusively to a single program. But it makes sense to designate one person as a resource for teachers and students in the program for the gifted, a person with the skills, background, or temperament to work effectively in this assignment. In-service training to acquaint this person with the nature and needs of gifted students would also be appropriate. It would not make sense to regard such a person as a miracle worker or to assume that such an allocation of personnel to the program for the gifted will forestall all difficulties. However, the provision of a consistent source of support and professional assistance and the prospect of a developing and sustaining relationship among counselor, program staff, and gifted students would constitute a positive feature of a program for the gifted that should be seriously considered by those involved in program planning.

However it is dealt with, this issue should be addressed in some manner. To try to ignore it in the planning stages only exacerbates the difficulties to be faced once the program is in operation. This is poor planning and poor education, and it will cause no end of problems in the long run.

CONCLUSION

Writing a book designed to serve as a guide for educators planning programs for the gifted is not the easiest of tasks. In trying to touch all the bases, in endeavoring to discuss the myriad of problems and concerns that program planners must confront, one inevitably faces the nagging realization that, as much as one has done, some things must have been omitted. I have tried to draw on my experience and that of others to anticipate a wide variety of situations, and I have tried to shed some light upon issues within the field that affect decisions that educators of the gifted must make. However, I advance no claim that this book is comprehensive in its coverage of the big and little questions that face us as a field. I realize that it is impossible to deal with every topic, to anticipate every contingency, to stay abreast of every development within the field, to maintain a perfectly consistent point of view, and to avoid perpetrating any stupidities or inanities whatever. I realize that all this is impossible, but I still worry about it.

I also worry about something else. In writing a book of this sort, it is necessary to focus on problematic situations with which program planners must deal, to describe some of the dangers that can result from ill-advised actions, and to derogate practices that one thinks are antithetical to the welfare of gifted students. In the present case, this means that at times I have been critical in these pages and that I may have given the false impression that the job of planning programs for the gifted is a thankless one, that most programs for the gifted are hopeless boondoggles, and that, as a field, we do not have a clue as to which way is up.

If I have given that impression, I regret it, for I am committed to our field, and I have a great and abiding respect for the many other educators who are equally committed to it. I do think we have a lot to learn, that we have at times countenanced some questionable practices, and that it is too early to pat ourselves on the back and say, "Well done." And I think that we could profit considerably from directing toward ourselves and our profession more of the critical thinking we urge on our students. However, this is true of every aspect of education. The problems and mistakes are many, perhaps in direct proportion to the importance of the calling.

The key to my attitude toward the field can be found in two pronouns I frequently use in discussing it in this book: *we* and *us*. If I have, in the course of dealing with the ins and outs of program design, cast a critical eye on some of what is done within the field, I do not wish to be seen as exempting myself from that criticism. It is my field, right or wrong, and I think it is more right than wrong.

We have quite a way to go before we can honestly claim that we have mastered our craft and met all our goals, but that should surprise no one familiar with the limits of human perfection. Programs for gifted children in this country are not always perfect, or even always good, but we are trying and we are making progress. We can look at the conditions facing gifted students in the schools today, compare the situation with that faced by gifted students 10 years ago, and deservedly feel pride over the fact that things are much better. The net effect of our exertions has been to do good, and that is no small accomplishment.

So it is appropriate to conclude that, despite my concerns and misgivings, I am proud to be a part of this field. I am proud of our cause and of what we have been able to achieve, often in the face of considerable opposition and misunderstanding. I am proud to be able to claim a shared purpose with some of the most dedicated and capable people in the educational profession. And I will be very proud if this book proves to be of assistance to any of them.

References

Alexander, P. A., & Muia, J. A. (1982). *Gifted education: A comprehensive roadmap.* Rockville, MD: Aspen Systems.

Alkin, M. C. (1969). Evaluation theory development. *Evaluation Comment, 2,* 2–7

Arieti, S. (1976). *Creativity: The magic synthesis.* New York: Basic Books.

Artaud, A. (1958). *The theater and its double.* New York: Grove Press.

Baldwin, A. (1978). The Baldwin identification matrix. In A. Baldwin, G. Gear, & L. Lucito (Eds.), *Educational planning for the gifted: Overcoming cultural, geographic, and socioeconomic barriers* (pp. 33–36). Reston, VA: Council for Exceptional Children.

Barclay, J. R. (1974). Needs assessment. In H. J. Walberg (Ed.), *Evaluating educational performance* (pp. 47–56). Berkeley, CA: McCutchan.

Baron, J. (1984). Criteria and explanations. *The Behavioral and Brain Sciences, 7,* 287–288.

Bayley, N. (1955). On the growth of intelligence. *American Psychologist, 10,* 805–818.

Begle, E. G. (1979). *Critical variables in mathematics education: Findings from a survey of the empirical literature.* Washington, DC: Mathematical Association of America.

Benbow, C. P. (1986). SMPY's model for teaching mathematically precocious students. In J. S. Renzulli (Ed.), *Systems and models for developing programs for the gifted and talented* (pp. 1–26). Mansfield Center, CT: Creative Learning Press.

Bishop, W. (1968). Successful teachers of the gifted. *Exceptional Children, 34,* 317–325.

Block, N. J., & Dworkin, G. (1976). *The IQ controversy.* New York: Random House.

Bloom, A. (1987). *The closing of the American mind.* New York: Simon & Schuster.

Bloom, B. S. (1956). *Taxonomy of educational objectives: The classification of educational goals. Handbook I: Cognitive domain.* New York: David McKay.

Bloom, B. S. (1980). The new directions in education research: Alterable variables. In W. B. Schrader (Ed.), *New directions for testing and measurement* (Vol. 5) (pp. 17–30). San Francisco: Jossey-Bass.

Borland, J. H. (1978). Teacher identification of the gifted: A new look. *Journal for the Education of the Gifted, 2,* 22–32.

Borland, J. H. (1986a). A note on the existence of certain divergent-production abilities. *Journal for the Education of the Gifted, 9,* 239–251.

Borland, J. H. (1986b). IQ tests: Throwing out the bathwater, saving the baby. *Roeper Review, 8,* 163–168.

Borland, J. H. (1986c). What happens to them all? A response to "What happens to the gifted girl." In C. J. Maker (Ed.), *Critical issues in gifted education: Defensible programs for the gifted* (pp. 91–106). Rockville, MD: Aspen Systems.

Brophy, J. E., & Good, T. L. (1974). *Teacher-student relationships: Causes and conse-quences.* New York: Holt, Rinehart and Winston.

Bruch, C. B., & Torrance, E. P. (1972). Mentioned in J. J. Gallagher, *Teaching the gifted child* (3rd ed.) (p. 384). Boston: Allyn and Bacon.

Bull, B. L. (1985). Eminence and precocity: An examination of the justification of education for the gifted and talented. *Teachers College Record, 87,* 1–19.

Burks, B. S., Jensen, D. W., & Terman, L. M. (1930). *Genetic studies of genius: Vol. 3. The promise of youth: Follow-up studies of a thousand gifted children.* Stanford, CA: Stanford University Press.

Buros, O. K. (1978). *The eighth mental measurements yearbook.* Highland Park, NJ: Gryphon Press.

Butler, C., & Borland, J. H. (1980). *Survey of programs for the gifted in New York State.* Unpublished manuscript.

Callahan, C. M. (1983). Issues in evaluating programs for the gifted. *Gifted Child Quarterly, 27,* 3–7.

Callahan, C. M., & Caldwell, M.S. (1986). Defensible evaluation of programs for the gifted and talented. In C. J. Maker (Ed.), *Critical issues in gifted education: Defensible programs for the gifted* (pp. 277–296). Rockville, MD: Aspen Systems.

Campbell, D. T., & Stanley, J. C. (1963). *Experimental and quasi-experimental designs for research.* Chicago: Rand McNally.

Carlberg, C. G., Johnson, D. W., Johnson, R., Maruyama, G., Kavale, K., Kulik, C. L., Kulik, J. A., Lysakowski, R. S., Pflaum, S. W., & Walberg, H. J. (1984). Meta-analysis in education: A reply to Slavin. *Educational Researcher, 13,* 16–23.

Carroll, L. (1968). Alice's adventures in wonderland and Through the looking glass. In M. Gardner (Ed.), *The annotated Alice* (pp. 17–345). Cleveland: Forum Books.

Case, R. (1974). Structures and strictures: Some functional limitations on the course of cognitive growth. *Cognitive Psychology, 6,* 544–573.

Clarizio, H. F., & Mehrens, W. A. (1985). Psychometric limitations of Guilford's structure-of-intellect model for identification and programming of the gifted. *Gifted Child Quarterly, 29,* 113–124.

Clark, B. (1983). *Growing up gifted* (2nd ed.). Columbus, OH: Charles E. Merrill.

Cochran, W. G. (1977). *Sampling techniques* (3rd ed.). New York: John Wiley & Sons.

Cohn, S. (1981). What is giftedness? A multidimensional approach. In H. A. Kramer (Ed.), *Gifted children: Challenging their potential* (pp. 33–45). New York: Trillium Press.

Colon, P. T., & Treffinger, D. J. (1980). Providing for the gifted in the regular classroom: Am I really mad? *Roeper Review, 3,* 18–21.

Cox, J., Daniel, N., & Boston, B. O. (1985). *Educating able learners.* Austin, TX: University of Texas Press.

Crockenberg, S. (1972). Creativity tests: A boon or boondoggle for education? *Review of Educational Research, 42,* 27–45.

Cronbach, L. J. (1963). Course improvement through evaluation. *Teachers College Record, 64,* 672–683.

Cronbach, L. J., & Furby, L. (1970). How should we measure "change"—Or should we? *Psychological Bulletin, 74,* 68–80.

Cronbach, L. J., Ambron, S. R., Dornbusch, S. M., Hess, R. D., Hornik, R. C., Phillips, D. C., Walker, D. E., & Weiner, S. S. (1980). *Toward reform of program evaluation*. San Francisco: Jossey-Bass.

DeLisle, J. (1988). The role of the gnome in gifted education: A response to "In defense of academic rigor." *Journal for the Education of the Gifted, 11,* 20–30.

Eisner, E. W. (1979). *The educational imagination*. New York: Macmillan.

Eisner, E. W., & Vallance, E. (1974). Five conceptions of curriculum: Their roots and implications for curriculum planning. In E. W. Eisner & E. Vallance (Eds.), *Conflicting conceptions of the curriculum*. San Francisco: McCutchan.

Ekstrom, R. B., French, J. W., & Harman, H. H. (1974). *Problems of replicating seven divergent production factors*. Princeton, NJ: Educational Testing Service.

Ekstrom, R. B., French, J. W., Harman, H. H., & Derman, D. (1976). *Manual for kit of factor-referenced cognitive tests*. Princeton, NJ: Educational Testing Service.

Elkind, D. (1981). *The hurried child: Growing up too fast too soon*. Reading, MA: Addison-Wesley.

Elkind, D. (1987). *Miseducation: Preschoolers at risk*. New York: Alfred A. Knopf.

Feldman, D. H. (1986). *Nature's gambit*. New York: Basic Books.

Fern, T. L. (1987). *Evaluation of gifted programs*. Unpublished manuscript, Teachers College, Columbia University.

Fine, T. W. (1969). Implementing a needs assessment program. *Educational Technology, 9,* 30–31.

Gagne, F. (1985). Giftedness and talent: Reexamining a reexamination of the definitions. *Gifted Child Quarterly, 29,* 103–112.

Galbraith, J. (1985). The eight great gripes of gifted kids: Responding to special needs. *Roeper Review, 8,* (15–18).

Gallagher, J. J. (1960). *Analysis of research on the education of gifted children*. Springfield, IL: Office of the Superintendent of Public Instruction.

Gallagher, J. J. (1985). *Teaching the gifted child* (3rd ed.) Boston: Allyn and Bacon.

Galton, F. (1869). *Hereditary genius*. London: Macmillan.

Gardner, H. (1983). *Frames of mind*. New York: Basic Books.

Gardner, J. W. (1961). *Excellence: Can we be equal and excellent too?* New York: Harper Brothers.

Gear, G. (1978). Effects of training on teachers' accuracy in the identification of gifted children. *Gifted Child Quarterly, 22,* 90–97.

Gerencser, S. (1979). The Calasanctius experience. In A. H. Passow (Ed.), *The gifted and the talented: Their education and development* (pp. 127–137). Chicago: University of Chicago Press.

Getzels, J. W., & Jackson, P. W. (1958). The meaning of "giftedness"—An examination of an expanding concept. *Phi Delta Kappan, 40,* 75–77.

Getzels, J. W., & Jackson, P. W. (1962). *Creativity and intelligence*. New York: John Wiley.

Glass, G. V. (1969). *The growth of evaluation methodology* (Research Paper No. 27). Boulder, CO: Laboratory of Educational Research, University of Colorado.

Gold, M. J. (1979). Teachers and mentors. In A. H. Passow (Ed.), *The gifted and the talented: Their education and development* (pp. 272–288). Chicago: University of Chicago Press.

Gordon, E., & Thomas, A. (1967). Children's behavior style and teachers' appraisal of their intelligence. *Journal of School Psychology, 5,* 292–300.

Guilford, J. P. (1950). Creativity. *American Psychologist, 14,* 469–479.

Guilford, J. P. (1967). *The nature of human intelligence.* New York: McGraw-Hill.

Hagen, E. (1980). *Identification of the gifted.* New York: Teachers College Press.

Hirsch, E. D. (1987). *Cultural literacy: What every American needs to know.* Boston: Houghton Mifflin.

Hirst, P. H. (1974). *Knowledge and the curriculum.* London: Routledge and Kegan Paul.

Hofstadter, R. (1963). *Anti-intellectualism in American life.* New York: Vintage.

Hollingworth, L. S. (1929). *Gifted children: Their nature and nurture.* New York: Macmillan.

Hollingworth, L. S. (1942). *Children above 180 IQ: Stanford-Binet.* New York: World Book Company.

Honzik, M. P., Macfarlane, J. W., & Allen, L. (1948). The stability of mental test performance between two and eighteen years. *Journal of Experimental Education, 17,* 309–324.

Horn, J. L., & Knapp, J. R. (197_.). On the subjective nature of the empirical base of Guilford's structure-of-intellect model. *Psychological Bulletin, 80,* 33–43.

House, E. R. (1980). *Evaluating with validity.* Beverly Hills, CA: Sage.

Howley, A., Howley, C. B., & Pendarvis, E. D. (1986). *Teaching gifted children.* Boston: Little, Brown.

Inhelder, B., & Piaget, J. (1958). *The growth of logical thinking from childhood to adolescence.* New York: Basic Books.

Jacobs, J. C. (1971). Effectiveness of teacher and parent identification of gifted children as a function of school level. *Psychology in the Schools, 8,* 140–142.

Jacobs, H. H., & Borland, J. H. (1986). The interdisciplinary concept model: Theory and practice. *Gifted Child Quarterly, 30,* 159–163.

Jarrell, R. H., & Borland, J. H. (in press). The research base for Renzulli's three-ring conception of giftedness: An exemplary analysis. *Journal for the Education of the Gifted.*

Johnson, M., Jr. (1977). Definitions and models in curriculum theory. In A. A. Bellack & H. M. Kliebard (Eds.), *Curriculum and evaluation* (pp. 3–19). Berkeley, CA: McCutchan.

Joint Committee on Standards for Educational Evaluation. (1981). *Standards for evaluations of educational programs, projects, and materials.* New York: McGraw-Hill.

Jones, R. L. (1972). Labels and stigma in special education. *Exceptional Children, 38,* 553–564.

Jones, R. L. (1974). Student views of special placement and their own special classes: A clarification. *Exceptional Children, 41,* 22–29.

Kaplan, S. N. (1974). *Providing programs for the gifted and talented.* Ventura, CA: Leadership Training Institute.

Kaufman, R. A. (1971). A possible integrative model for the systematic and measurable improvement of education. *American Psychologist, 26,* 250–256.

Kaufman, R. A., & English, F. W. (1976). *Needs assessment: A guide to improve school district management.* Arlington, VA: American Association of School Administrators.

Kelley, T. L. (1928). *Crossroads in the mind of man: A study of differentiable mental abilities.* Stanford, CA: Stanford University Press.

Keogh, B. K., & Smith, C. E. (1970). Early identification of educationally high potential and high risk children. *Journal of School Psychology, 8,* 285–290.

Kerlinger, F. N. (1973). *Foundations of behavioral research* (2nd ed.). New York: Holt, Rinehart and Winston.

Kontos, S., Carter, K. R., Ormrod, J. E., & Cooney, J. B. (1983). Reversing the revolving door. *Roeper Review, 6,* 41–42.

Krueger, M. L. (Ed.). (1978). *On being gifted.* New York: Walker.

Kulik, C. L., & Kulik, J. A. (1982). Effects of ability grouping on secondary school students: A meta-analysis of evaluation findings. *American Education Research Journal, 19,* 415–428.

Lombroso, C. (1895). *The man of genius.* New York: Scribners.

Maddux, C. D., Scheiber, L. M., & Bass, J. E. (1982). Self-concept and social distance in gifted children. *Gifted Child Quarterly, 26,* 77–81.

Maker, C. J. (1982a). *Curriculum development for the gifted.* Rockville, MD: Aspen Systems.

Maker, C. J. (1982b). *Teaching models in education of the gifted.* Rockville, MD: Aspen Systems.

Marland, S. P. (1972). *Education of the gifted and talented. Report to Congress.* Washington, DC: U.S. Government Printing Office.

Meeker, M. N., & Meeker, R. (1977). *SOI learning abilities test.* El Segundo, CA: SOI Institute.

Meyerowitz, J. H. (1962). Self derogations in young retardates and special class placement. *Child Development, 33,* 443–451.

Mitchell, B. M. (1988). The latest national assessment of gifted education. *Roeper Review, 10,* 239–240.

Nevo, D. (1983). The conceptualization of educational evaluation: An analytical review of the literature. *Review of Educational Research, 53,* 117–128.

New York State Education Department. (1982). *Educating gifted pupils in the regular classroom: Training manual.* Albany, NY: New York State Education Department.

Newland, T. E. (1976). *The gifted in socio-educational perspective.* Englewood Cliffs, NJ: Prentice-Hall.

Parnes, S. J., Noller, R. B., & Biondi, A. M. (1977). *Guide to creative action.* New York: Scribners.

Pascual-Leone, J., & Smith, J. (1969). The encoding and decoding of symbols by children: A new experimental paradigm and a neo-Piagetian model. *Journal of Experimental Child Psychology, 8,* 328–355.

Passow, A. H. (1984). *Reforming schools in the 1980s: A critical review of the national reports.* New York: ERIC Clearinghouse on Urban Education.

Pegnato, C. W., & Birch, J. W. (1959). Locating gifted children in junior high schools: A comparison of methods. *Exceptional Children, 25,* 300–304.

Perkins, D. N. (1981). *The mind's best work*. Cambridge, MA: Harvard University Press.

Phenix, P. H. (1964). *Realms of meaning*. New York: McGraw-Hill.

Pintner, R. (1931). *Intelligence testing, Methods and results* (2nd ed.). New York: Henry Holt.

Pollins, L. D. (1983). The effects of acceleration on the social and emotional development of gifted students. In C. P. Benbow & J. C. Stanley (Eds.), *Academic precocity* (pp. 160–178). Baltimore: Johns Hopkins University Press.

Renzulli, J. S. (1977). *The enrichment triad model*. Mansfield Center, CT: Creative Learning Press.

Renzulli, J. S. (1978). What makes giftedness? *Phi Delta Kappan, 60*, 180–184, 261.

Renzulli, J. S. (1981). Identifying key features in programs for the gifted. In W. B. Barbe & J. S. Renzulli (Eds.), *Psychology and education of the gifted* (3rd ed.) (pp. 214–219). New York: Irvington.

Renzulli, J. S. (1986a). The three-ring conception of giftedness: A developmental model for creative productivity. In R. J. Sternberg, & J. E. Davidson (Eds.), *Conceptions of giftedness* (pp. 53–92). New York: Cambridge University Press.

Renzulli, J. S. (Ed.). (1986b). *Systems and models for developing programs for the gifted and talented*. Mansfield Center, CT: Creative Learning Press.

Renzulli, J. S., & Hartman, R. K. (1981). Scale for rating the behavioral characteristics of superior students. In W. B. Barbe & J. S. Renzulli (Eds.), *Psychology and education of the gifted* (3rd ed.) (pp. 157–164). New York: Irvington.

Renzulli, J. S., & Owen, S. V. (1983). The revolving door identification model: If it ain't busted, don't fix it; If you don't understand it, don't nix it. *Roeper Review, 6*, 39–41.

Renzulli, J. S., Reis, S. M., & Smith, L. H. (1981). *The revolving door identification model*. Mansfield Center, CT: Creative Learning Press.

Richert, E. S., Alvino, J. J., & McDonnel, R. C. (1982). *National report on identification*. Sewell, NJ: Educational Improvement Center—South.

Ronvik, R. (1989). An essay on education for the gifted. In J. VanTassel-Baska & P. Olszewski-Kubilius (Eds.), *Patterns of influence on gifted learners: The home, the self, and the school* (pp. 231–240). New York: Teachers College Press.

Ross, J. D., & Ross, C. M. (1976). *Ross test of higher cognitive processes*. San Rafael, CA: Academic Therapy Publications.

Runco, M. A. (1985). Reliability and convergent validity of ideational flexibility as a function of academic achievement. *Perceptual and Motor Skills, 61*, 1075–1081.

Sawyer, R. (1988a). In defense of academic rigor. *Journal for the Education of the Gifted, 11*, 5–19.

Sawyer, R. (1988b). Response from Robert Sawyer. *Journal for the Education of the Gifted, 11*, 31–34.

Scriven, M. (1967). The methodology of evaluation. In R. E. Stake (Ed.), *AERA monograph series on curriculum evaluation*, No. 1. Chicago: Rand McNally.

Silverman, L. K. (1986a). What happens to the gifted girl? In C. J. Maker (Ed.), *Critical issues in gifted education: Defensible programs for the gifted* (pp. 43–90). Rockville, MD: Aspen Systems.

Silverman, L. K. (Ed.). (1986b). *The IQ controversy* [Special issue]. *Roeper Review, 8* (3).

Slavin, R. E. (1984). Meta-analysis in education: How has it been used? *Educational Researcher, 13,* 6–15.

Sosniak, L. A. (1987). Gifted education boondoggles: A few bad apples or a rotten bushel? *Phi Delta Kappan, 69,* 535–538.

Spearman, C. (1927). *The abilities of man.* New York: Macmillan.

Stanley, J. C. (1980). On educating the gifted. *Educational Researcher, 9,* 8–12.

Stanley, J. C. (1981). Rationale of the study of mathematically precocious youth (SMPY) during its first five years of promoting educational acceleration. In W. B. Barbe & J. S. Renzulli (Eds.), *Psychology and education of the gifted* (pp. 248–283). New York: Irvington.

Sternberg, R. J. (1979). The nature of mental abilities. *American Psychologist, 34,* 214–230.

Sternberg, R. J. (1981). A componential theory of intellectual giftedness. *Gifted Child Quarterly, 25,* 86–93.

Sternberg, R. J. (1982a). A schism has arisen [Letter to the editor]. *Roeper Review, 4,* 52.

Sternberg, R. J. (1982b). Lies we live by: Misapplication of tests in identifying the gifted. *Gifted Child Quarterly, 26,* 157–161.

Sternberg, R. J. (1984). Toward a triarchic theory of human intelligence. *The Behavioral and Brain Sciences, 7,* 264–316.

Sternberg, R. J. (1986). A triarchic theory of intellectual giftedness. In R. J. Sternberg & J. E. Davidson (Eds.), *Conceptions of giftedness* (pp. 223–246). New York: Cambridge University Press.

Sternberg, R. J., & Davidson, J. E. (Eds.). (1986). *Conceptions of giftedness.* New York: Cambridge University Press.

Stufflebeam, D. L. (1972). The relevance of the CIPP evaluation model for educational accountability. *SRIS Quarterly, 5,* 3–6.

Stufflebeam, D. L. (1974). *Meta-evaluation* (Occasional Paper No. 3). Kalamazoo: Western Michigan University.

Stufflebeam, D. L., Foley, W. J., Gephart, W. J., Guba, E. J., Hammon, R. L., Merriman, H. O., & Provus, M. M. (1971). *Educational evaluation and decision-making.* Itasca, IL: Peacock.

Tannenbaum, A. J. (1979). Pre-Sputnik to post-Watergate concern about the gifted. In A. H. Passow (Ed.), *The gifted and the talented: The education and development* (pp. 5–27). Chicago: University of Chicago Press.

Tannenbaum, A. J. (1983). *Gifted children: Psychological and educational perspectives.* New York: Macmillan.

Tanner, D., & Tanner, L. N. (1980). *Curriculum development: Theory into practice* (2nd ed.). New York: Macmillan.

Terman, L. M. (1925). *Genetic studies of genius: Vol. 1. Mental and physical traits of a thousand gifted children.* Stanford, CA: Stanford University Press.

Terman, L. M., & Oden, M. H. (1947). *Genetic studies of genius: Vol. 4. The gifted child grows up.* Stanford, CA: Stanford University Press.

Terman, L. M., & Oden, M. H. (1959). *Genetic studies of genius: Vol. 5. The gifted group at midlife.* Stanford, CA: Stanford University Press.

Thorndike, R. L. (1966). Some methodological issues in the study of creativity. In A. Anastasi (Ed.), *Testing problems in perspective* (pp. 436–448). Washington, DC: American Council on Education.

Torrance, E. P. (1962). *Guiding creative talent.* Englewood Cliffs, NJ: Prentice-Hall.

Torrance, E. P. (1966). *Torrance tests of creative thinking: Technical-norms manual.* Princeton, NJ: Personnel Press.

Torrance, E. P. (1972). Can we teach children to think creatively? *Journal of Creative Behavior, 6,* 114–141.

Torrance, E. P. (1984). *Mentor relationships: How they aid creative achievement, endure, change, and die.* Buffalo, NY: Bearly Limited.

Treffinger, D. J. (1982). Gifted students, regular classrooms: Sixty ingredients for a better blend. *Elementary School Journal, 82,* 276–273.

Tremaine, C. D. (1979). Do gifted programs make a difference? *Gifted Child Quarterly, 23,* 500–517.

Tyler, R. W. (1950). *Basic principles of curriculum and instruction.* Chicago: University of Chicago Press.

Wallach, M. A. (1970). Creativity. In P. H. Mussen (Ed.), *Carmichael's manual of child psychology* (pp. 1211–1272). New York: John Wiley.

Ward, V. (1961). *Educating the gifted: An axiomatic approach.* Columbus, OH: Charles E. Merrill.

Wechsler, D. (1974). *Wechsler intelligence scale for children* (Rev. ed.). New York: The Psychological Corporation.

Whitmore, J. R. (1980). *Giftedness, conflict, and underachievement.* Boston: Allyn and Bacon.

Witty, P. A. (1958). Who are the gifted? In N. B. Henry (Ed.), *Education of the gifted* (pp. 41–63). Chicago: University of Chicago Press.

Yoder, A. H. (1894). The story of the boyhood of great men. *Pedagogical Seminary, 3,* 134–156.

Index

About the Author

James H. Borland is Assistant Professor of Education and Coordinator of the graduate programs in the Education of the Gifted and Early Childhood Special Education in the Department of Special Education at Teachers College, Columbia University. Before assuming his current position, he was the codirector of the Center for the Study and Education of the Gifted at Teachers College and the director of the college's Hollingworth Preschool. He has served as consultant for program development, program evaluator, and teacher trainer with nearly one hundred public and private educational agencies in the United States and abroad. In addition to being the author of this book, he is the editor of the series of which it is a part. He currently resides in Manhattan with his wife, Marcia, and his son, Max.